# How People Harness Their Collective Wisdom and Power

## To Construct the Future in Co-Laboratories of Democracy

# How People Harness Their Collective Wisdom and Power

## To Construct the Future in Co-Laboratories of Democracy

### Alexander N. Christakis

**with**

### Kenneth C. Bausch

INFORMATION AGE
PUBLISHING

Greenwich, Connecticut 06830 • www.infoagepub.com

Library of Congress Cataloging-in-Publication Data

Christakis, Alexander N.
  How people harness their collective wisdom and power to construct the
future in co-laboratories of democracy / Alexander N. Christakis with
Kenneth C. Bausch.
      p. cm. – (Research in public management)
  Includes bibliographical references and index.
  ISBN 1-59311-482-6 (hardcover) – ISBN 1-59311-481-8 (pbk.)
  1. Interactive management. 2. Public administration. I. Bausch, Kenneth
C., 1936- II. Title. III. Research in public management (Unnumbered)
  HD30.29.C47 2006
  658.4'01–dc22

                                                          2006002400

Printed in the United States of America

*To my five children:*
*Quan Yang Duh*
*Nicholas A. Christakis*
*Dimitri A. Christakis*
*Anna-Katrina S. Christakis*
*Nora A. Christakis*

*And my eleven grandchildren:*
*Kathryn and Emily Duh*
*Sebastian, Lysander, and Lena Christakis*
*Alexandra and Bianca Christakis*
*Alexander and Ariana Christakis*
*Ronan Alexander Hussar*
*Maddox Nicholas Hussar*

*For the joy they give me whenever and wherever*
*I see them on the planet*

# CONTENTS

## PART I
### Evolution of Dialogue   1

## PART II
### Architecture of the Structured Design Process (SDP)   23

# PART III

## Co-laboratories in Action   63

# PART IV

## A Science of Dialogic Design   127

# PART V

## Constructing the Future   189

# APPENDICIES

# FOREWORD

## Dr. Enrique G. Herrscher

**F**ew books present an idea that might change the world. This is one of the few.

The emphasis here is on the word "might." Two things are *always* needed to change the world, or an organization, or oneself, or anything: *intent and procedure.* That is: a serious desire to change, and an adequate methodology. Alexander (Aleco) Christakis' book presents one such methodology. It is called *dialogue.*

Not a "natural" dialogue, not any kind of human interaction, not even—important as it is—the recommendation to "put oneself in someone else's shoes," certainly not "just talking." But a highly structured dialogue, said (with exciting examples) to have been applied successfully for over thirty years. In fact, the whole book is based on the thesis (in my simplified version, not in Aleco's words) that *(a) dialogue is important; (b) dialogue is difficult; and (c) the only way to overcome the difficulties is through an adequate methodology,* such methodology being basically the contents of the book.

But methodology alone does not produce change, and Aleco's book fully acknowledges the difficulties, constraints and pathologic situations to be overcome. Therefore, the book is not only about methodology. In my view (and I am not following the book's structure but my own), *its gist is fourfold: (a) an attitude; (b) a philosophy; (c) a call for action; and (d) a methodology.* Let me explain what I mean by these interrelated parts, expressed in my own words, surely less rigorous than Christakis'.

*How People Harness Their Collective Wisdom and Power*, pages xi–xvi
Copyright © 2006 by Information Age Publishing

## AN ATTITUDE

A collaborative spirit, *a true regard for "the collective wisdom of the group,"* the power of "mutual persuasion and respect," permeate Christakis' book. This goes beyond participative democracy within the hierarchical model, that often gets stuck mid-road because power or bureaucracy (structure) work in the shadows.

You will read the book and find more about both the ethical and practical roots and their far reaching effects in an increasingly complex web-world, but let me add two personal notes.

When I first met Aleco Christakis, at the 49th annual meeting of the International Society for the Systems Sciences (ISSS) at Crete in 2003, his all-embracing personality did more to show me how a group consciousness through dialogue is generated, than the axioms and laws you will read here. Particularly strong was the message delivered at the last plenary by representatives of native tribes. While most of us selected one or two spokespersons to present conclusions in the name of the group, in their case the whole group came forward, and each person expressed his or her thoughts and experiences.

When I read (chapter 20) the wonderful Winnebago tribe chairman's account of the essence of the pipe ceremonial, I was reminded of a similar tradition we had as young boys and girls at the local YMCA camp site in Argentina. At the last campfire, a half burned stick was passed around, and each one holding it "opened his/her heart" and expressed their feelings towards the camp experience and their interaction with others. A beautiful forerunner of what is said in this book.

## A PHILOSOPHY

By this perhaps presumptuous term, I refer to what Christakis calls "Science of Dialogue Design" or "People Science," based on the "Wisdom of the People" ("Demosophia") paradigm, a Weltanschauung from which the above "attitude" derives. It resembles what I once termed "Science of Dialogue," characterizing that way the essence of systemics (in my incoming presidential speech at the 2004 ISSS annual meeting).

I won't reproduce the axioms, definitions, laws and measurements that, as with any science, characterize this one, because you will find them, well worded and orderly, in the text. But I do consider it a valid contribution to state here what I consider the ten major assumptions of this science, because they are the building blocks of the proposed methodology that follows:

- That the self-organizing model is spreading in all kinds of organizations in the post-industrial world
- That in a world where influence increasingly replaces control, dialogue and teamwork will be more and more the preferred methods
- That commitment, shared responsibility and real change can only be achieved by democratic participation
- That mutual purpose and a collective leadership are necessary to link the group's work with the organization and its external environment
- That practices based on the hierarchical model have only limited effectiveness because they generate negative feedback
- That without a proper process, individuals do not learn from each other (they often use the debate to persuade others, stick to a zero-sum mode or simply voice their beliefs)
- That while the generation of ideas is comparatively easy, relating them to each other is complex
- That stakeholders possess the requisite knowledge for defining and resolving systemic problems
- That stakeholders are however generally programmed to see situations in terms of the mechanistic paradigm
- That computers lessen the cognitive demands on designing participants, and therefore are an essential aid for easing consensus.

## AN ACTION PLAN

The dialogue proposed here is not a case of neutral collection of observer-independent data, but rather a proposal to "enable people from all walks of life to experience participative democracy in national, international, organizational and inter-organizational settings."

To translate above attitude and philosophy into action in the real world is no easy task. Reading the book makes it clear—at least for me—that this is an instance of "necessary but not sufficient." I have my doubts—and believe Aleco would share this view—whether this kind of dialogue would succeed in the face of strong negative forces arising from power relations or vested interests. But the point I want to make is that often the situation is not so bad. However, even in a favorable setting , a positive outcome can only be assured if the right tools are applied.

In other words, numerous opportunities are lost not because those who oppose change are too powerful but because those who are in favor fail to make it happen. The story of President Clinton and the failure of the Northwest Forest Conference (1993) illustrates the point. A project sponsored by a U.S. President should not be weak, but lack of an adequate procedure makes it so.

Rather than commenting on the action plan itself, it may be of interest to extract the 20 major problems the action is supposed to solve, and how:

- To achieve, through a preliminary "White Paper," a common understanding of the problem situation
- To generate, by disciplined discussion, a common language
- To open the door, thanks to such common ground, to true teamwork
- To bring together key stakeholders who identify barriers, provide a hierarchy of issues and develop a plan of action
- To give a voice to those who are rarely heard, by "patient honoring of stakeholder autonomy"
- To empower "those who do the job"
- To equalize power relations among the stakeholders
- To integrate, through interaction, diverse viewpoints
- To " elicit ideas and points of view from all stakeholders"
- To have stakeholders "to think clearly and outside their preconceived mental boxes"
- To avoid "premature closing", jumping too early at conclusions
- To severely restrict "power-grabbing activities" by stakeholders trying to monopolize attention or exercising the role of experts
- To view problems/solutions without a winner –loser perspective
- To heighten the "appreciation for the scope of responsibilities that each person has"
- To establish "salient priorities for design"
- To uncover unexpected solutions
- To lessen, by use of interactive software, the cognitive demands on designing stakeholders
- To reverse, by participation and dialogue, "the dismal trends of decline and discontent prevalent in most societies and organizations today"
- To create " an atmosphere of serenity, equity, authenticity and empathy"
- To "learn to have fun together as a community·

The reader will find (and enjoy) the practical ways to achieve these goals through the diverse examples furnished in the book.

## A METHODOLOGY

There is no need, in a Foreword, to go into the steps of the process which is, as said at the beginning, the gist of the book, Suffice to mention here the one salient characteristic, in my view, of the methodology: *a clear distinction between process and contents,* between the rules of the meeting, the voting methods and the consensus reaching procedures on the one hand, *man-*

*aged exclusively by the facilitator team,* and the actual opinions, discussions, conclusions and proposals on the other hand, that remain within *the exclusive power of the stakeholders.*

I had the privilege to witness this separation twice: years ago, at an ISSS conference, with John Warfield, and recently (2005), at the ISSS annual meeting in Mexico, with Allenna Leonard, and consider that it is the most powerful feature of the methodology. It not only saves a lot of trouble and time: it provides the procedural discipline that in many cases marks the difference between success and failure.

## THE LATIN AMERICAN CASE

Let me finish with a "contextual" note (nothing in systemic thinking is context-free!). I once said that there are two regions where the systems approach is bound to grow significantly in the next decades: the Eastern European countries and the Latin American ones. When writing these lines for these two wonderful systemic thinkers Aleco Christakis and Ken Bausch, I venture to state that the one region that would and should benefit most from the contents of this book is Latin America.

Due to historical, sociological, cultural and economic reasons too complex to describe here, the problems of reaching consensus in a truly democratic way in most (or all) Latin American countries, as well as in many (or most) of their public, social and private organizations, are enormous.

Asking for forgiveness for possibly unjust generalizations, here are a few items that appear in the book as exceptions but that in Latin American countries are usual:

- The self organizing model is still a minority
- Hierarchy and privileges are prevalent
- There is very little disposition to learn from each other
- The suspicions about what management really wants is typical both at the corporate and public level
- Valuable proposals often trigger concerted opposition from entrenched power structures.

These negative traits, notable exceptions and improvement efforts notwithstanding, conform the extremely low "social capital" that is the object of extensive research and awareness action by Inter American Bank expert Bernardo Kliksberg.

In addition, the present inevitable world-wide globalization process means, for a number of reasons beyond the scope of this Foreword, more disadvantages than advantages for the peoples of this region. The increasing tension between the need to be "part of the world," and the equally important need to preserve local identities, creates dilemmas impossible to solve without a credible end equitable procedure for reaching consensus on public issues.

In a similar way, organizations both in the corporate arena and in the entrepreneurial context face post-industrial changes and challenges impossible to cope with if not by dialogue practice suited to web world requirements and participative management modes.

Thus, the "structure of dialogic design" put forward in this book, would be a most urgently needed tool, its enormous difficulties notwithstanding.

—Dr. Enrique G. Herrscher
University of Buenos Aires
Past president of International Society for the Systems Sciences

# PROLOGUE

**M**y commitment to developing a new model for the practice of disciplined dialogue can be traced to an insight I had while sitting in a bus in Paris, France in 1974. The bus was taking me back to my hotel after the end of the second day of a conference on the subject of "New Towns," organized by the French government. I was one of five "expert consultants" retained by the French to offer advice on an urban development design project for the greater Paris Region. There were three Americans and two Europeans in the consulting group. One of the Europeans was an Austrian, named Erich Jantsch, who was a leader in the social systems design movement in Europe. I had met Erich during one of his visits to Greece during a conference organized by a famous Greek Architect-Planner, Dinos Doxiadis. Doxiadis was the man responsible for changing my professional orientation from theoretical nuclear physics to systems design and planning in 1967.

In the 1970s, Erich Jantsch had made profound contributions to the design of social systems and to evolutionary theory. Unfortunately, Erich's work was not at that time appreciated by the dominant social science paradigm, especially in the USA. In the 1970s most social scientists were interested in explaining and predicting the dynamics of social systems, such as American cities, rather than designing them. Like many other revolutionary scholars throughout history, Erich was not part of the "normal social science" community, primarily because of his advocacy of the need for a paradigm shift in the design of social systems.

As Erich and I rode the bus back to the hotel together, we struck up a conversation about the proceedings of the French conference on urban design. We were both frustrated with the inability of the conference participants to effectively communicate among themselves. We were also dissatis-

*How People Harness Their Collective Wisdom and Power*, pages xvii–xx
Copyright © 2006 by Information Age Publishing

fied that our consultant role was mainly to be window dressing for promoting the Paris urban development plan. The French planners were doing most of the talking. They were enamored with their "master plan" for the future of Paris. We the consultants were supposed to listen and give the master plan our blessing as the "best plan" for the people of Paris. It became clear that the "voice of the external consultants" was more important to the French planners than the voice of the people of Paris.

Both Erich and I were formally educated in theoretical physics. As a result of our education, we knew the elegance and rigor of scientific communication as it is practiced in the world of physics. The rigor is primarily due to the powerful language of mathematical equations and symbols that physicists use to explain and predict physical phenomena and their dynamics in a transparent, concise, and rigorous manner. No self-respecting physicist would have been able to survive the information overload, cognitive dissonance, and linguistic confusion that were prevalent during the deliberations of the participants at this French conference. We were both very troubled by that experience, and yet we could not offer a better alternative for transparent and productive dialogue among the conference participants.

As the bus was taking us from the remote country site where the conference was being held to the center of Paris, which was full of activity and glitter in the early evening, I watched the Parisians taking their strolls through the streets. The city of Paris clearly belonged to them, and yet their voices were not heard at the conference. The planners and expert consultants were planning Paris without input from the Parisians. They were using an esoteric and confusing language, which ordinary Frenchmen would not have understood, even if they had been invited to participate.

I thought about these two distinct issues—the exclusion of the Parisians and the poor communication amongst the disparate experts—and I drifted into silent reflection on the learning experiences I had during the three years in the '60s that I worked for Doxiadis.

Doxiadis was formally trained as an architect and engineer in Greece and Germany in the 1930s. After a distinguished career in various government positions in Greece during and after World War II, he established his own urban design consulting firm. Beyond this very successful consulting business, Doxiadis had a vision. He wanted to invent the science of human settlements, or "Ekistics," the Greek word he coined for this science. With this science, he wanted to improve the elegance and rigor of design communications among urban planners, people from all walks of life, and policy makers. He was, in essence, as frustrated about design communications as Erich and I were during our participation at the French conference. He was convinced that the only way to improve the quality of human settlements for all their inhabitants was to introduce scientific principles in the same way that physicists had done for physical phenomena. He believed

that the invention of the science of Ekistics would improve the communication among all the stakeholders, and consequently ameliorate the urban
design disasters that were happening in the latter half of the 20th century
in cities around the world.

In 1965, immediately after the completion of my PhD dissertation in
theoretical physics at Yale University, and upon my return to Greece to
serve in the Greek army, Doxiadis hired me as his personal adviser. My
assignment was to help him invent the new science of Ekistics. I accepted
the assignment and started introducing concepts from physics, including
the development of mathematical models, in the context of Doxiadis'
research and consultancy projects. After working on this task for about two
years, I recognized that the theoretical physics approach could not make
Doxiadis' vision a reality. A truly human science of design would have to be
built upon a different basis.

What urban design needed was not an emulation of the esoteric mathematical language of physics but a "new" language that people could use to
engage in a dialogue for democratically designing their communities. The
availability of such a language would have made it possible both for the citizens of Paris to participate in the French conference and for the experts
to communicate among themselves and with the stakeholders. The inhabitants of a city are, after all, the principal users of any urban design or redesign project. Any urban design that would not be informed by their voices
would not be democratic. Their voices, however, cannot have a significant
impact on the design of their cities unless they are engaged in participative
democracy.

Participative democracy has undergone major transformations throughout history, going back to the model practiced during the Golden Age of
Athens in 500 B.C. These changes have increased the speed in the decision-making process, but have done so by compromising the value and virtues of citizen participation. In the history of Western government, we have
pro- (or re-) gressed from participative democracy, to representative
democracy, to government by experts, to government for corporate lob-
bies. In effect, we have returned to the plutocracy model from which the
Athenian democracy strove to free us. There must be ways that we can
engage in democratic dialogue to attain designing efficiency while retaining participative openness and fairness. We need a workable human science, one that honors and uses the authentic voices of people to design
their futures.

In the Paris bus, I felt that my credentials in theoretical physics, my
expertise in urban design, and my engagement over a year with the French
project as a consultant, did not qualify me to render any advice about the
quality of the Paris master plan, especially since "the wisdom of the people
of Paris" was not solicited during its design. This insight ultimately con-

vinced me to resign from this position. It became crystal clear to me that the notion of the "expert" in designing social systems had to be reinvented. I felt that, by playing the role of the expert in the absence of the voices of the people of Paris, I had become part of the problem and not part of the solution for this city.

The Paris conference, the bus conversation with Erich Jantsch, and my three years of apprenticing with Doxiadis' urban design firm, convinced me that what was needed was a "new science" that would enable people to engage in human design and to experience participative democracy through dialogue, as it was practiced in the agora of Athens during its Golden Age. I also recognized that, in light of the complexity of the Information Age, the challenges of participative democracy through dialogue in the modern agoras are formidable. This insight was the beginning of the journey of collaborative effort with other researchers to find a model of dialogue to bring the wisdom of people to the surface, making this model the ideal of participative democracy by all citizens an achievable objective in the Information Age.

After thirty years of research and testing in the arena of practice, the ideal of a science of human settlements that Doxiadis was envisioning in the 1960s became the Structured Design Process (SDP) paradigm, which is the main focus of this book. This new process enables citizens from all walks of life to participate on equal footing with experts in designing their social systems. It enables all stakeholders to construct visual patterns of problems and solutions systemically, collaboratively, and collectively.

My intention in writing this book is to present an axiomatic practical approach of social design. I do not wish to deprecate traditional democratic and managerial methods. There is, however, sufficient empirical evidence that leaders and managers, even when they espouse the democratic ideal for their organizations, cannot implement it in the situations they are confronting. A root cause for these failures, I believe, is a false presupposition that an approach in the Information Age could be founded on a paradigm that is similar to the one used in the agora of Athens 2,500 years ago.

This belief led me to commit thirty years of my professional life to developing and applying a new process for the practice of design that is useful to all people independent of their educational or power status. I call it the Structured Design Process (SDP). The process works across disciplines and cultures. It has been practiced all over the world in a variety of settings ranging from the emancipation of oppressed indigenous people to the development of safer pharmaceutical products and health care services for patients.

# ACKNOWLEDGMENTS

It is difficult to mention and acknowledge all the partners on the road of this journey, who have contributed significantly in terms of philosophical, theoretical, methodological, and practical ideas in the development of the dialogue process described in the book in the last thirty years. By confining myself to personal experiences, and disregarding historical influences going back to Greek philosophers such as Aristotle, I start by acknowledging the incredible inspiration provided to me when I was a young man in the late '60s by my friend, Hasan Ozbekhan, who was the first person to expose me to the general theory of planning and design. Hasan, of Turkish heritage, and me of Greek heritage developed an instant intimacy from the first time we met during his visit to Greece in 1966. This friendship surprised and astonished our friends. The relationship led to our collaboration in the early phases of the Club of Rome, which will be described later on.

The inspiration for writing this book came from my friend Ken Bausch who pushed me to put down in writing some of the experiences and stories I was sharing with him during our three years of collaboration. Ken also contributed some organizing principles and sections of the book in its early version, for which I am very grateful. The chapter on leadership in Part V, is the result of a very productive collaboration for over ten years with Larry Magliocca of The Ohio State University. LaDonna Harris, my Native American friend for fifteen years, has provided me with the spiritual energy and the emotional and intellectual support to continue this work, even when the continuing was hard and lonely. She has always been and will always be very special in my life, as in so many other lives. Two early adopters and practitioners of the methodology, who were also early sponsors in a variety of government projects, were David Mackett of the

*How People Harness Their Collective Wisdom and Power*, pages xxi–xxiii
Copyright © 2006 by Information Age Publishing
xxi

National Oceanic and Atmospheric Administration (NOAA), and Robert McDonald of the US Forest Service. I have wonderful memories of stories from the design arena of fisheries research and national forest planning that we shared together for over twenty years.

I would like to thank Robert Menapace, Norma Romm, Beth Steenwyk, Debie Canza, Robin Gibbs, Bill Shearer, and Nicholas Christakis, for taking the time to review parts of the manuscript and offer their constructive comments. Their comments helped me improve the quality and transparency of the ideas I was trying to share with the readers. In this capacity Helen Weisz, my wife, has endured the review of many drafts with good humour and lots of love. The book was actually written during our visits in the last two summers to our home in Archanes, Crete, which Helen has designed in a way that we can be together and yet have separate working spaces. I am very grateful for her design work, in which I did not participate, and for her dedicated partnership for ten years of our marriage.

I also want to express my sincere gratitude to Diane Conaway, who has been my loyal partner on the road as a member of the CWA, Ltd consultancy (www.CWALtd.com) for over twelve years. Without Diane's dedication and hard work it would have been impossible to sustain the CWA consultancy and to perform more than one hundred projects with clients from all over the world. Diane and I have travelled many places together, even working together with Greek stakeholders, even though Diane does not understand Greek. She has always been my competent and loyal colleague, and has never failed to offer her support and dedication to the vision of a dialogue process for participative democracy

The following people have engaged the methodology in the arena of application and continue to be a source of inspiration as reflective practitioners in its community of science: Marian Godfrey, Pew Charitable Trusts; Doug Bauer, Pew and Smith-Kline Beecham; Julie Carlston, Alexander Fleming, Margaret Porter, and Janet Woodcock, US Food and Drug Administration; Bela Banathy, Far West Research Laboratory and Saybrook Graduate Institute; Bela Antal Banathy of the International Society of the Systems Sciences; Wilfred Shearer, The Franklin Group Inc., Eleanor Vogt and Lou Diamond, National Patient Safety Foundation; LaDonna Harris and Laura Harris, Americans for Indian Opportunity; Larry Magliocca, Caroline Coston and Cesar D'Agord, The Center for Populations with Special Needs of The University of Ohio; Theodoros Tsekos, Hellenic National Center for Public Administration; Alexander Lane and William Darrow, Schering Plough Research Institute, Robert McDonald of the US National Forest Service, Marios Michaelidis and Noni Diakou of The Cyprus Academy for Public Administration, Janet Crow and Lisa Taylor of the Forum of ESRD Networks, Tom Parker of the Chronic Kidney Disease Initiative, Karen Sanders of Leading Design International, Tom Watkins, Jackie

Thompson, Beth Steenwyk, Karen Rockhold, David Smith, and Nancy Mincemoyer of the Michigan Department of Education.

Among associates special thanks are due to Tom Flanagan, Kevin Dye, Ali Geranmayeh, Hasan Ozbekhan, Matthew Shapiro, Dimitri Christakis, University of Washington; Chris Feudtner, University of Pennsylvania, Reynaldo Trevino-Cisneros, Roxana Cardenas, Instituto Technologica Estudios; Nicholas Christakis, Harvard University; Ken Bausch, Institute for 21st Century Agoras, Surinder Batra, Center for Interactive Management–India; and Gary Alexander, University of Idaho.

Finally, I want to express my gratitude to the Editor of the Public Management series of the Information Age Publishing, Inc., Professor Nancy Roberts, who gave me intellectual and emotional encouragement and support throughout the hard work of producing the book and meeting the deadlines. Nancy was instrumental in making the book more readable and more transparent to the readers, hopefully. In the final analysis, however, I am fully responsible for the delivery of the concepts included in the book.

—Alexander N. Christakis
Archanes, Crete

# INTRODUCTION

The practice of dialogue should be distinguished from conversations, discussions, debates, or town-hall meetings of the type that have become very fashionable during political campaigns in the USA. Dialogue comes from the Greek work *Dialogos*. *Dia* means "through" and *logos* means "meaning." It implies deep understanding and appreciation of the variety of perspectives and interests surrounding complex issues, such as redesigning public education, reforming health care to insure uninsured people, learning how to promote social and economic development in poor urban communities, preserving the quality of life and environment, to mention a few. The definition of dialogue adopted in this book is: *the participation of observers engaged in creating meaning, wisdom, and action through communicative and collaborative interaction.*

Dialogue, democracy, philosophy (science), and design all grew together in the soil of ancient Greece. Dialogue was the essence of its participative democracy. Plato's *Dialogues* set the exemplar for Western thought. This dialogue was oriented toward designing a good political and social life. The confluence of dialogue, democracy, deep thinking, and design that flowered after the reforms of Solon (c. 600 B.C.) fueled Athens' greatness for centuries.

Eventually, however, democracy was derided as mobocracy because demagogues had led Athens into devastating wars. Plato, for instance, considered it to be better only than chaos. Preferring tyrants and aristocracies, he proposed the ideal of the philosopher king. He and Aristotle believed that political and design decisions needed to be made by experts.

Experts also took over philosophy. Practical philosophy, dealing with individual and social behavior, was advanced by Stoic philosophers, Roman and Canon law, and by Renaissance philosophers and authors. Some of this thought was idealistic, like Thomas More's *Utopia*; some of it was descriptive, like Jonathan Hobbes *Leviathan*; and some of it was ruthlessly practical, like Nicolai Machievelli's *The Prince*.

The desire for certainty evidenced by Descartes has led in our day to a narrowing of the topics upon which philosophy focuses. Social and political philosophy is narrowly functionalist, interested in how things work, not in what a good society would be like. Natural philosophy has morphed into modern science, which abhors moral issues and treats social ones mainly by describing them from the outside.

Today, participative democracy is limited to small select situations. Governments and academia are ruled by experts and power politics. Surprising, perhaps, is the emergence of participative democracy in capitalist enterprises, which are striving to re-invent themselves. This emergence is led by what can be loosely termed "soft systems" facilitators and theoreticians who deal with the human side of social organization.

People all over the world aspire to participative democracy. Unfortunately today, due to the escalating complexity of the Information Age, the participative planning and design of any social system, from cities to national health care programs, is too often not feasible. All of us as observers have experienced information overload and our incapacity to understand and embrace all the aspects of multidimensional social, economic, environmental, political, and technological issues. This phenomenon, when coupled to the increasing lack of the ability to engage stakeholders in meaningful and productive dialogue for defining and resolving complex issues, makes participative democracy an ideal that cannot be realized now and in the future, unless we adopt a new approach.

We want to engage in dialogue in order to gain understanding and build consensus among stakeholders with diverse interests and perspectives. This effort requires the use of a new approach for resolving the complex issues challenging us in the Information Age. Over 30 years ago, a group of researchers began developing and testing a dialogue model for meeting this challenge. Learning about the theory, methodology, and practice of this form of dialogue is the main objective of this book.

The thesis advocated and elaborated in the chapters that follow is:

> *As human evolution is experiencing the complex challenges of the Information Age, humanity cannot take responsibility for guiding its evolution without the capacity to surface the will and wisdom of the people by engaging them in meaningful dialogue in the context of the emerging Agoras (meeting spaces) of the 21st century Global Village.*

It is my intent to make this thesis transparent to the reader.

*Part I* of this book, *Evolution of Dialogue*, recounts the origins of Greek democracy that establish the image of people freely deciding their future. It also tells of the demise and weaknesses of that democracy. It describes the allure of participative democratic design and the problems it faces in the context of globalization. It also indicates the unshakeable burdens of dialogue that wreak havoc on undisciplined design efforts.

*Part II, Architecture of the Structured Design Process (SDP)*, spells out the components of SDP: its consensus methods, distinctive language patterns, role responsibilities, stages of inquiry, software, collaborative facility, and dialogue laws.

*Part III, Co-Laboratories in Action*, describes successful applications of SDP that exemplify the workings of SDP in redesigning a large organization, introducing a new product, developing ecological strategy. The cases come from the domains of health care, ecology, and non-profit organizations.

*Part IV, A Science of Dialogic Design*, describes the context of this science. It expounds its axioms, key definitions, and six dialogue laws. It explains the kind of science underlying the SDP Architecture and offers metrics for measuring observer diversity and situational complexity. The metrics are useful in determining the relevancy and applicability of the SDP to a particular complex situation.

*Part V, Constructing the Future*, describes the transformational leadership that enables construction of the future initiatives and proposes a framework for developing that leadership.

"Developing meaningful Take-aways from Co-op Experience"?

# Part I

## EVOLUTION OF DIALOGUE

Participative dialogue is the essence of democratic design. Its origin in the Agora of Athens is the iconic forerunner of the Structured Design Process (SDP). SDP is a designing process that updates participative democracy so that it can function in the agoras of the Information Age.

Governments, corporations, and other groups have failed to master the participative democracy and interdisciplinary dialogue that they espouse. This failure trumpets the need for an effective structured dialogue process that will enable stakeholders to design their futures. The largely unstructured dialogue in the Greek agoras was a wonder for its time, but it had great weaknesses. When we try to guide our Information Age organizations with the same unstructured dialogue, those weaknesses increase exponentially.

CHAPTER 1

# CLASSIC ATHENIAN DEMOCRACY

## Many Thanks to Plutarch

The Greeks emerged from their Dark Ages in the 8th century B.C. with the appearance of Homer and monarchical city-states. They plunged into cut-throat mining and commerce with no regard for the rights of the disenfranchised. They were pursuing the ancient virtues of *habrosyne,* which valued wealth, power, and ostentation as supreme goods. They even resorted to enslaving their countrymen. As the rich prospered, the poor grew desperate.

In 632 B.C., the wealthy aristocracy replaced the Athenian monarch with their own government in which they elected one of themselves *Archon* (ruler) each year and appointed a council of ex-Archons as an advisory council. In 621, Dracon, the ruling *Archon,* established severe laws to bring order to Athens' civil strife. These Draconian laws prescribed death for many crimes. Dracon is reported by Plutarch to have said, "We need the death penalty to prevent small crimes, and for the big ones I cannot think of any greater punishment." These same laws authorized a creditor to enslave a defaulting debtor and his family to get money to pay off the debt. The cruelty and arrogance (*habrosyne*) of the rich caused the poor to form into gangs to save themselves and rescue those who had been made slaves through usury.

*How People Harness Their Collective Wisdom and Power,* pages 3–5
Copyright © 2006 by Information Age Publishing

3

Solon, a well-traveled merchant and poet grew up in this Draconian Athens. He was noted for his moderation (*sophrosyne*). He wrote:

> The man whose riches satisfy his greed
> Is not more rich for all those heaps and hoards
> Than some poor man who has enough to feed
> And clothe his corpse with such a God affords.
>
> I have no use for men who steal and cheat:
> The fruit of evil poisons those who eat.
>
> Some wicked men are rich, some good men poor,
> But I would rather trust in what's secure;
> Our virtue sticks with us and makes us strong,
> But money changes owners all day long.
>
> —recorded by Plutarch

In 580, both rich and poor were sick of the constant civil strife. The aristocrats of Athens saw Solon as someone who was partial to neither the rich nor the poor, and they asked him to lead. The rich consented because Solon was wealthy, and the poor consented because he was honest.

Solon's first reform was forbidding mortgages on bodies. Even with the consent of the debtor, the creditor could no longer legally enslave him and his family. Those who had already become slaves were liberated, and those who had been sold to foreigners returned to Athens as free men. Solon also ordered that all outstanding debts were forgiven, so all mortgages on land disappeared. He went on to repeal the death penalty for all crimes except murder and manslaughter.

Neither the rich nor the poor got what they wanted from Solon's reforms. The poor did not get complete redistribution of wealth and the wealthy were angry over the loss of money they were owed. With time and success, however, he won their forgiveness. When the Athenians saw the good result of the release of debts, they appointed Solon general reformer of their law.

With the replacement of *habrosyne* by *sophrosyne* (moderation, Golden Mean) advocated by Solon, the Athenians did not renounce competition (*eris*); they even deified it in the goddess Eris, but they demanded a level playing field. This combination of fairness and moderation created an environment in the *agora* of Athens for the growth of democracy.

Although Solon's democracy was interrupted by Peristratus, a tyrant whose family ruled until 508 B.C., Cleisthenes restored representation and put Athenian democracy on a sound footing. From this foundation, the Athenians constructed a democracy that ushered in a glorious century of sculpture, architecture, drama, philosophy, citizen army and navy, and all the vigorous achievements of a free people.

Athenians experienced the liabilities of democracy along with its achievements. For example, they had no structured safeguards to protect them from demagogues. The intrigue of Alcibiades (a student of Socrates) who incited Athens to attack Syracuse, another democratic city-state in Sicily, is an outstanding example. After ten years of indecisive leadership, missed opportunities, deception, the intervention of Sparta, and unbelievably bad luck, Athens was defeated. They were utterly and entirely defeated; their sufferings were on an enormous scale; their losses were, as they say, total; army, navy, everything was destroyed, and out of many, only a few returned. So ended the events in Sicily (Thucydides).

At the same time in Athens, Plato and Aristotle endured this civic agony and neither of them had anything good to say about democracy. Plato ranked democracy just above chaos as a form of government, putting even tyranny above it with aristocracy higher still and the Philosopher King at the acme of good government. Aristotle considered democracy to be "mob rule." An Athenian known as the Old Oligarch in about 420 makes the case against democracy this way: "Democracy is appalling, since it represents the rule of the poor, ignorant, fickle, and stupid majority over the socially and intellectually superior minority, the world turned upside down" (Cartledge, 2005).

The indecisiveness displayed by democracy in endeavors such as the disaster at Syracuse led many Athenians to favor aristocratic, oligarchic, and even tyrannical forms of government over democracy. For that reason, tyrants ruled Athens intermittently for centuries. Eventually, warfare between Athens and Sparta, spurred largely by pride and democratic bellicosity, brought Athens to ruin.

The Athenians were a proud, vigorous, combative, and maritime people. Their strength and glory stemmed largely from their dedication to the state that they had democratically put together. This strength was never so evident as in their defeat (aided by Sparta) of the Persians under Cyrus the Great, in which they pitted their volunteer army and navy against the massive might of Cyrus' mercenaries. Citizen volunteer foot soldiers (hoplites) and sailors, such as Socrates, fought with a cleverness and fierceness that turned the tide.

\* \* \*

Our civilization faces a crisis much more complex than that posed to the Greeks by the Persian invasion. Will we invent a form of dialogue to support democracy that is up to the challenges of the Information Age?

CHAPTER 2

# THE ALLURE
# OF PARTICIPATIVE
# DEMOCRACY

The dialogue that is integral to participative democracy attracts us because it is necessary for personal and organizational health. This kind of dialogue gives us meaningful input into the direction of our lives and the design of our futures.

## WE WANT TO BE HEARD

We all want to be heard. We seek a welcoming audience for our ideas, feelings, and plans. How frustrating is it when people reject our observations, won't even hear them, or worse, ignore us completely.

We all need to be heard. If our cries as babies had not been heard, we would not now be alive. If parental figures had not reacted to us with approval and disapproval as we were growing up, we would never have formed a stable personality. If people ignore and reject us, they deny our importance and even our autonomy.

Healthy families and high-performance work teams listen to all their members and honor each member's autonomy. They draw upon their collective wisdom. This wisdom is more than the sum of their parts.

In a larger context, organizations and societies must be responsive to their stakeholders if they are to sustain their viability and vigor. Even dictatorships have to meet minimal standards of responsiveness if they are to avoid revolutions. The movement toward "flat hierarchies" in business recognizes the importance of wisdom that a company possesses everywhere in its chain of command. For example, in the context of the postmodern management paradigm, to increase productivity management gurus urge companies to practice varieties of participative democracy by establishing cross-functional teams that share leadership in order to meet the demands of change more efficiently.

The virtues of participative democracy stem from its openness to all kinds of opinions from all kinds of stakeholders. When people and their positions are respectfully listened to in an activity, they are involved. When decisions are made on an equitable basis, people support those decisions and are likely to work for their implementation. Democracies since the heyday of Athens have surpassed their adversaries with the vigor of their convictions. Such openness and fairness unleashes the wisdom and the power of a people.

There are two related vices of participative democracy. One is its vulnerability to abuse. Certain people tend to dominate the discourse by reason of their riches, power, prominence, expertise or insistence. The autonomy of many stakeholders is not respected. Factions develop. Debate trumps dialogue. Power dominates over reason, common sense, and community wisdom.

The other vice of democracy is its inability to transact complex business in an efficient way. We have all sat through endless meetings that never came to a rational conclusion, where nothing was decided or decisions were made not on the basis of reason, but simply out of fatigue. We all have experiences of disengaging from the discussion and letting others dominate the discourse and make the decisions.

Because of the cumbersome nature of participation, democracy has undergone historic transformations that speed the decision-making process but lose its participative virtues. In the history of Western government, we have pro- (or re-) gressed from participative democracy, to representative democracy, to government by experts, to government for corporate interests. In effect, we have returned to the plutocracy from which democracy strove to free us. There must be ways that we can engage in democratic dialogue to attain decision-making efficiency while retaining participative openness and fairness.

The vices of undisciplined dialogue were painfully evident to me when, as a young man (c. 1970), I participated in the Delos Conversations organized by the Greek architect Dinos Doxiadis, the formative processes of the Club of Rome under the leadership of the Italian industrialist Aurelio Peccei, and the Academy for Contemporary Problems established and sponsored by the Battelle Memorial Institute in the early 1970s. I observed outstanding authorities in economics, sociology, biology, psychology, anthropology, environmental science, philosophy, and politics as they came together to address looming world crises, envision fruitful responses, and strive for a conscious evolution toward a humane future. These authorities conversed efficiently within their own disciplinary boundaries, but were frustrated in their attempts to span boundaries. Their differences in expectations and semantics stunted productive communication.

## THE MOVE TOWARD TEAMWORK

In the Fall of 1992, an issue of *Business Week* magazine on "Reinventing America" advocated a postmodern paradigm for managers. The major emphasis of this paradigm is on teamwork over individualism. Leading business thinkers and top executives argued that interdisciplinary teams, which meld the skills, experiences, and insights of several people, would outperform any individual in the Information Age. The "quality movement" of the '90s, in which teams played a key role, required companies to organize interdisciplinary teams for accomplishing specific tasks and to abandon the traditional manner of organizing around functions such as marketing and finance. Major corporations like IBM, General Motors and others, tried at that time to reinvent themselves and to embody the postmodern paradigm of cross-functional teams. Most of these well-intentioned efforts, however, failed because the leadership of these organizations did not grasp how difficult it is to engage team members in true dialogue on complex interdisciplinary issues (Roberts, 2002). Without productive cross-functional dialogue these teams were not able to collectively converge on a consensus action plan for implementation.

During the same decade, President Clinton aspired to "reinvent government." He encouraged dialogue among critical governmental agencies and set up inter-agency teams for managing complex public policy issues. Major newspapers in the United States, like the *Philadelphia Inquirer*, constantly reported on the government's inability to solve acute social problems, such as inner city deterioration and drug use, organizing the health care system to provide insurance for all Americans, the failure of urban schools to provide good quality education, and many other problems. During that decade, many editorials called for measures to improve the quality of dialogue among the relevant stakeholders to help them build consensus. Again, as we will see in many examples of citizen participation, not much was accomplished because the citizen/stakeholders were unable to engage in productive dialogue.

Thus, even in the face of acute problems, the best intentions in management thought and governance style have had little impact in bringing about the desirable changes advocated by the postmodern management paradigm. What is needed is to reinvent participative democracy. The new democracy for the Information Age should enable people from all walks of life to participate in a true dialogue focused on designing their communities and achieving their goals. In most social systems today, true dialogue among people with diverse, and sometimes conflicting interests, does not happen. This book aims to change that.

## INTERDISCIPLINARY DIALOGUE

In the early '70s at a prominent research institute, researchers observed the deliberations of an interdisciplinary team of managers, political and social scientists, psychologists, architects and engineers working on the design of a hypothetical city of one million people. The researchers concluded that the team of participants was not capable of producing a consensus design of the hypothetical city even though the requisite disciplinary expertise was represented on the team. It became apparent to the researchers that the language used in interdisciplinary team meetings was inferior—in terms of discipline and depth of meaning—to the language used in single-discipline team meetings.

In the single discipline teams, participating experts used scientific terminology and models that provided rigor and transparency to their deliberations. During interdisciplinary team meetings, however, the experts lacked a common scientific language and used ordinary language by necessity as their means of interaction and communication. As a result, they could not engage in *science-based interdisciplinary dialogue;* could not integrate their diverse knowledge across disciplines; and, as a result, were unable to adequately design the hypothetical new city.

The researchers concluded that participation by the various disciplines, although necessary, was not sufficient. What was needed, they said, were aids that would help members of the interdisciplinary team to engage in high quality dialogue across disciplinary boundaries, just as they do within the boundaries of individual disciplines. Without new process methodologies and models, experts could not engage in interdisciplinary dialogue, and therefore could not integrate their diversity of knowledge and wisdom.

These findings triggered the search for a new process. The principal utility of the process would be to enable all people to participate in finding solutions to complex problems affecting the quality of their lives independent of their discipline, experience, or educational background. It also would lead to cooperation with the other stakeholders of a particular situation, by excavating the wisdom of the people through structured dialogue. Thirty years of research, development, and testing, in a variety of complex situations, both in the private and public sectors, have produced the Structured Design Process (SDP) that engages stakeholders in participative democracy through disciplined dialogue. Workshops using SDP are called Co-Laboratories of Democracy because they enable people to harness their collective wisdom and power to construct the future.

As mentioned before, the thesis advocated in this book is that disciplined dialogue can excavate the wisdom of the people, and therefore it is the necessary prerequisite for the guided evolution of society. Furthermore, without people's participation in dialogue they are not likely to exercise their "community power," which is the meaning of the Greek word "Democracy." This is the essence of participative democracy. On account of the escalating complexity of the Information Age, however, it is much more difficult now to engage people in dialogue than it was during the Golden Age of the Athenian Republic, 2,500 years ago. As we will see in Part IV by using a quantitative metric to measure the complexity of a situation, the complexity of issues addressed in the Agoras of Athens during the Golden Age was at least one order of magnitude less than the complexity of issues facing stakeholders in the Information Age.

The level of complexity confronting the citizens and the leadership of ancient Athens was much lower than that confronting the citizens of the Information Age. For example, two thousand five hundred years ago Pericles, the leader of the Athenian Republic during its Golden Age, could stroll from one end of the city of Athens to the other in fifteen minutes. During his stroll Pericles could capture the pulse of the city by talking to the Athenians, and did not need any sophisticated polling techniques of the type political leaders are using today. The President of the United States could not stroll today in the capital city of Washington, D.C., even if he wanted to interact with the citizenry. In addition to the larger scale of Washington, as compared to ancient Athens, the President today would have to be accompanied by numerous Secret Service Agents for safety reasons, which is another indicator of the complexity we are facing today.

The critical question is: *Given the complexity of political, social, economic, and technological issues of the Information Age, and the strong linkages among those issues, is it reasonable to expect that the approach for engaging people in dialogue 2,500 years ago during the Golden Age of the Athenians would work today?*

## THE PROMISE OF DEMOCRACY

In a classic article in the *Harvard Business Review,* published in March–April 1964, and re-published twenty-six years later, titled *Democracy is Inevitable,* Philip Slater and Warren Bennis write:

> Democracy (whether capitalist or socialist is not an issue here) is the only system that can successfully cope with the changing demands of contemporary civilization. We are not necessarily endorsing democracy as such; one might reasonably argue that industrial civilization is pernicious and should be abolished. We suggest merely that given a desire to survive in this civilization, democracy is the most effective means to this end.

The authors declare that the inhabitants of the modern world need to become adaptive to change because of the momentum created by increasing technological innovation. Change has become a permanent and accelerating factor of life. If citizens and organizations are to survive, they need to adapt. To do that, their best strategy is to discard the military-bureaucratic model and to adopt the more suitable scientific model. To the question "why is science gaining acceptance as a model?" Slater and Bennis offered a prophetic answer over a quarter-century ago:

> Science is winning out because the challenge facing modern enterprises are knowledge-gathering, truth-requiring dilemmas. Managers are not scientists, nor do we expect them to be. But the processes of problem solving, conflict resolution, and recognition of dilemmas has great kinship with the academic pursuit of truth. The institution of science is the only institution based on and geared for change. It is built not only to adapt to change, but also to overthrow and create change. So it is and will be with modern industrial enterprises.

Slater and Bennis further explain what they mean by "democracy." For them, democracy is neither capitalism nor socialism. They see no linkage to the free-market economy in their definition. They stress the values of the democratic ideal. Democracy for them is a system of values—a climate of beliefs governing behavior—that people affirm by their deeds as well as their words. These values include:

- Full and free communication, regardless of rank and power;
- A reliance on consensus rather than coercion or compromise to manage conflict;
- The idea that influence is based on technical competence and knowledge rather than on the vagaries of personal whims or prerogative of power;

- An atmosphere that permits and even encourages emotional expression as well as task-oriented behavior;
- A basically human bias, one that accepts the inevitability of conflict between the organization and the individual, but is willing to cope with and mediate this conflict on rational grounds.

These democratic values resonate around the world. They have, for example, commonality with Middle Eastern values. Emotional expression is encouraged, community consensus is esteemed, and mechanisms are sought for balancing power so that it is not abused. These values are points of agreement with people outside the Western democratic framework and are a good starting point for cross-cultural dialogue.

These values resonated for Mikhail Gorbachev whose *glasnost* opened Russia to the transforming power of democracy and loosened its hold on its satellite countries. He presided over the break-up of the Soviet Empire and emerged as an advocate for a "multi-polar, multi-centric" democratic, humanistic new world order.

In a speech given in Philadelphia on April 14, 1993, Gorbachev said: "I firmly believe that the civilization of the 21st century should be built on a balance of interests rather than a balance of forces." He added that by interests he did not mean just economic interests but the broader interests of humankind. He and his colleagues at the Gorbachev Foundation, a Moscow think-tank he heads, have been making a blueprint of the kind of New World order that should evolve. They also believe in the inevitability of democracy. They visualize a new order in which neither a few states nor a group of states would dominate totally. The new order would be based on respect for individual rights and on collective responsibility. To be sure, this is not the new order that has emerged in the beginning of the 21st century where the forces of western style globalization impacts on indigenous people around the world.

Valuable as the blueprints from the Gorbachev Foundation might be, Information Age democracy will not emerge unless people from all walks of life engage in disciplined dialogue. For example, people need to address the issue of globalization along with all the experts—the economists, lawyers, journalists, think-tank analysts, and ex-politicians. The public itself— civic organizations, trade unions, environmentalists, ethnic and racial minorities, businessmen, scientists, and social systems scientists—need to weigh in and be heard. To meet this challenge for inclusivity, a grand transformation is needed in the ways people engage in dialogue. We need the new process in order to construct and experience the new 21st century Agoras.

## DEMOCRACY IN THE CONTEXT OF GLOBALIZATION

Thomas Friedman (2000) in his book *The Lexus and the Olive Tree* writes:

> In the Cold War system, the most likely threat to your olive tree was from another olive tree. It was from your neighbor coming over, violently digging up your olive tree and planting his on its place. That threat has not been eliminated today, but, for the moment, it has been diminished in many parts of the world. The biggest threat today to your olive tree is likely to come from the Lexus—from all the anonymous, transnational, homogenizing, standardizing market forces and technologies that make up today's globalizing economic system. There are some things about this system that make the Lexus so overpowering it can overrun and overwhelm every olive tree in sight— breaking down communities, steamrolling environments and crowding out traditions—and this can produce a real olive tree backlash. But there are other things about this system that empower even the smallest, weakest political community to actually use the new technologies and markets to preserve their olive trees, their culture and identity.

The world has changed since the end of the Cold War. In the misleading shorthand of the time, we used to frame the world as a battleground between Democracy and Communism. In our naiveté, we conveniently overlooked a deeper global division between the unstoppable force of Westernizing globalization and the immovable object of traditional culture.

The current debates over globalization bring this conflict into central focus. It is described in various dichotomies:

- The Lexus and the Olive Tree—Friedman (2000)
- Jihad vs. McWorld—Barber (1995)
- Business Class (existing Washington consensus) and Prism (sectarian traditionalism)—Shell's Global Scenarios to 2020.

To many Westerners, globalization is an unstoppable and benign force that will spread understanding, freedom, and global harmony. To other Westerners and most traditional peoples, globalization is a steamroller that threatens their culture and livelihood.

How we handle these ideological clashes determines the prosperity, sustainability, and humaneness of the world's future. If we are to take responsibility for our evolution, and avoid being pawns of a monolithic system, we need powerful new tools for dialogue and democracy (Banathy, 1996). We need to enlarge our capacity to engage multi-lingual, multicultural, and geographically dispersed stakeholders in boundary-spanning dialogue among civilizations (Lopez-Garay, 2001).

As Banathy (2000) writes:

Dialogue is a vehicle for understanding cultures and subcultures in organizations. And organizational learning depends upon such cultural understanding. It facilitates the development of a common language and collective mental models. Thus, the ability to engage in dialogue becomes one of the most fundamental and most needed human capabilities. Dialogue becomes a central component of any model of evolutionary transformation.

Western people who engage in boundary-spanning dialogue and work toward a global-spanning value system see democratic values as the starting point. They do not, however, give blanket endorsement to the democracy we know and practice today. They challenge us to practice what can be defined as an Information Age democracy, where every person has the opportunity to participate and to influence the evolutionary process of humanity, and is responsible for it. This kind of democracy has deep roots in many traditional cultures, such as the Native Americans. It provides a welcome open space where all cultures can engage in productive dialogue for evolutionary transformation.

The Internet provides an example of the lifting power of a non-factional style of globalization. It offers democratic access to all points of view. As important as television has been in democratizing information all over the planet, the Internet is at the pinnacle of this trend. The Internet is totally decentralized, no one owns it, no one can turn it off; it has the potential of reaching in every home in the world. Internet technology, if properly utilized for the conscious evolution of humanity, has a major role to play in the Information Age democracy. It can do so because it promotes boundary-spanning dialogue across geographically dispersed civilizations and communities.

If we assume that the trend towards globalization is irreversible, we face the major challenge of finding the appropriate social balance that will democratize globalization (Friedman, 2000, p. 444). At the minimum, we must as a people discover a new social compact that embraces both the free markets of globalization and cultural-sensitivity to the needs of as many people as possible. In this process, we will be embracing conscious evolution and help the civilizations of planet Earth to engage in a dialogue as defined by Herman Lopez-Garay (2001, p. 18):

> Intercultural dialogue should aim at disclosing the foundation of the way of being of the participating cultures—their particular cultivation of their collective way of life—so that in the context of such display of ways of being human, "we" the human race can discover our humanity as a whole and hence disclose a new way of transcendence, a new way of being together at a global scale.

CHAPTER 3

# THE UNSHAKEABLE HUMAN BURDENS OF DIALOGUE

**W**ithout a framework of disciplined inquiry that permits organizational learning in an explicit way, the theories-in-use by individuals engaged in dialogue are undisciplined and muddling. Lacking disciplined inquiry to prevent this situation, the authenticity of the stakeholders is compromised and their voices are silenced, and inferior designs are produced. This muddling should not be attributed to the bad will of individuals or groups. It is caused by the unshakeable human burdens of dialogue.

Three decades of research have revealed unshakeable human burdens that undermine successful dialogue. The first two types of burdens include well-documented research into (a) human limitations of cognition, and (b) group pathologies (individual, group, and collective). The third burden relates to (c) the current focus of critical theorists, namely: the impact of power relations (Ulrich, 1983).

## THE LIMITS OF HUMAN COGNITION

"7 ± 2" (Miller, 1956) expresses the limits of human short-term (working) memory, that our working memory can handle only 5–9 items at a time. These limits on our working memory place severe constraints on the practice of community decision-making and design. If these constraints are not honored, we overload our cognitive capacities and lose our capacity to rec-

*How People Harness Their Collective Wisdom and Power*, pages 17–21
Copyright © 2006 by Information Age Publishing

ognize differences that make a difference. In our overloaded state we overlook important information and cripple our ability to create good designs. As a consequence, in any social system designing situation, however complex, the design dialogue should not require the designers to deal with more than nine items simultaneously, and usually should involve fewer.

In the fast pace of today, the leisurely pace set in traditional democracy and academic research is a luxury we cannot afford. How then can we carefully include the views of all stakeholders, let them explain what they mean, and simultaneously honor the limits of short-tem memory and keep pace?

## GROUP PATHOLOGIES

Group dialogue work may become seriously frustrating when several types of social-emotional problems occur. Bales (1951) identified how individuals can disrupt the work of groups through expressing negative social-emotional behaviors. For a host of reasons individuals in group situations:

- Vent their anger and frustration;
- Perceive the situation as a threat to their self-interests;
- Use the situation to get attention;
- Dominate the group; or
- Follow some inappropriate strategy to meet a social or emotional need.

Most groups find it difficult to confront these types of issues without assistance.

Tuckman (1965) characterized a typical pattern of group activities consisting of four stages:

1. Forming (group members begin to develop initial stages of group identity);
2. Storming (the inherent conflicts of differing views and approaches to the task surface);
3. Norming (consensual arrangements permit the group to proceed); and
4. Performing (group members may now contribute to the group task).

Unaided group dynamics is a developmentally fragile process. Many groups do not develop beyond the storming stages. This fact has contributed to the increased use of facilitators for group meetings. An "outside" facilitator may be successful in reaching the Norming stage of group process since that may be the implicit justification for bringing in a facilitator. However, putting aside the individual fallibilities for the moment, a group addressing a complex design situation most likely will not be able to reach the Performing stage even when the goal of redesigning the situation is embraced by all. This in fact was the phenomenon observed early on in the interdisciplinary dialogue of the hypothetical city project and the Club of Rome initiative, as discussed earlier. In neither one of those designing situations were the teams able to perform.

Since most group dialogue work is done either within or between organizations, the context of change is fundamentally important. What are the operational beliefs about change expressed or implied by the top managers of participating organizations? Do these managers see change as systemic, episodic, or expedient?

If systemic, the context of change will be more comprehensive and inclusive of stakeholders. Systemic change takes time and requires acknowledgement that the time scale for design will need to be adjusted.

If managers see the need for change to be episodic, they send a clear message to the group that they should quickly reach a solution. In this situation, a group will feel rushed. They will experience considerable pressure to hold questions and to avoid proposing untested ideas. The group dialogue may short circuit on the question, "What does management want?" The group may believe that management knows what it wants, but is going through the motions of securing others' inputs.

In short, groups under this kind of pressure use rough strategies that attempt to avoid threat or embarrassment (Argyris, 1982). Rather than creating knowledge, these strategies fatigue and intimidate stakeholders. They induce people to agree with those members of the group who dominate the discourse.

## UNEQUAL POWER RELATIONS

The third burden, the impact of power relations, is the least understood pathology. The conveners of dialogue may overlook its influence since most organizations assume the hierarchical power structures of positional authority that have dominated the industrial era. Organizational managers in the upper levels of authority are assumed to know more about what should be done. They expect deferential treatment and are given it in designing situations by most conventional dialogical processes. In a similar fashion, those individuals with superior communicative competence dominate group processes by intimidating others through the ease and quantity of their wordsmithing. This phenomenon has been referred in the literature of group dynamics as the "prima donna effect." In the social systems designing literature (Banathy, 1996), the issue becomes: Who is responsible for designing the system? When experts design social systems for the stakeholders, instead of stakeholders designing their own social systems, stakeholder ownership and commitment to implementation is marginalized.

Dialogue is not substantively possible in a group situation where unequal power relations permeate the consciousness of the group. Power for the individual will be equated with the capacity to act. If people perceive that they are powerless, their involvement will be superficial and their commitment to action inconsequential. An acceptable design process needs to build in equitable power relations.

Michel Foucault's work, *Power/Knowledge* (1980), presents a liberating vision of power relations as a constructive, positive force. For him, power occurs in a relational mode through the events of dialogue, which construct the social reality of the participants. Power is an emergent characteristic in the complex behavioral relationships of people. To the extent that knowledge is shared and created, the relational affinity is empowering to all. Power is not about "agency." It is a social reality of relational affinities constructed through dialogue. As Foucault states it:

> In thinking of the mechanism of power, I am thinking of its capillary form of existence, the point where power reaches into the very grain of individuals, touches their bodies and inserts itself into their actions and attitudes, their discourses, learning processes and everyday lives. (p. 39)

In this capillary form, power is manifested in the distinctions made by individuals and accepted by groups. Through the group construction of high quality observations, individuals and groups are transformed. Experience has shown, that this transformational effect cannot be induced by posting "rules of equitable power relations" on the wall of a meeting facility, or lecturing a group on how to be empowered. It must become the social fabric of the dialogue process. The stakeholders must experience equitable power relations in the context of the transformative power of dialogue as described by Roberts (2002).

## A FUMBLED OPPORTUNITY

Many golden opportunities for significant change have been met with well-intentioned efforts that floundered for the lack of proper scientific practice. An example of such an opportunity was offered by President Clinton when he invited a community of stakeholders to attend the Northwest forest conference held on April 2, 1993. The purpose of this conference was to search for a consensus in the economy vs. environment conflict. Without action by the government, timber harvesting in the coastal forests of Northern California, Oregon and Washington was about to come to a standstill; but any decision that resumed logging at high levels could drive the northern spotted owl and a number of other forest animals into extinction. The President convened the forest conference in order to hear the views of the stakeholders first hand. The day before the conference he told the Portland *Oregonian* newspaper: "The prospect that these meetings might actually be used as a method of governing . . . is quite exhilarating."

Unfortunately, three months after President Clinton, Vice President Gore and the Administration's domestic cabinet officers convened the one-day Northwest forest conference, the situation got worse. At this conference, President Clinton predicted that he would probably make no one happy in the end. It is hard to believe that when the President of the United States personally moderates and listens to the different points of view of the stakeholders, the decisions made by the Administration would not please the majority. However, assuming that bringing the parties of interest to the table is sufficient for the resolution of a *complex issue* is erroneous. Twenty years of experience in the development and testing of the "science of complexity" has shown that unless the parties participate in a process of a true dialogue, enabling them to collectively define the complex issue, the situation usually gets worse.

After the conference, employing the "conventional wisdom" paradigm of fragmentation of the complex system, President Clinton appointed three working teams, one to focus on the science of the issue, one to look at the economics, and one to try to un-knot all the complex and intertwined responsibilities among governmental agencies. In other words, he trusted the knowledge of experts instead of the wisdom of the people.

In June 1993, after the three teams gave the White House their initial recommendations, it was reported in the *Los Angeles Times* that major interest groups on all sides began voicing their dissatisfaction with the findings and recommendations of the working teams. In light of the approach used to engage the interested parties, the escalation of the conflict is not a surprise to those familiar with the management of complexity.

Logger, Buzz Eades, made the most profound statement at the forest conference. Sitting next to the President, he said at one point that he was not always convinced by biological science or economic science in the dispute between trees and jobs. Then he told the President, "I am full of hope because I believe I am sitting beside a man who believes in people science." The hopes of Eades and the President were dashed because the "people science" they attempted to employ did not sufficiently trust people and was inappropriate science.

# Part II

## ARCHITECTURE OF THE
## STRUCTURED DESIGN PROCESS (SDP)

---

**O**ver the last 30 years, researchers have applied, sometimes invented, and tested various components that would enable effective large group dialogue. They experimented with various combinations of those components in designing situations. They have settled on the following as essential components of SDP architecture. Part II details the SDP components and their evolution. Part III will then describe how the architecture is actualized in Co-Laboratories of Democracy

### TABLE 4–1
### COMPONENTS OF SDP

The Architecture of SDP is composed of 31 component constructs, which have been grouped into seven modules. The seven modules, and the approximate time period of their development, are:

A. **6 Consensus Methods:** (1) Nominal Group Technique, (2) Interpretive Structural Modeling, (3) DELPHI, (4) Options Field, (5) Options Profile, and (6) Trade-off Analysis (Years 1972–1982);

B. **7 Language Patterns:** (1) Elemental observation, (2) *Problematique*, (3) Influence tree pattern, (4) Options field pattern, (5) Options profile/scenario pattern, (6) Superposition pattern, and (7) Action plan pattern (Years 1970–1989);

C. **3 Application Time Phases:** (1) Discovery, (2) Designing, and (3) Action (Years 1989–2001)

D. **3 Key Role Responsibilities:** (1) Context—Inquiry Design Team, (2) Content—Stakeholders/Designers, and (3) Process—Facilitation Team (Years 1982–2002);

E. **4 Stages of Interactive Inquiry:** (1) Definition or Anticipation, (2) Design of Alternatives, (3) Decision, and (4) Action Planning (Years 1989–1995); *Test SDP theory and put into practice!*

F. **Collaborative Software and Facility** (Years 1981–1995); and

G. **6 Dialogue Laws:** Requisite: (1) Variety (Ashby), (2) Parsimony (Miller), (3) Saliency (Boulding), (4) Meaning and Wisdom (Peirce), (5) Authenticity and Autonomy (Tsivacou), and (6) Evolutionary Learning (Dye) (Years 2001–2003).

*Bringing it all together in application*

These component constructs strongly interact in the practice of SDP, as will become transparent in the following chapters. For example, the Discovery phase of Module C is a prerequisite in determining the context for the four stages of interactive inquiry of Module E. Also, in terms of roles and responsibilities, i.e. Module D, the determination of the context through the Discovery phase is the responsibility of the inquiry design team, while the management of the focused and open dialogue during the four interactive inquiry stages (Module E) is the sole responsibility of the facilitation team. In the majority of cases, there are overlaps in terms of roles and responsibilities among the members of the inquiry design and the facilitation team. However, the lead facilitator of the facilitation team should avoid interviewing and interacting with stakeholders during the Discovery phase in order not to compromise his or her neutrality in the eyes of the participants to the co-laboratory.

# CHAPTER 4

# SIX CONSENSUS METHODS

The first task the researchers set for themselves in the '70s while observing the work of the interdisciplinary team designing the hypothetical city was to identify consensus methods that would work in social systems design situations. They borrowed some methods and developed new ones, all the while testing them in the arena of practice. The following consensus methods were developed and/or tested in the years 1972-1982: (1) Nominal Group Technique, (2) Interpretive Structural Modeling, (3) DELPHI, (4) Options Field, (5) Options Profile, and (6) Trade-off Analysis.

## NOMINAL GROUP TECHNIQUE (NGT)

The Nominal Group Technique (NGT), originally invented by Delbecq (1975), asks people to write down their responses to a triggering question, and then share them with the group. It is similar in its intent to ordinary brainstorming techniques, except for a step requiring the participants to silently record their ideas before sharing them with the group. In SDP, it is used instead of brainstorming because it slows down the pace of generation and assimilation of observations, thus enabling all the participants, not just the most dominant ones, to offer their ideas in their own words. If properly applied, the NGT protects the authenticity and autonomy of every observer during the application of SDP.

*How People Harness Their Collective Wisdom and Power*, pages 25–29
Copyright © 2006 by Information Age Publishing

After the initial introductions and socializing in a typical SDP session, the context of the present situation and the process to be employed in the sessions are discussed. Then the triggering question is proposed, clarified, and opened to comment using NGT.

The participants, sometimes arranged 4 or 5 to a table, are given ten minutes to write down their responses to the triggering question. They are given another 10 minutes to discuss those contributions with their tablemates. Then in round robin style one table at a time describes one of its contributions to the whole group. The process continues until all contributions have been heard and recorded.

As these contributions are presented they are projected onto a screen for visual inspection by the group. They are also printed out and posted on a wall. In addition, they are labeled and entered into a database for later recall and use.

In a second round robin, each contribution is clarified by its author who answers clarifying questions proposed by the group. No criticism or altering of a contribution without its author's consent is allowed. Any different interpretation can be entered as a new original contribution.

The result of this use of NGT is a palpable reduction of tension in the room as people realize that their ideas are being heard. Dialogue is actually occurring. Team cohesion is forming.

## INTERPRETATIVE STRUCTURAL MODELING (ISM)

Interpretive Structural Modeling (ISM) is a method invented by John Warfield (1976). It creates the influence trees that identify the crucial root sources among a set of observations that constitute a *Problematique,* or a "mess" of a deeply enmeshed situation. Discovering the root sources of a *Problematique* has major implications in terms of stakeholders identifying a set of truly effective corrective actions.

In SDP, ISM makes explicit the perceived relationships among proposed problems or solutions in complex situations. Using the tools of mathematical set theory and logic, it tracks the long and deep logic expressed by stakeholder/designers as they decide whether the accomplishment of proposal **A** would significantly help in accomplishing proposal **B**. If it would, then $A \rightarrow B$. If **B** would significantly help to accomplish **C**, then $B \rightarrow C$. Therefore, $A \rightarrow C$. This propagating relationship (mathematic transitive property) is augmented by using the cyclical relationship: if $A \rightarrow B$ and $B \rightarrow A$, then $A \leftrightarrow B$, in which case, **A** and **B** are said to cycle on each other.

In SDP co-laboratories, a programmed computer keeps track of the long and deep logic between decisions made on the basis of the paired relational judgments by the participants. Long logic is of the form: if A influences B; and B influences C; therefore, A influences C. Deep logic is more complicated. For instance,

if C ==> D and E, and D =/=> C but E ==> C, and also E ==> D,
then C <==> E and are basically equivalent in their influencing
and together (C + E) ==> D.

In doing this logic for the stakeholders, the software frees them to deal with matters that really concern them without needing to constantly reorganize their conceptual maps.

With a few added premises, our deliberations on paired relationships would produce a "tree of meaning" such as the following. It depicts the most influential agent(s) (A in our example) at the root of the tree, with B the second from the bottom row, C and E, on the third row, and D (and F) on the fourth. This primitive tree might look like this:

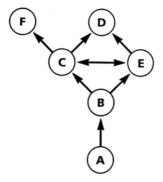

A more complex tree produced in an actual design situation would have a similar structure. As in this example, it would indicate the roots and "deep drivers" of a messy situation and indicate where action needs to be taken to achieve an organization's objectives.

A tree of meaning, or influence tree, indicates the *influence* that observations, such as problems or solution actions, have on each other. It is a vast improvement over any mere *importance* ranking because it actually indicates what needs to be addressed to really change a situation, i.e., to really do conscious evolution. Usually, the observations that are deemed most important are not nearly as influential as are other more mundane alternatives. [See next chapter for a graphic representation of an influence tree.] Importance voting identifies symptomatic problems, while influence voting identifies the root causes for these problems.

## DELPHI

DELPHI, invented by researchers at the RAND Corporation in the 60's, is a widely used method for gathering responses to key questions from panels of experts/participants who are geographically dispersed. In SDP, DELPHI is used to engage participants remotely in reviewing products of group work generated during the Design phase, i.e., usually after they have experienced a face-to-face interaction as a group.

DELPHI can be used to develop the views of a panel of individuals relative to some issue. It minimizes the role of dominant personalities, removes geographic limitations, allows input from persons who otherwise might not be able to participate, and allows anonymity.

## OPTIONS FIELD

The Options Field method is a computer-assisted learning process that portrays the conceived dimensions of a complex situation, including the simple options available in each dimension and the clusters of interdependent dimensions. It emerges as participants discover relationships of affinity among their observations, and cluster them into similarity categories. The Options Field provides a basis for group dialogue on the saliency of the proposed action options concerning a design, and the means whereby a group design can be continuously updated. [See next chapter for a graphic representation.]

## OPTIONS PROFILE

In the Options Profile method, participants select from the Options Field options that fit within certain contextual action scenarios. Each options profile is a representation of one action scenario developed by the group of participants within the context of the Options Field relevant to the particular design situation. [See next chapter for a graphic representation.]

## TRADE-OFF ANALYSIS

Trade-off analysis enables participants to compare alternative action scenarios, two at a time, and converge on the preferred alternative for implementation. It portrays graphically the central ideas behind a selection. The method is intended to provide for the public sector of government a way of developing a choice through the use of a prescribed set of techniques that allow for broad participation, while at the same time providing a way to reveal all of the steps and procedures that led to a final choice. It is ideal when a choice is a major one, involving a substantial and possibly long-term commitment, with many people wanting to know the basis for the ultimate choice. [See next chapter for a graphic representation.]

All six of these consensus methods are presented in extended and explicit form in Appendix A. With the exception of Trade-off Analysis, they are also illustrated in various stories from the design arena presented in Part III.

# CHAPTER 5

# SEVEN LANGUAGE PATTERNS

Language in this chapter refers to words, graphics, and the verbal/ graphic interface. The ordinary verbal language of elemental observation and dialogue is extremely practical in it's enabling us to exist as social, intelligent humans. In its unaided state, however, it is not adequate for cross-disciplinary research, as was pointed out in the prologue. For that reason, each co-laboratory spends its initial sessions to build up a consensual linguistic domain in which participants come to understand what people mean by their words and the emotions behind them.

In addition to ordinary verbal language, the rigorous language of mathematical logic is employed in SDP sessions, but principally by the software programmed into the computer. This logic can be expressed verbally, in mathematical symbols, or just as sequences in a software program.

Graphic language can convey complex ideas with an immediacy missing from verbal language. The *problematique* language pattern, which portrays the strong interactions among a set of problems or issues giving rise to a "mess, is such a graphic. (A "mess" is a convoluted problem where tinkering with one of its aspects results in changes to all of its aspects, which is the original meaning of Problematique as used by the Club of Rome). A graphic example of a *Problematique* and its deconstruction in elemental observations, which are graphically displayed by geometric shapes, is shown in Figure 5.1.

*How People Harness Their Collective Wisdom and Power*, pages 31–36
Copyright © 2006 by Information Age Publishing

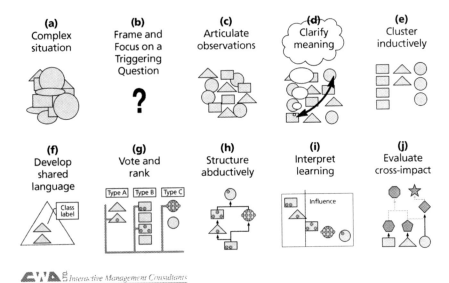

Figure 5.1. A *Problematique* and its deconstruction.

The influence tree pattern, also called a tree of meaning, is the hybrid graphic/textual interpretive construct that visually displays and interprets the relationships discovered with computer assistance during SDP. It is the computer-generated depiction of the results of Interpretative Structural Modeling. A schematic of an influence tree pattern for a set of goals relevant to a situation is shown in Figure 5.2.

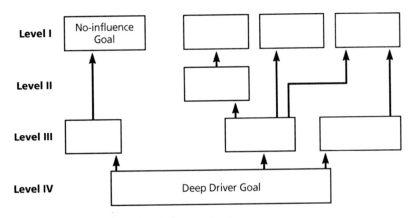

The example shown above is an influence structure.
▲ demonstrates the direction of influence.

Figure 5.2. Influence Tree pattern.

An Options Field pattern is a hybrid depiction of the patterns developed using the Options Field method to categorize action options. An Options Field from Appendix A is shown in Figure 5.3:

| Cluster #1— Redesign | Cluster #2— Priority | Cluster #3— Productivity | Cluster #4— New Business | Cluster #5— Sales Force |
|---|---|---|---|---|
| • **(Option 2)** Develop a clear understanding of roles, responsibilities, and accountability | • **(Option 1)** Adopt a transparent process for project selection and prioritization | • **(Option 5)** Maximize productivity in areas such as R&D | • **(Option 6)** Develop two new business opportunities that are a strategic fit and generate new revenue | • **(Option 8)** Train, motivate, and mobilize field sales force |
| • **(Option 4)** Simplify the organization to make it functional | • **(Option 3)** Develop milestones and a sense of urgency for meeting the milestones | • **(Option 9)** Redesign product development and commercialization and process | • **(Option 12)** Merge with Company XYZ | • **(Option 13)** Reduce sales force by 20% |
| • **(Option 7)** Emphasize everyone's role as a stakeholder in the achievement of strategic objectives | • **(Option 16)** Apply new problem-solving approaches | • **(Option 15)** Discontinue R&D in medical instrumentation | | • **(Option 14)** Design an "idealized" sales force automation system |
| • **(Option 10)** Consolidate certain functions to reduce or eliminate redundancy | | | | |
| • **(Option 11)** Adopt a team-based organization paradigm | | | | |

Figure 5.3.    An Options Field.

An Options Profile is a selection of options from the Options Field that fit with a specific scenario or strategy. In this representation, the options chosen are linked to a "Tie line" to indicate their selection. In Appendix A, interactive and reactive scenarios for a hypothetical case of strategic management are each represented, with their own Options Profile. As shown in Figures 5.4 and 5.5, the chosen options are printed in italics and tied to the tie line. A narrative of the scenario corresponding to the selected Options Profile is also composed to illustrate the translation of the graphic profile to a more conventional prose description. This is the one reason why all the graphic patterns of the SDP are called "translatable graphics."

The Superposition pattern combines the Influence Tree among issues, generated in the Definition stage of the interactive inquiry, with the action options of the Design Alternatives stage, as presented in the Options Profile, to graphically display the impact of selected action options on the roots of the Tree by means of a color-coded master Influence Tree combining problems and solutions. An example from Appendix A is presented in Figure 5.6.

| Example of Interactive Alternative Profile | | | | |
|---|---|---|---|---|
| **Cluster #1—Redesign** | **Cluster #2—Priority** | **Cluster #3—Productivity** | **Cluster #4—New Business** | **Cluster #5—Sales Force** |
| • **(Option 2)** Develop a clear understanding of roles, responsibilities, and accountability | *(Option 1)* Adopt a transparent process for project selection and prioritization | • **(Option 5)** Maximize productivity in areas such as R&D | *(Option 6)* Develop two new business opportunities that are a strategic fit and generate new revenue | *(Option 8)* Train, motivate, and mobilize field sales force |
| • **(Option 4)** Simplify the organization to make it functional | • **(Option 3)** Develop milestones and a sense of urgency for meeting the milestones | *(Option 9)* Redesign product development and commercialization and process | • **(Option 12)** Merge with Company XYZ | • **(Option 13)** Reduce sales force by 20% |
| *(Option 7)* Emphasize everyone's role as a stakeholder in the achievement of strategic objectives | *(Option 16)* Apply new problem-solving approaches | • **(Option 15)** Discontinue R&D in medical instrumentation | | *(Option 14)* Design an "idealized" sales force automation system |
| • **(Option 10)** Consolidate certain functions to reduce or eliminate redundancy | | | | |
| *(Option 11)* Adopt a team-based organization paradigm | | | | Tie Line |

**Alternative A:** *Emphasize everyone's role as a stakeholder in the achievement of strategic objectives while adopting a team-based organization paradigm. Adopt a transparent process for project selection and prioritization and apply new problem-solving and design approaches. Redesign product development and commercialization process. Develop two new business opportunities that are a strategic fit and generate new revenue. Train, motivate and mobilize field sales force and design an "idealized" Sales Force Automation System.*

Figure 5.4.   An Interactive Alternative profile.

| Example of Reactive Alternative Profile | | | | |
|---|---|---|---|---|
| **Cluster #1—Redesign** | **Cluster #2—Priority** | **Cluster #3—Productivity** | **Cluster #4—New Business** | **Cluster #5—Sales Force** |
| • **(Option 2)** Develop a clear understanding of roles, responsibilities, and accountability | • **(Option 1)** Adopt a transparent process for project selection and prioritization | • **(Option 5)** Maximize productivity in areas such as R&D | • **(Option 6)** Develop two new business opportunities that are a strategic fit and generate new revenue | • **(Option 8)** Train, motivate, and mobilize field sales force |
| • **(Option 4)** Simplify the organization to make it functional | *(Option 3)* Develop milestones and a sense of urgency for meeting the milestones | • **(Option 9)** Redesign product development and commercialization and process | *(Option 12)* Merge with Company XYZ | *(Option 13)* Reduce sales force by 20% |
| • **(Option 7)** Emphasize everyone's role as a stakeholder in the achievement of strategic objectives | • **(Option 16)** Apply new problem-solving approaches | *(Option 15)* Discontinue R&D in medical instrumentation | | • **(Option 14)** Design an "idealized" sales force auto-mation system |
| *(Option 10)* Consolidate certain functions to reduce or eliminate redundancy | | | | |
| • **(Option 11)** Adopt a team-based organization paradigm | | | | Tie Line |

**Alternative A:** *Consolidate certain functions to reduce or eliminate redundancy while developing milestones and a sense of urgency for meeting the milestones. Discontinue R&D in medical instrumentation. Merge with Company XYZ and reduce sales force by 20%.*

Figure 5.5.   A Reactive Alternative profile.

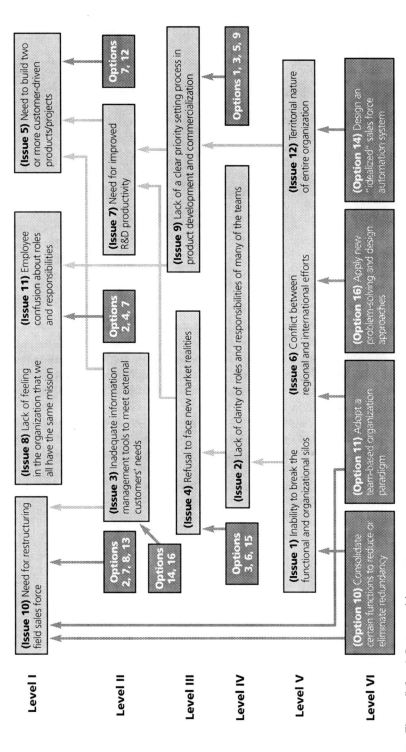

Figure 5.6. A Superposition pattern.

**Level I**
(Issue 10) Need for restructuring field sales force
(Issue 8) Lack of feeling in the organization that we all have the same mission
(Issue 11) Employee confusion about roles and responsibilities
(Issue 5) Need to build two or more customer-driven products/projects

**Level II**
Options 2, 7, 8, 13
Options 14, 16
(Issue 3) Inadequate information management tools to meet external customers' needs
Options 2, 4, 7
(Issue 7) Need for improved R&D productivity
Options 7, 12

**Level III**
Options 3, 6, 15
(Issue 4) Refusal to face new market realities
(Issue 9) Lack of a clear priority setting process in product development and commercialization

**Level IV**
(Issue 2) Lack of clarity of roles and responsibilities of many of the teams
Options 1, 3, 5, 9

**Level V**
(Issue 1) Inability to break the functional and organizational silos
(Issue 6) Conflict between regional and international efforts
(Issue 12) Territorial nature of entire organization

**Level VI**
(Option 10) Consolidate certain functions to reduce or eliminate redundancy
(Option 11) Adopt a team-based organization paradigm
(Option 16) Apply new problem-solving and design approaches
(Option 14) Design an "idealized" sales force automation system

35

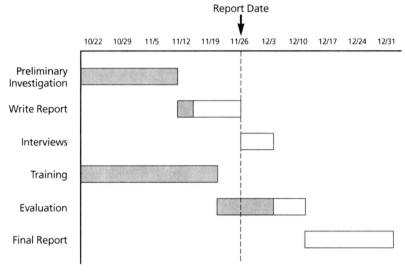

Figure 5.7.   A Gantt chart.

The Action Plan embodies the assigned responsibilities, time lines, interaction patterns, and monitoring activities decided by the participants. This plan may take many forms depending on the preference of the participants and the needs of the action plan. Part of this plan is often presented as a Gantt chart. A Gantt chart is a horizontal bar chart developed as a production control tool in 1917 by Henry L. Gantt, an American engineer and social scientist. Frequently used in project management, a Gantt chart provides a graphical illustration of a schedule that helps to plan, coordinate, and track specific tasks in a project. A simple Gantt chart is shown in Figure 5.7.

These Seven Language Patterns are integral parts of SDP. They integrate the deliberations done in co-laboratories, make them understandable and translatable to participants, accelerate decision-making, and enable the successful design of Collaborative Action Plans.

CHAPTER 6

# THREE PHASES AND THREE KEY ROLE DISTINCTIONS

In experimenting with ways to lessen the cognitive overload of participant designers, researchers discovered that there are three phases and three key roles in SDP that vastly reduce the cognitive burden if they are explicitly recognized and honored by all the actors involved. The three application time phases relate to the time sequence for engaging the actors, namely: (1) Discovery, (2) Designing, and (3) Action. The three role distinctions relate to context, content, and process. The three primary actors of any SDP engagement are: (a) the inquiry design team that sets the context during the Discovery phase (b) the facilitation team that guides the focused and open dialogue process during the Designing phase, and (c) the stakeholder/designer team that controls the content of the social design and has the primary responsibility during the Action phase. These SDP actors satisfy the distinctions between context, content, and process in the following manner.

The Discovery phase focuses on defining the boundaries of relevance, the framing of triggering questions, and the planning of the anticipated activities during the face-to-face interactive inquiry of the stakeholders. The Discovery phase, which is completed by the inquiry design team in collaboration with representatives of the client organization(s), is usually the most challenging one. In fact, experience has taught us that if this phase is done well the probability of not deriving useful products by engaging the stakeholders in interactive inquiry is minimal. In the Designing phase, the

*How People Harness Their Collective Wisdom and Power*, pages 37–45
Copyright © 2006 by Information Age Publishing

stakeholders participate in disciplined dialogue so that they can make contributions in terms of observations and explanations, make distinctions and decisions, and generate alternative action scenarios. In the Action phase, responsibilities are assigned to the stakeholders and their organizations. And progress in implementing the collaborative action plan is usually monitored by a steering committee with special attention to actions of high leverage.

The inquiry design team working with representatives of the client organization(s) interviews a sample of stakeholders of the situation and identifies the *context* of a design. It also frames the triggering questions to be discussed by the participants. The inquiry design team prepares a paper describing the general parameters of the situation and presenting the perspective of representative stakeholders. This paper is distributed to all participants of the social system designing team prior to their engagement in the Designing phase of the SDP (see Appendix D for an example of a White Paper).

The stakeholder/participants alone determine the *content* of the design during the four stages of the interactive inquiry (Module E). Within the context and the triggering questions that have been decided upon in the Discovery phase, the participants make their observations, distinctions, and relational judgments on the basis of their individual and collective knowledge and wisdom.

The facilitation team is in charge of the *process* during the Designing phase. The team sees that the dialogue process works smoothly with everyone being heard and everyone's authenticity and autonomy being honored. The team records the proceedings, displays observations, operates the computer software, and publishes the results of the deliberations in collaboration with the inquiry design team. In so doing, the team liberates the participants to concentrate solely on the content of the social system-designing situation that they are concerned with.

As a consequence of these role distinctions, participants are not burdened with cognitive overload. In most cases, they are engaged in deliberating on the basis of paired relational judgments, thus staying well within the rule of "7 ± 2." Working in this way they do not have to laboriously fit each observation into their existing mental models. The group mental model emerges by means of individual and collective learning and successive approximations. They can do this responsibly because the long and deep logic programmed in the software keeps track of their relational judgments. This long and deep logic enables stakeholders to transcend their cognitive limitations and to converge on consensual action scenarios systematically, collaboratively and systemically.

## SETTING THE CONTEXT

As mentioned, the inquiry design team is charged with discovering the context for SDP co-laboratories during the Discovery phase. In cooperation with the sponsor, it establishes a tentative definition of the boundaries of relevance, frames the triggering questions, and plans co-laboratory activities and agenda for the stakeholders for the Designing phase. These tasks are usually the most difficult ones.

### Determining Boundaries of Relevance

The contexts in which SDP is used span government and social policy issues, corporate governance, community and non-profit organizations. They encompass complex blends of finance, ethics, health, morale, and sustainability. Careful preparation is taken to ensure effective stakeholder participation in designing goals and strategies in these situations. Good preparation combined with efficient and disciplined dialogue reduces the cognitive pressure placed upon stakeholder/designers, and enables them to make high quality observations and decisions about what really concern them, the content.

The inquiry design team works first with representatives of the client organization and involved professionals to identify the stakeholder interests and likely stakeholder representatives. Then it interviews those stakeholders to elicit their viewpoints on what the problems and possible solutions might be, all the time on the lookout for unexpected stakeholders and viewpoints. It may employ an open-ended survey as part of its investigations.

Then the inquiry design team prepares a White Paper that lays out scenarios of the situation as viewed by these various stakeholders. It touches upon stakeholder issues that are identified by the Soft Systems CATWOE acronym.

- **C**ustomers of the situation (those who would be victims or beneficiaries of the system were it to exist;
- **A**ctors who would carry out the activities of this system;
- **T**ransformation process answers the question: What input is transformed into what output in this system?
- **W**eltanschauung answers: What image of the world makes this meaningful?
- **O**wner is the one who could abolish this system;
- **E**nvironmental constraints identifies the external limits that this system takes for granted (Checkland, 1991, p. 69).

The White Paper is then shared with the sponsor and revised if necessary. It is presented to all stakeholder/designer participants prior to their engagement in the Designing phase (Module C) for their orientation and to gather comments from their peers.

The time required for this preparation of the White Paper varies according to the complexity of the project as regards to science, politics, and diversity of stakeholder concerns. Less complex situations may require only a week or two. Very complex situations may require months. An example is the paper prepared for the World Health Organization event in Geneva (1998) that sought to build an international partnership to eliminate Lymphatic Filariasis (LF), a parasitic disease afflicting 73 nations whose most notable symptom is elephantiasis. The preparation of this White Paper required an inquiry design team of three individuals working for three months.

During the Discovery phase, it became reasonably clear that the successful implementation of the Global Program to Eliminate Lymphatic Filariasis by the year 2020 faces many challenges. Divergent viewpoints and concerns voiced by a wide variety of stakeholders and organizations were found to be interlinked. A cascade of linkages were discovered that connected international agencies, philanthropic organizations, non-government organizations (NGOs), national government agencies, academic research communities, professional healthcare associations, health service oversight bodies, pharmaceuticals suppliers, monitoring and testing system suppliers, primary healthcare providers, public health field workers, training and education programs, patients, and the media. The full participation of each of these groups during the implementation of the co-laboratory conducted in Geneva was seen as crucial to the long-term success of such a large public health initiative. No single organization alone had the capacity to address such a complex issue without the design of a Collaborative Action Plan spelling out roles and responsibilities for the partners.

Seventy-two representatives from over thirty international organizations participated in the Geneva Forum, whose aim was to support efforts to eliminate this highly stigmatizing and devastating disease from 73 endemic countries, where 119 million people are already afflicted with Lymphatic Filariasis (LF) and 1.1 billion are at risk of infection. One LF patient from Ghana, Victoria, was invited to participate at the Forum on an equal basis with public health experts, Medical Doctors, WHO officials, representatives of national governments, and the like. Victoria's participation and contribution was crucial to the deliberations of the participants and the final outcome of the Forum, as acknowledged by most of the participants during the Forum. During this Discovery phase prior to the engagement of the stakeholders a very thoroughly researched White Paper was prepared and distributed to the invited participants.

The time devoted to the production of the White Paper was well spent. The three-day forum identified the leverage points for the campaign and established a comprehensive working network for combating the disease. In 2002, 59 million people ingested Lymphatic Filariasis drugs. The Global Alliance for Eliminating Lymphatic Filariasis, *www.filariasis.org*, is on target to meet its 2020 goal.

An example of a White Paper is presented in Appendix D.


## Triggering Question

On the basis of the completion of the Discovery phase, an appropriate triggering question is framed. The wording of this question is crucial to the success of the SDP co-laboratories. For the Lymphatic Filariasis Forum, the question was: *What barriers do you anticipate to our goal of eliminating LF by the year 2020.* For a National Mental Health Association (NMHA) 2001 co-laboratory on how to improve the quality of Mental Health Information, the triggering question was: *What are the important principles for improving the quality of mental health information?* For a 2001 co-laboratory with the Northwest Energy Efficiency Alliance, the triggering question was: *What national/ regional trends/events would you consider as having the greatest impact on electric energy efficiency over the next fifteen years?*

If the framing of the triggering question is not done well, the risk of failed stakeholder engagements is very high. Sometimes, just adjusting one word or one prefix in a triggering question is all it takes for a co-laboratory to become a success story or a failure. The framing of the triggering question is the most challenging and critical aspect of any application of SDP in the arena.


## Anticipating Activities of the Design Co-Laboratory

The logistics of the design co-laboratory include the usual items for any meeting: time, place, participation, facilitators, equipment, supplies, and support. The makeup of the participating stakeholders, their continual participation, the sequence of sessions, the specifications of the designing room (see Chapter 8), and SDP software (Chapter 8) are especially important.

## PRODUCING THE CONTENT

Stakeholder/participants collectively determine the content of their design. They are the "content experts" who generate, clarify, and construct relational maps for a large number of succinct elemental observations (two or three lines of prose) representing their knowledge and wisdom. Through successive approximations, they recursively converge to the interactive design of a Collaborative Action Plan (CAP), which is co-owned by them because it has been co-created.

Stakeholders engaged in these focused and open dialogues perform three principal activities recursively:

- Generate elemental observations and explanations of the meaning of these observations in response to properly framed *triggering questions*. For example, in response to a triggering question like "What barriers stand in the way of worldwide cooperation for our organization?" an observation might be "We lack sufficient asset base and resources."
- Produce relational graphic maps of observations and explanations in the context of carefully framed *generic questions*. For example,

"In the context of designing a regional alternative future for the adoption of energy efficiency, does

Option-X

have *significant* characteristics in common with

Option-Y?"

- Interpret, analyze and evaluate relational maps (influence trees, affinity clusters, etc.) and alternative action scenarios in response to agreed-upon *criteria*. The criteria-based evaluation of design alternatives is not performed prematurely; it is deliberately reserved for the third stage of the interactive inquiry module of Table 4.1 (Module E).

Stakeholders are free to give total attention to the content that is their concern because the context is already fixed and the process is being managed by the facilitation team. They make their observations freely in response to triggering questions without fear of censure or criticism, because the facilitation team blocks this from happening. Their autonomy is totally respected and protected. They are also free to consider the opinions of "technical experts" and evaluate the worth of those opinions. In the end, stakeholders have complete control over the content of the design.

In addition, computer software is limiting the velocity of information for their consideration to ordered pairs and keeping track of the logic of their decisions, thus relieving them of the burdens of trying to fit new information into their cognitive maps. This freedom to give full attention to just a few things at a time allows them to think clearly and outside their preconceived mental boxes.

Process control is a subtle strategy of inequitable power relations that is averted in SDP. A stakeholder or a small group of stakeholders can attempt to control the design process by inserting their own process. This would of course set up a control situation that the other stakeholders would find almost impossible to surmount. There are numerous experiences in social system designing situations that are described in other writings that identify the nature of these power relation strategies (cf. Magliocca & Christakis, 2001).

To prevent such power grabs and to insure stakeholder freedom, designer/stakeholders need to trust the facilitation team to handle the process. They must refrain from trying to meddle with the components of the SDP architecture.

## GUIDING THE PROCESS

For SDP to work properly, the facilitation team must not meddle with the content of the dialogue. They guide the process, valuing everyone's autonomy, accurately recording their observations and clarifications, competently working the SDP computer program, producing graphics, projecting and posting them for examination by the stakeholders. They generate interim reports so that stakeholders are kept abreast of what they have decided. The three key people on the facilitation team are a lead facilitator, a recorder, and a computer software operator.

### Lead Facilitator

The lead facilitator sets the tone for the design co-laboratory. He or she explains the process and the schedule, lays down ground rules for the dialogue in its various phases, and shows utmost respect for all participants, respecting their autonomy by not altering their observations and not allowing others to do so. He or she reviews the context of the work and introduces the triggering question making sure that everyone understands it. Then he or she keeps the dialogue moving, enforcing the principles of disciplined dialogue, and maintaining the group's empathy, authenticity, and equity. Ten guidelines for the performance of the SDP facilitator role are presented in Table 6.1. Adherence to these guidelines, which have been called the "Ten Commandments," is very crucial for the success of the co-laboratory. My experience from training other people all over the world in

performing the SDP facilitator role has been that the hardest commandments to practice in the arena are: (a) #5, prohibiting participants from
premature valuations of the contribution of other participants so that the
autonomy and authenticity of the authors of observations is protected, and
(b) #7, avoiding compromising the neutrality of the role of the facilitator
in terms of content statements by him or her.

### Table 6.1.   Decalogue of the SDP Dialogue Facilitator
### (The Ten Commandments)

1. The less you say the more effective you are.

2. Remember that Dialogue for the SDP paradigm is defined as: The participation of
   observers engaged in creating meaning, wisdom, and action through communicative
   and collaborative interaction.

3. Remember the three axioms, the six laws of Dialogue, and the Tree of Meaning (to be
   discussed in detail in Part IV), and make sure you practice them.

4. Never sacrifice the group for the individual.

5. Ask for ""questions and comments" during clarification dialogue; Prohibit premature
   valuations of observations.

6. Doing the wrong thing is worse than doing nothing.

7. Avoid compromising your neutrality by making content or value statements.

8. Never negotiate the process with the participants; Process is what you know and do best.

9. When in doubt take a break and talk with the sponsor.

10. Create a climate of equity, authenticity, and empathy.


## Recorder

The recorder captures the observations of stakeholders as they are trying to formulate them. He or she also captures the dialogue as they are
clarifying their observations and other stakeholders are questioning them.
The observations and the clarifying dialogue bring about a commonly
shared linguistic domain that enables genuine mutual understanding. The
observations and dialogue are printed out and shared with the stake-
holder/designers. This provides an audit trail of the group work to be
revisited and updated as the evolution of the situation dictates.


## Computer Software Operator

The operator of the computer software captures the synopsis of each
response to a triggering question, projects it upon a screen, and corrects it,

if necessary, to the satisfaction of the person making the observation. He or she also codes the observation for later recall and logical operations. He or she prints out each response and posts it on the wall of the Collaborative facility for later clustering, voting, and display of influence patterns.

The facilitation team works smoothly with each other, with facility staff and assorted volunteers. Every effort is made to make the co-laboratory a success. After the session, one or more members of the facilitation team in collaboration with the inquiry design team and the sponsor produce a report that describes what happened and presents the findings in a transparent manner to the participants, always honoring the consensual language that emerged during the co-laboratory.

CHAPTER 7

# FOUR STAGES OF INQUIRY

In the Designing phase, SDP enables participants to offer observations and explanations, make distinctions and decisions, and generate alternative action scenarios. In this brief chapter, we describe the four stages of interactive inquiry by the participants to the co-laboratories. Extended descriptions of the four stages are saved for Part III, Chapter 11, with the dynamic interactions among them as experienced in specific co-laboratories in the arena of practice.

SDP is a specialized process aimed at problem solving and design through collaborative teamwork and the participation of stakeholders. The intent is to build *patterned* interactions among stakeholders in a socially produced linguistic domain (shared vocabulary) and to engage them in designing social systems that integrate their diverse cognitive realities into communal wisdom. The designs emerge with the practice of focused and open dialogue and as a consequence of successive approximations from one stage of the inquiry to the next. Understanding the significance of the concept of successive approximations is critical in appreciating the theory and practice of the SDP paradigm.

These dialogical activities are immersed in four distinct but interrelated stages (Module E of Table 4.1):

1. Defining and anticipating the intent of the design challenge, or "What *should we do?*"

*How People Harness Their Collective Wisdom and Power*, pages 47–48

2. Designing alternative designs for action, or *"*How *can we implement the intent of the design?"*

3. Choosing the preferred action alternative, or "*Which* alternative is the best for implementation and *why?"*

4. Planning for action, or *"*When *will we do what we can do?"*

# CHAPTER 8

## COLLABORATIVE SOFTWARE AND FACILITY

### SDP SOFTWARE

The interactive software used in SDP sessions is either CogniSystem or its new streamlined version Root Cause Mapping (see Appendix B). Under either name this software is a refined version of the software that was worked on from the very beginning of SDP research back in the early '70s. From the beginning, the researchers developed ways to use interactive software. The researchers goals in developing the software were: (1) to lessen the cognitive demands on designing participants; (2) to generate better designs; (3) to speed the designing process; and (4) to maintain participant-driven rather than expert-driven deliberations.

The use of computer software in the intensely human endeavor of designing good living and working situations raises hackles for some distrusters of technology. Such suspicion is warranted when "experts," working with concepts of their choosing and fixed structures built by programmers, pontificate on how people and societies should behave. But in SDP, stakeholders are the experts and the evolving structures of the computer-aided system are shaped by interactions (Bausch and Christakis, 2002). The following quotation captures the philosophy underlying the SDP computer software and how it is used in design co-laboratories.

> We treat other people not as merely "rational beings" but as "responsible beings." An essential part of being human is the ability to enter into commitments and to be responsible for the courses of action that they anticipate. A

*How People Harness Their Collective Wisdom and Power*, pages 49–53

computer can never enter into a commitment (although it can be medium in which the commitments of its designers are conveyed), and can never enter as a participant into the domain of human discourse. (Winograd and Flores, 1986)

The purpose of SDP software is to act in a support function to the deliberations of the stakeholders. It is designed to provide an idealized symbiosis between the human being and the computer. It essentially enables the stakeholders to practice focused and open dialogue without violating cognitive limitations.

The software keeps track of participant observations, recording them, displaying them, arranging them in accord with participant decisions, and organizing the efficient delivery of products to participants.

This software records observations and meanings, produces, iteratively, representations resulting from the design dialogue, and enables stakeholders to review the representations and amend them through additional discourse. It keeps track of the logic expressed in stakeholder pair-wise decisions, produces the graphic language patterns of relationships among observations, and displays them on a large screen, with the flexibility to amend the observations and the patterns continuously. The software handles the long and deep logic involved in complex social design instantaneously and effortlessly.

In SDP applications, the software is always operated by the facilitation team in order to free participant/designers to concentrate on the content, which is the area of their expertise. The primary role of the stakeholders is to engage in dialogue and to interpret the representations as displayed in the Collaborative facility. A printer is used to produce hard copies of all the representations for review and amendment by the stakeholders.

One of the principal advantages of using the SDP software is the efficiency gained in the exploration of relationships among a large number of ideas. In the SDP application with the U.S. Food and Drug Administration, to be discussed in Chapter 13, stakeholders would have had to spend 75 working days to explore all the relationships necessary to complete a Collaborative Action Plan. With SDP, they were able to produce a plan for action in 6 dedicated days of teamwork.

The SDP software is an integral component of SDP architecture of Table 4.1 and must coexist with four other components in order to be effective during the co-laboratory. The other four components are: (a) Community of Stakeholders, (b) SDP Facilitation Team, (c) Consensus Methods, and (d) Collaborative Facility. These five components, when they co-exist, provide a set of capabilities for engaging stakeholders in focused and open dialogue and produce the types of graphic/textual products described in Chapter 5.

The software is capable of producing and displaying automatically a variety of reports including: lists of observations; influence representations among observations; classification of observations into affinity groupings; superposition representations; options field representations; priority representations; sequence representations; and histograms resulting from trade-off evaluation of alternative designs. Easily understood textual and graphic reports are available at any point within SDP co-laboratories. The final reports of SDP co-laboratories are utterly transparent in their goals, procedures, mutually agreed upon value criteria, and derivation of results.

Note: CogniSystem software is an integral part the author's CogniScope commercial application of SDP. Root Cause Mapping © is a more user-friendly version of the software recently developed by Leading Design International, Inc. (*www.leadingdesign.org*).

## COLLABORATIVE FACILITY

The last component of a well-designed and conducted SDP co-laboratory is a facility with the following physical characteristics:

- Comfortable chairs;
- Proper seating arrangements;
- Sufficient wall space to display the results of participant observations and decisions;
- A screen or wall on which developing information such as triggering questions, definitions, observations, influence patterns, and option profiles can be projected; and
- Computers, projectors, and printers.

A floor plan displaying a configuration of a Collaborative facility with 48 participants is displayed in Figure 8.1.

If the sponsors of a design co-laboratory are unable or unwilling to find an appropriate Collaborative facility for it, they increase the risk of failure of the co-laboratory experience for the stakeholders. This component of the SDP architecture is the most difficult to explain to potential clients, most of whom are accustomed to assembling their stakeholders in ordinary meeting facilities that lack the comfort and the display requirements of the SDP paradigm. Experience tells us that anytime we compromise on the requirements of the Collaborative facility, we diminish the creativity and productivity of the participants, thus increasing the risk of under-conceptualization of the design situation.

In a story to be presented in Chapter 14 as an illustration of an SDP co-laboratory, the sponsor never understood the importance of following the specifications of a floor plan similar to that shown in Figure 8.1, even

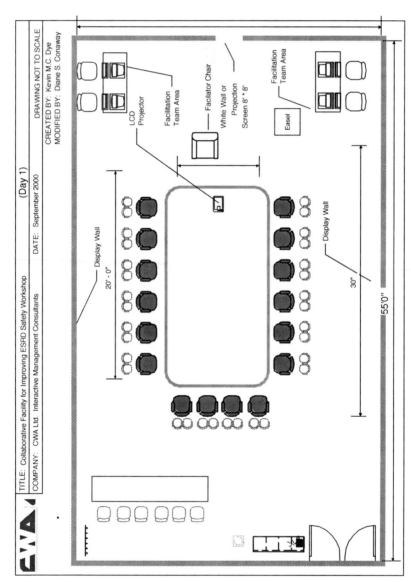

Figure 8.1. An example of a floor plan for a collaborative facility accommodating forty-eight participants.

though the floor plan was shared with the sponsor during the Discovery phase. When the facilitation team arrived at the scene of the event and saw the meeting facility it became apparent that, although it was very elegant in terms of décor, it was totally inappropriate for SDP dialogue. The problem was the large size of the room and the lack of display space visible to the participants. Since no other facility was available at that particular hotel, it was necessary at that last minute to bring in panels for displaying the information in visual proximity to the participants and in conformity with the predetermined dimensions of the Collaborative facility. The final outcome of this project was successful, as described by Dr. Tom Parker's statement about the outcome quoted in Chapter 14. Dr. Parker himself was amazed, however, at his staff's lack of understanding of the criticality of an adequate Collaborative facility for engaging in participant design.

# CHAPTER 9

# SIX DIALOGUE LAWS

These six laws will be discussed intensively in Part IV that deals with the science of dialogic design. They are briefly described here to complete the components of the SDP architecture (Table 4.1).

1. The law of *requisite variety* demands that an appreciation of the diversity of perspectives and stakeholders is essential in managing complex situations.
2. The law of *requisite parsimony* states that structured dialogue is needed to avoid the cognitive overload of stakeholder/designers.
3. The law of *requisite saliency* states that relative salience of observations can only be understood through comparisons within an organized set of observations.
4. The law of *requisite meaning* states that meaning and wisdom are produced in a dialogue only when observers search for relationships of similarity, priority, influence, etc. within a set of observations.
5. The law of *requisite autonomy in distinction-making* states that during dialogue it is necessary to protect the autonomy and authenticity of each observer in drawing distinctions.
6. The law of *requisite evolution of observations* states that learning occurs in a dialogue as the observers search for influence relationships among the members of a set of observations.

# CHAPTER 10

# RELIEVING THE BURDENS OF DIALOGUE

**C**hapter 3, the unshakeable human burdens of dialogue, discussed the limits of human cognition, group pathologies, and unequal power relations. This chapter discusses how the architecture of SDP, just described, relieves those burdens.

Several ways that SDP lessens the burdens of dialogue are obvious:

1. The seven Consensus Methods are proven ways to facilitate design dialogue.
2. The seven graphic language patterns use a graphic-prose hybrid language (displayed in visual form) to enhance the ongoing linear nature of dialogue. This graphic-prose language enables the stakeholders/observers to construct efficiently relational patterns so that many observations may be displayed and understood within the cognitive capacity of human information processing.
3. The three role responsibilities remove the chores of defining context and managing process from the stakeholders, so that they can concentrate on the content of their dialogue. The facilitation team relieves the participants from the nuisance work of recording, reporting, and displaying their observations.
4. The computer software keeps track of the logic of the deliberations and thereby releases participants from the burden of continually needing to integrate new knowledge and information with previ-

*How People Harness Their Collective Wisdom and Power*, pages 57–62

ously derived cognitive maps. It also speeds convergence to an action plan with deep understanding and collective agreement by all participants.

5. The Collaborative facility minimizes the discomfort involved in long meetings and makes the products of stakeholder deliberations immediately available for viewing, discussing, and amending.

These measures increase stakeholder capacity to explore relationships among observations three-at-a-time (paired judgments with regard to a third consideration), as stipulated by the Law of *Requisite Parsimony* to be discussed in Chapter 23. The measures enable participants to relate the diversity of ideas through elemental observation and personal dialogue while, at the same time, SDP software provides formal reasoning with real-time products during their SDP dialogue experience.

In addition, the manner in which influence trees are constructed is carefully paced so that stakeholders have sufficient time to process information, keeping their tasks well within the limits of human information processing capabilities. First, stakeholders are asked to write their observations silently in response to a triggering question. Second, each stakeholder articulates his or her ideas (which are displayed on a large screen, and then printed and posted on the wall in large print). Third, the authors of each idea are asked to explain the meaning of their observation. Fourth, clarification questions or comments are encouraged from others. Research has shown that stakeholders will begin their dialogue believing that others see the design situation as they do. As they are asked in SDP to explain their contribution so that it can be recorded, they will simply say there's no need for an explanation; everyone knows what they mean. Other participants invariably indicate they are not sure what the author means.

In fact, experience shows that even after the observations by individual authors are clarified to the satisfaction of all participants during the round-robin generation and clarification of ideas, when the participants are asked to make relational judgments among the ideas two-at-time, they suddenly recognize that they are in need of additional clarification by the authors of the ideas. This patient honoring of stakeholder autonomy pays off big in participant enthusiasm for the work of designing. One participant in an inner-city co-laboratory stated:

> I have been to a lot of meetings, and sometimes I have a fair amount to say, but what made this special is that I really felt that I have been heard. The CogniScope [SDP] dialogue approach really works to protect people's autonomy in a way that I have never before experienced. My ideas were my own, and they were understood. It was very exciting.

Note: CogniScope in the name used for SDP in the author's commercial consultancy.

As previously indicated, it is fundamental to its success that SDP protects and enhances the autonomy and authenticity of the participants. One way of promoting this in conventional group dialogue sessions is by the convener and/or the facilitator opening the group session by explaining to participants the desirability of open expression of thoughts during the dialogue. One way to enforce this requirement is to ask participants to refrain from making evaluative comments of others contributions in the initial stages. However, as the dialogue unfolds it requires discipline to prevent the emergence of group pathologies, which may be quite subtle in their effect.

SDP insists that all stakeholders at the table have a voice. If top managers or other persons of authority or expertise sit at the table, their views are given no more consideration or weight than the views of others. To bring this equality about, the facilitation team works very closely with top managers prior to SDP workshops. These managers must be convinced in their minds and hearts that the process will not work if people are unable to contribute their best observations in an authentic fashion. During the SDP dialogue session the facilitation team works hard to ensure that nobody's authenticity and autonomy is violated. Without the help of the facilitation team, many stakeholders would not be able to express their authentic voices. As a result, they would disengage from the process and stop their active participation.

The context role within the SDP paradigm, as identified in Chapter 6, is an extremely important component for preventing individual or group pathologies during design work. The interviews by the inquiry design team during the Discovery phase give all the stakeholder/designers ample opportunity to consider the situation and frame their observations. The preparatory White Paper provides a summary of different positions. The triggering question focuses attention on the agreed-upon critical considerations.

SDP uses the Nominal Group Technique (NGT) to solicit individual contributions in response to the triggering question. This method of generative dialogue is slower than more free flowing methods such as "brainstorming." The slower pace is deliberate. It establishes a process of thoughtful and reflective dialogue. Individual stakeholders will vary considerably in the level of communicative competence. The slower pace is particularly important for individuals who are less verbal and more reticent in expressing their viewpoints.

Many group pathologies creep into group dialogue when some individuals begin to monopolize the group's attention:

- by producing long lists of ideas and expressing them in a loud or forceful way,
- by being superior in an organization's chain of command, or
- by being an "expert."

In the opening stages of SDP, these power-grabbing activities are severely restricted because each observer is allowed to contribute only one observation at a time in round-robin fashion. At all points in the co-laboratory, observers are assured of a proper hearing of their observations and explanations because they have the floor to themselves, with the facilitation team protecting their voice and autonomy. From the start of a co-laboratory, SDP respects and supports individual autonomy and diversity of perspective.

As mentioned in Part I, Michel Foucault, in *Power/Knowledge* (1980), presents a liberating vision of power relations as a constructive, positive force. For him, power occurs in a relational mode through the events of dialogue, which construct the social reality of the participants. Power is an emergent characteristic in the complex behavioral relationships of people. To the extent that knowledge is shared and created, the relational affinity is empowering to all.

According to Foucault, power is manifested in the distinctions made by individuals and accepted by groups. Through the group construction of high quality observations, individuals and groups are transformed. In the SDP paradigm, the equitable power relations that are generated have a transformational effect on the stakeholders, which will be discussed in more detail in Chapter 26. Experience has shown that this transformational effect cannot be induced by posting "rules of equitable power relations" on the wall of a meeting facility, or lecturing a group on how to be empowered. It must become the social fabric of the dialogue process. The stakeholders must experience equitable power relations in the context of the transformative power of dialogue as described by Roberts (2002). The SDP paradigm accomplishes this experience by adhering to the eight activities shown in Table 10.1.

As mentioned earlier, the six dialogue laws will be extensively covered in Chapter 23.

Finally, the role responsibilities identified in Chapter 6, especially the distinctions between "process" and "content," seem to be unique to the SDP when compared to conventional approaches to dialogue facilitation. Every SDP co-laboratory begins with the sponsor and the stakeholders understanding the distinctions between "context," "content," and "process." The facilitation team is completely responsible for the process role. They are the process experts in the application of the SDP approach for disciplined inquiry. As process experts, they do not provide any opinions on the validity of any content observations whatsoever. They offer no contributions or

**Table 10.1.  SDP Design Activities that Validate the Application
of the Six Dialogue Laws**

| | *Activity* | *Laws* |
|---|---|---|
| 1 | SDP enables observers to draw distinctions in response to a "triggering question" that has been carefully framed in preparation for the design dialogue; | Diversity<br>Autonomy |
| 2 | SDP provides the opportunity for all observers to explain their distinctions. i.e., they "unpack the meaning" of specific observations by selecting the explanatory path that is meaningful to the praxis of their life; | Diversity<br>Saliency<br>Meaning |
| 3 | Participants construct patterns among their observations and employ focused and open-dialogue methods of inquiry to discover relationships among the variety of observations generated; | Parsimony<br>Meaning<br>Learning |
| 4 | Participants systematically discover categories of similarity and dissimilarity among observations; | Meaning<br>Parsimony<br>Learning |
| 5 | Participants interpret patterns of observations and discover interdependencies and the strength of interactions among them; | Saliency<br>Meaning<br>Learning |
| 6 | Participants select alternative pathways to action in a multidimensional design space; | Saliency<br>Meaning<br>Learning |
| 7 | Participants evaluate alternative "action pathways" and select the preferred one for implementation; | Saliency<br>Learning |
| 8 | Participants design an action plan by exploring the temporal relationship among the observations selected for inclusion in the preferred action pathway. | Autonomy<br>Learning<br>Saliency |

observations related to content. This excludes the facilitation team entirely from assuming a dominant role in the dialogue around content.

The stakeholders are identified as the "content experts." They engage in the generation of observations, the distinctions and descriptions of observations, and the selection of design pathways to action. They are free of the obligation of maintaining an equitable group process, because this is the responsibility of the facilitation team. They can expect to make their observations freely in response to the triggering question without fear of censure or criticism, since the facilitation team will block this from happening. They are also free to consider the opinions of "technical experts" and evaluate the implications of their statements on the desired outcome. However, in the end, the stakeholders have complete control over the content of the design. They also must accept that they will not be able to influence how the process will be conducted because this is the role of the facilitation team.

Process control is another subtle strategy of inequitable power relations that is averted in the SDP paradigm. A stakeholder or a small group of stakeholders can attempt to control the design process by inserting their own process. This would of course set up a control situation that the other stakeholders would find almost impossible to surmount. There are numerous experiences in social system designing situations that are described in other writings that identified the nature of these power relation strategies (Magliocca & Christakis, 2001).

For example, during a co-laboratory for redesigning a government agency department composed of 70 lawyers, the designing team members initially attempted to control the process of the dialogue, which they found, too disciplined. With the intervention of the leader of the department the integrity of the process was preserved. As a result the participants were enabled by the end of the first day of group work to transcend their self-referentiality. As a community of learners they drew agreed-upon distinctions in their dialogue, which gradually and iteratively led to a consensual linguistic domain. By understanding the distinctions drawn by others, they chose time and again to expand their horizons and to gain a richer appreciation of the variety of viewpoints and of their mutual orientation about their situation.

It has been observed from over eighty-one applications in the arena during the 1980s that, independent of the group of stakeholders and of the subject matter, the average number of observations generated during one-day of an SDP co-laboratory is equal to sixty-four. In this government department redesign case, the stakeholders exceeded that average and generated ninety-four distinguishable observations during the first day of group work. As we will see in Chapter 25 this case corresponds to one of the highest complexity measures.

In the interactions among the members of the designing team they created a common framework for understanding the design situation. Eventually they were speaking the same language. They generated communicable observations and explanations that were recorded by the Facilitation team for future reference, relational graphic language patterns of their observations similar to those shown in Figures 5.1 to 5.7, new categories of observations constructed inductively, amendments of earlier representations, etc.—ultimately converging upon the Collaborative Action Plan, which included a time sequencing of actions chosen by supermajority vote displaying "what to do when and by whom."

In the beginning of their engagement, the team members put the preoccupation with taking immediate action into the background of their consciousness, and so avoided premature closure. By focusing on understanding each other's observations and explanations they actually increased the horizon of action options that they might choose to implement. During the SDP co-laboratory they proposed distinctions based upon contemplated action options, and those distinctions sparked new ideas for action, and so on in an iterative pattern until agreement was reached.

# Part III

## CO-LABORATORIES IN ACTION

In discussing the SDP architecture, I mentioned my intention to revisit Module E, the Four Stages of Interactive Inquiry, because it represents the integration of the entire component constructs of SDP theory in the arena of practice with the engagement of stakeholders in disciplined dialogue. These four stages test SDP theory and put it into practice. They engage stakeholders in co-laboratories in the following stages, mentioned briefly in Chapter 7, namely: (1) Definition or Anticipation, (2) Design of Alternatives, (3) Decision, and (4) Action Planning. The other six modules of the SDP architecture (Table 4.1) are essential and integral parts for successful application in the arena of the Four Stages of Inquiry. In fact, experience tells us that if all the other components of the SDP architecture have been performed in accordance with the principles of the theory, Module E guarantees the success of stakeholder engagements in co-laboratories.

Part III shows how co-laboratories have implemented these four stages of SDP. It offers:

- A detailed overview of SDP methodology;
- A customized SDP Application;
- Case: Designing a front-end master plan for a new product;
- Case: Re-designing a large organization;
- Case: Anticipating alternative futures in energy efficiency;
- Case: Indigenous wisdom of the people forum;
- Cases: International boundary-spanning dialogue;
- Case: Community-based co-laboratory.
- Case: Development of meaningful take-aways from Co-op Experience?

CHAPTER 11

# OVERVIEW OF THE METHODOLOGY

I start by presenting a generic description of the SDP dialogue methodology. Each specific application in the arena of practice requires an appropriate modification of the generic methodology in order to satisfy the requirements of the particular situation, such as number of participants, number of workshop days, desirable outcomes from the co-laboratory work, resources allocated to the project, and the like.

The duration of the projects implemented over the last fifteen years with CWA Ltd. (*www.CWALtd.com*) clients varied from a two-week to a six-month period, depending on the complexity of the situation. The number of stakeholders participating in the co-laboratories ranged from 10 to 200 participants. The number of workshop-days per co-laboratory ranged from two days to six days. The six-day co-laboratories were implemented by engaging the stakeholders in three two-day workshops conducted within a period of approximately six weeks.

An SDP project is launched with the implementation of the Discovery phase during which the inquiry design team gathers intelligence through a review of extant literature and interviews with a representative sample of stakeholders. Usually ten to twelve interviews are held with different representatives of the community of stakeholders. Experience shows that after the completion of the tenth interview the knowledge generation about the situation from the interviewees becomes repetitive. This knowledge base is

*How People Harness Their Collective Wisdom and Power*, pages 65–74

documented and distributed to the participants prior to the workshop as a White Paper (See Appendix D for an example of a White Paper).

Also during the Discovery phase the inquiry design team frames the triggering question(s) in collaboration with a representative(s) from the sponsor. When the triggering question has been agreed upon, the identification of representatives of the community of stakeholders to participate in the co-laboratory is initiated. The three key criteria for identifying the representatives of the community are: (a) Variety of perspectives about the design situation, (b) Content knowledge and sensitivity in the context of the triggering question framed for the situation, and (c) Capacity to make a commitment to contribute to the implementation of the Collaborative Action Plan (CAP).

During the Definition stage of the Designing phase of Table 4.1, the participants are asked to define/anticipate the situation by addressing the question *"What should we do?"* In response to this question they generate a set of observations relevant to the situation. The observations are recorded and displayed in real time on the screen of the Collaborative facility. The authors of the observations are asked to clarify their statements through focused and open dialogue. During the Definition stage, the group inductively explores similarities among the observations and constructs affinity clusters, and abductively discerns the most influential observations by producing and interpreting an influence tree-pattern among important observations.

The second stage of interactive inquiry in the Designing phase focuses on the Design of Alternatives. The participants are asked the question *"How can we do what we should do?"* They propose and clarify action options for addressing the roots of the influence tree-pattern displayed on one of the walls of the Collaborative facility. Participants again construct affinity clusters by exploring the relationship of similarity among pairs of action options, and proceed to select those options that are the most salient to them for the third stage of the process, which is Decision. The most salient options are superimposed onto the influence tree-pattern, thus demonstrating the potential leverage of actions on ameliorating the situation.

In the third stage of the inquiry, participants decide on a Consensus Action Scenario by designing alternative scenarios that focus on the question *"Which are the preferred options and why?"* They usually work in small teams to identify and select the most salient options within and across each of the affinity clusters produced in the second stage of inquiry. The small teams present in a plenary session their action scenarios and the rationale for their selections. After all team scenarios have been presented and discussed at the plenary session, the facilitation team helps the participants to converge on a consensus action scenario. The facilitation team ensures that the Law of *Requisite Saliency* is not violated during the decision process.

In the fourth stage of the inquiry, i.e., Action Planning, the participants are engaged in answering the question *"When will we do what we can do and who will do it?"* thus completing the design of the Collaborative Action Plan.

The generic description of the four stages of inquiry (Module E) conducted during a co-laboratory is schematically depicted in the following three figures. Figure 11.1 summarizes graphically the four stages of inquiry.

## DEFINITION

The *Definition/Anticipation* stage begins with a complex, messy situation, depicted graphically in Figure 11.1 by overlapping geometric shapes representing the variety of perspectives among the stakeholders, all of which are strongly interacting to produce the *Problematique* of the situation. For example, in employing SDP to a strategic management situation for the US Forest Service the team of twenty-five participants was asked to respond to the triggering question: "What are short-term Annual Performance Goals based on a draft annual performance plan derived from the Strategic Plan (2000 Revision)?" Employing SDP dialogue, the strategic planning team efficiently generated and clarified the meaning of the 83 proposed goals, prioritizing them by voting on relative importance, and finally assigning them to affinity categories of similar goals on the first day of group work. On the following day the team constructed a tree of influence showing the interrelationships among the Goals by means of series of votes of influences among the Goals, two-at-a-time. These three process steps are shown graphically in Figure 11.1 on the left side under the title of *Definition*. The influence tree produced through structured dialogue focusing on the influences among the goals enabled the participants to discover the "deep rooted" goals, i.e., those goals which, if achieved, would exert strong leverage in achieving other goals, as shown schematically in Figure 11.2. In this schematic, these deep-rooted goals of the influence tree are located at Level IV, with arrows propagating upward to less influential goals located at Level I.

Figure 11.2 illustrates what an influence tree of goals dealing with a complex strategic management situation might look like after the participants have had the opportunity to engage in SDP dialogue. Supported by the computer groupware, the participants are engaged in discovering relationships among goals, efficiently producing influence and affinity patterns among goals (i.e., graphic patterns as shown in Figure 11.2). They can amend the statements of goals and relational patterns continuously and automatically, with maximum flexibility and adaptability of thought and structure.

68

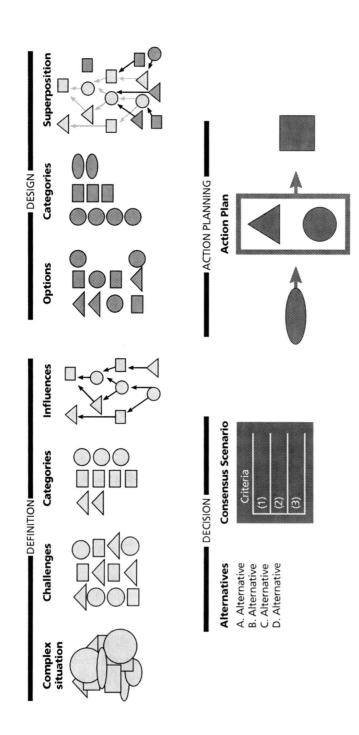

Figure 11.1.   Generic inquiry stages of the SDP Co-laboratory.

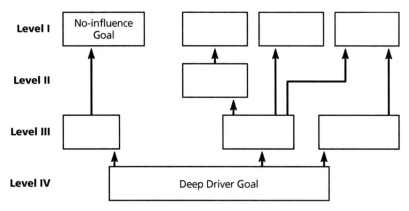

The example shown above is an influence structure.
↑ demonstrates the direction of influence.

Figure 11.2.   A schematic of a leverage map of the influence structure of goals

## DESIGN

In a generic application of SDP dialogue the *Definition stage* is followed by the *Design of Alternatives stage,* i.e., the identification of options that, if implemented, would meet the deep-rooted goals and contribute to achieving the system of goals exhibited in Figure 11.2. The options proposed by the participants are clarified, prioritized and assigned to similarity categories as shown schematically in Figure 11.1 under the title of DESIGN.

Figure 11.3 displays another product of the generic methodology, namely the identification of those options that, if implemented, would address the deep-rooted goals. Identifying those *options* (or actions) that, according to the majority of stakeholders participating in the dialogue, have the strongest leverage in terms of the system of goals is another benefit of the methodology. Figure 11.3 is a schematic of the Superposition Pattern mentioned in Chapter 5.

## DECISION

Referring again to Figure 11.1, the third stage of SDP dialogue provides the participants with an integrated, systemic model of evaluating alternatives in the context of a set of criteria, and converging on the preferred alternative during the *Decision Stage.* In some applications of SDP dialogue the rigorous trade-off Consensus Method is employed for evaluating alternative designs (see Appendix A for details on the trade-off method).

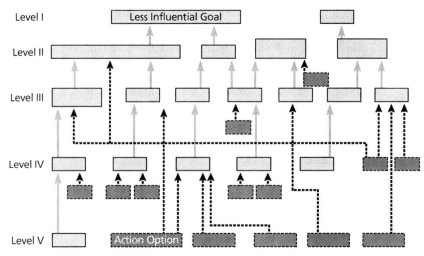

Figure 11.3.   Actions with high leverage become apparent. Illustrating superposition of action options (dark) and goals (light).

Indeed, all things considered, this is precisely where such a collaborative design forum of stakeholders ought to converge when dealing with the implementation of collaboratively designed action plans in the context of the challenges of the Information Age.

## ACTION PLANNING

Action Planning is done according to standard management practices. Stakeholders accept responsibilities; lines of communication are established; schedules are set etc., often using Gantt charts. Action Planning is sometimes done after the face-to-face meeting is over if there are time restraints.

## DETAILS FOR THE DEFINITION STAGE OF INQUIRY

The details for the Definition stage of inquiry are schematically depicted in Figure 11.4. As stated above, the inquiry begins with a complex, messy *Problematique* situation, as depicted graphically by overlapping geometric shapes (Figure 11.4a) representing the variety of perspectives among the observers. A review of eighty-one applications, completed during the decade of the 1980s, found that for the Definition stage the average number of observation generated by groups of approximately twelve participants, independent of the composition of the group and of the subject matter being addressed, is equal to sixty-four.

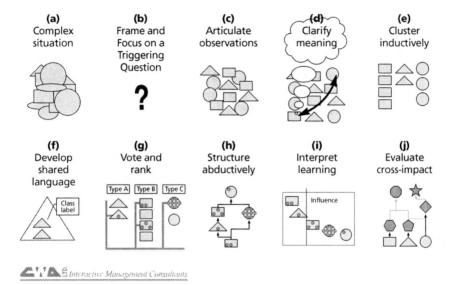

Figure 11.4.    The linguistic graphic patterns of the definition stage.

A detailed elaboration of the SDP dialogue steps of inquiry as depicted in Figure 11.4 is offered below:

Step (a) is the geometric representation of the *Problematique* that structured dialogue is asked to address. It consists of many interrelated institutions, cultures, economic, political and social factors, etc. During the Discovery phase the inquiry design team investigates this "mess" with the intent to prepare a White Paper, and to frame the triggering question.

In step (b), the triggering question defines the context of the dialogue. A typical triggering question might read:

"What are critical current and anticipated issues to be addressed in order to achieve our strategic vision?"

In response to this question, the participants articulate their ideas in their own words to the full attention of the other participants, step (c). Their words are posted on a wall of the Collaborative facility and everyone agrees not to alter them. In a second round robin, step (d), the authors of the statements are given the opportunity to respond to questions by other participants in order to explain the meaning and intent of the their observations. This approach authenticates each person irrespective of his or her education level or position of power. It produces a palpable reduction of tension. People seem surprised as they are being heard, perhaps for the first time, in important designing matters affecting their lives.

In step (e), the participants collaborate to inductively cluster the observations they have made. Then in step (f), they agree upon labels for the clusters they have created. These steps enhance the understanding of the meaning of the observations and build a consensual language and a sense of shared competence within the group. The Law of *Requisite Meaning* and the Law of *Requisite Parsimony* are implemented during this step.

In step (g), participants rank the ideas presented in the affinity clusters according to individual and subjective relative saliency. This step brings into sharp relief the different priorities and values within the group. In the ensuing discussion about the distribution of votes, stakeholders come to understand where their co-participants are coming from, which leads to a respectful working relationship based on defined mutual interest. The Law of *Requisite Saliency* is implemented in this step.

In step (h), participants explore influence relationships among the observations and construct abductively a tree of influence. Charles Peirce is credited with the invention of abductive reasoning, which is a combination of inductive and deductive thinking. It is the type or reasoning that contributes to the construction of hypotheses. In this step, they relate their observations in paired judgments asking whether observation *A* really influences observation *B*, and vice-versa. The Law of *Requisite Meaning* and the Law of *Requisite Parsimony* are implemented in this step.

In steps (i) and (j), the stakeholder/designers examine the "tree of meaning" they have constructed in step (h). As a group, they analyze and interpret the cross-impacts existing among the observations they have made. If there is a need to amend the preliminary pattern of influences after the interpretation, they can do this efficiently again with computer assistance, and produce a new version of the tree-pattern. In many cases participants volunteer to share their interpretations of the tree of meaning in the context of their experience, thus contributing to the richness of the dialogue.

In this manner, step-by-step, SDP dialogue progressively clarifies the situation and opens the way to greatly enhanced decision-making and action planning. In addition it:

- Authenticates every stakeholder/participant;
- Elicits ideas and points of view from all stakeholders;
- Moves toward effective and meaningful consensus;
- Elicits and deals with the different priorities of stakeholder/participants;
- Equalizes power relations among the stakeholders; and
- Goes beyond identifying factors that are important, to specifying those that are most influential in addressing the social system-designing situation.

Figure 11.5 displays some pictures from a recent application of the SDP with a group of stakeholders representing parents, teachers, students, administrators, and consultants from a middle school in Michigan. These stakeholders focused their dialogue on the issue of improving the performance of students with disabilities in terms of the Average Yearly Progress (AYP) in mathematics. AYP is a measure of accountability based on the No Child Left Behind (NCLB) Legislation passed by the US Congress in 2002. This team of twenty-five representative of the community of stakeholders allocated five days of dedicated group work and converged on a Collaborative Action Plan that includes twelve effective priorities to be implemented by task forces in the next two years (Belay, et al., 2005). The twelve priority actions were selected from an original set of more than fifty proposed by

Figure 11.5.   Illustrating the SDP Design of a Collaborative Action Plan (Photos courtesy of David Smith of the Michigan Department of Education)

the workshop participants. The pictures of Figure 11.5 are indicative of how the stakeholders, through the SDP approach of learning by iteration and by graphic representations, were able to converge to the high priority actions for implementation.

# CHAPTER 12

# CUSTOMIZED SDP APPLICATION

In this chapter, as a means to make the Four Stages of Inquiry more transparent, I will discuss a customized version of the methodology using as an example a co-laboratory in February of 2003 involving 48 participants representing 38 different organizations. More stories from the design arena are presented in the following chapters. Those stories from the design arena, however, will not discuss methodological aspects, as I will do in this chapter.

The case described here represents an inter-organizational initiative focusing on Chronic Kidney Disease (CKD) patients. It is estimated that there are about 20 million CKD patients in the USA alone today. This means that CKD is a very serious and multidimensional public health policy problem requiring the engagement of the community of stakeholders in a meaningful and productive dialogue. CKD patients eventually end up in dialysis units suffering form End Stage Renal Disease (ESRD), costing the US taxpayers billions of dollars every year to keep them alive (see White Paper in Appendix D).

## THE CHALLENGES OF COLLABORATION IN THE CKD SITUATION

From the outset, the sponsors of the CKD project (Parker et al., 2004) recognized that any group of people, when trying to solve a complex problem

*How People Harness Their Collective Wisdom and Power*, pages 75–86
Copyright © 2006 by Information Age Publishing
All rights of reproduction in any form reserved.

such as improving patient outcomes for the CKD situation, confronts three challenges that, if properly addressed, represent opportunities.

1. First, the problem often seems vast, unwieldy, bewildering. Individual stakeholders often understand one aspect of the problem, but the entire problem to each person is overwhelming. If all the individual understandings could be somehow joined together, real progress would occur.

2. Second, individual stakeholders—depending on their backgrounds, experiences, and training—perceive the problem differently, and use different terms or language to describe their perceptions. Again, uniting these differing perspectives could be a real opportunity to improve everyone's understanding of the problem. Often, however, groups do not allow individuals enough time to clarify their perspective so that others understand them sufficiently. This cuts short the group learning that is so essential to resolving complex problem situations.

3. Finally, while no one in the group comprehends the entire complex problem, the group as a whole possesses a collective understanding of the problem that would enable them to map out how different components of the problem are related to each other. The challenge is to employ a methodology that facilitates a group tapping into this collective understanding and wisdom in a constructive, goal-oriented manner.

The SDP co-laboratory addressed each of these challenges, striving to turn them into collective opportunities through the four basic stages of inquiry (Module E)—the first three of which were conducted during the face-to-face co-laboratory, the fourth completed in a follow-up DELPHI study in which the participants were asked to respond to survey questions regarding their specific roles and responsibilities in implementing the agreed upon Collaborative Action Plan.

## STAGE ONE: GAIN A DEEPER APPRECIATION OF BARRIERS

The first stage—gaining a better appreciation of the situation by identifying component barriers to resolving the problem—proceeded in six steps:

1. Before the co-laboratory, a White Paper describing the problem situation is produced by interviewing fourteen knowledgeable people (see Appendix D). These interviews were used as a means to provide participants at the co-laboratory with a rough sketch of the problem, to

frame the triggering question that starts the SDP dialogue, and sensitize the 48 participants to the diversity of opinion on the situation.

2. At the co-laboratory, the complexity of the CKD problem was described by articulating its component barriers, with participants individually listing separate barriers that they think are important factors of the complex problem situation. The total number of barriers generated during the first day of group work was eighty-four.

3. Clarify individual perceptions about these 84 barriers in order to promote group learning.

4. Categorize barriers within affinity clusters, i.e., categories of similar characteristics, and compile individual judgments (by voting) to further understand which barriers are of higher relative saliency.

5. Use group judgments (through strong majority votes) to understand how the nineteen relatively more important barriers are interrelated in terms of their influence upon one another.

6. Use this collective understanding to identify the most influential of the nineteen important barriers of the problem situation.

The products of these steps can also be viewed as a diagram. Figure 12.1 depicts how the group deconstructed the *Problematique* into component barriers, worked to understand exactly what these barriers meant to the individual who authored them, and then deepened their collective understanding of these barriers by seeing how they were interrelated. This results in the identification of barriers, which are considered "deep drivers" of the situation (indicated by an ! in Figure 12.1) that influence the outcome of many other barriers. Resources committed to the deep drivers attain the highest overall leverage.

## Methodology: Determining Influences among the Barriers

After describing a complex problem in terms of its component barriers to resolving the situation, and the variety of perspectives on the barriers,

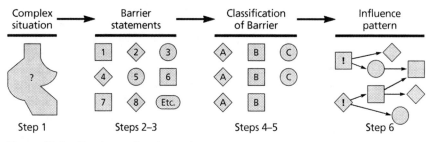

Figure 12.1.    Products of each step in stage one.

people can better plan what to do if they take the time to understand how various barriers influence other barriers. Often, through this disciplined inquiry, people are able to discover that a seemingly insignificant barrier in fact directly and indirectly affects our ability to address a wide range of other barriers; meanwhile, a barrier that initially looked to be critical in fact has little influence on any other parts of the overall problem.

In the CKD case, the 48 participants were engaged through this dialogue process by focusing the group on the question: "if we surmount this barrier, will we be better able to surmount another barrier?" This question was asked repeatedly with pairs of barriers. The group collectively decided yes or no by voting, and slowly a graphic pattern of influence emerged. The computer support groupware helped the group to discern this pattern by taking the results of the voting and using the basic inference logic of transitivity. (For example, if surmounting $A$ helps us tackle $B$, and surmounting $B$ helps us tackle $C$, then surmounting $A$ helps us tackle $C$ and the question "does $A$ influence $C$" does not have to be posed to the group). In the CKD case, this inference logic saved the group 75% of the time required to complete this step in a robust fashion, as compared to not having such computer support.

## Findings: The Pattern of Influence among the CKD Barriers

In constructing the graphic pattern of influence by means of abductive reasoning, participants were asked relational questions that followed the following format:

> Suppose the community of stakeholders is able to make progress
> in addressing:
> (Barrier X)
> will this help *significantly* in addressing:
> (Barrier Y)
> in the context of designing an action agenda for improving patient
> outcomes in CKD?

The entire group explored the influences among the nineteen most important barriers. Based on a strong majority opinion of participant judgments about the interdependence between pairs of barriers, an Influence Tree was produced and is depicted in Figure 12.2: Influence Pattern of Barriers for Improving Patient Outcomes in CKD. Arrows show cases where surmounting one barrier will help significantly in surmounting another barrier. This diagram represents the compilation of a strong consensus. It was generated by the assertions of at least thirty-two of the forty-eight participants for each of eighty-five relational questions. Unanimous opinions

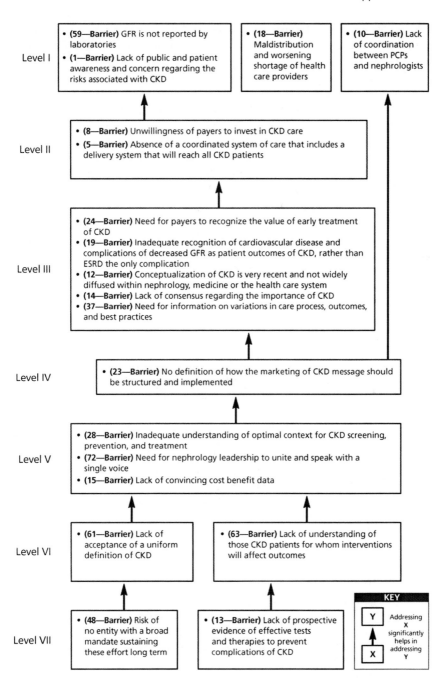

Figure 12.2.    Influence graphic pattern of barriers for improving patient outcomes in CKD.

grew in frequency as the inquiry progressed. Given that nineteen barriers were selected as being more important, the participants without computer support would have to answer 342 questions, instead of 85. Hence, the efficiency gain in terms of speed of converging on the Influence Tree shown in Figure 12.2 is a factor of four. The 48 participants were able to complete the task of influence mapping in two hours of group work instead of eight hours required if the computer support groupware of SDP (*CogniScope*™) was not available. It is doubtful that this very busy group of stakeholders, composed primarily by Medical Doctors, would have allocated eight hours of dedicated group work to discover the interconnections among the 19 more important barriers, and as a result identify the "root cause barriers" in the context of designing an action agenda for improving patient outcomes in CKD.

Addressing barriers that appear lower in the Influence Pattern, such as those at Level VII in Figure 12.2, have more wide-ranging effects than addressing ones that are higher, and thus the deeper barriers are the ones to tackle preferentially.

Below I quote from the paper by Dr. Tom Parker, published in the Nephrology Annals in the spring of 2004, offering the authors' interpretation of Figure 12.2 (Parker et al, 2004):

> This Figure depicts the results: the influence pattern arrows show situations where surmounting one barrier will help significantly in surmounting another barrier. In order for a barrier to have influence on another barrier, at least 32 of the 48 stakeholders had to assert this effect. Indeed, as convergence in the process proceeded, there was often unanimous opinion. Barriers that appear lower in the influence pattern in Figure 12.2 have more influence on other barriers that appear higher in the pattern. The hypothesis posited by CWA is that this pattern can help to form the CKD Initiative's subsequent strategy, since preferentially addressing the deeper barriers is likely to have more wide ranging affects than addressing higher barriers on the "tree". In a sense, the deeper barriers can be interpreted as having more "leverage"—that is, the power to move and ameliorate other barriers—and thus the resolution of these deeply leveraging barriers could have cascading benefits for addressing the entire set of barriers that constitute this complex problem.

The Figure shows that the stakeholders determined, summarily, that:

1. There isn't a group with a broad mandate to sustain the overall effort to improve the outcomes for CKD patients and that the varied parties and societies working on their own could not maintain the effort, acting independently. Level VII of the Figure shows that this is the very root of the barrier tree. Essentially, the stakeholders determined that the various societies, agencies, corporations, physicians and others, working individually as they are currently doing, are the root barrier. There needs to be a systematically coordinated effort to sustain a solution.

2. That there is not uniform definition that was understandable by the varied parties (caregivers, public, payers, etc.). This, too, is determined to be a basic "root" problem, as noted in the Figure, Level VI. Unless we understand what the definition of chronic kidney disease might be, how can we set about dealing with who to treat and how to treat them?

3. We don't know which therapies are the most effective—another Level VII very basic barrier.

4. Finally, we must know which patients to whom we should apply the therapy (Level VI).

Figure 12.2 takes the barriers to higher levels on the tree. But these 4 root barriers must be managed in order to sustain any solution to the others. Noteworthy, too, is the interpretation that the human resources issue on Level I stands alone. It is a barrier that cannot be dealt with through resolution of other barriers. Another way of saying this is that any solution will have to be made "around" the human resources issue.

This interpretation, quoted from the paper by Dr. Tom Parker, is indicative of the type of stories delivered by stakeholders at co-laboratories after the production of similar influence- tree patterns. These stories, delivered from a variety of stakeholder perspectives while interpreting the specific influence tree-pattern of that situation, significantly enhance the understanding by all the participants of the complexity of the social-system-designing situation they are confronting.

## STAGES TWO AND THREE: GAIN A BETTER APPRECIATION OF POSSIBLE ACTIONS

### Methodology: Designing Alternative Action Scenarios

Having gained a deeper appreciation of the components of the *Problematique* as articulated by different participants, and their interdependencies, the group next moves on to consider what can be done to surmount these barriers. The second stage proceeds in four steps:

1. Envision parts of the solution in relation to the overall problem, with participants individually listing separate potential action options that address specific barriers.

2. Clarify individual perceptions about each action option, in order to promote group learning.

3. Cluster action options based on their similarity and compile individual judgments (by voting) to further understand which action options are of higher relative saliency.

4. Use this collective understanding to identify the most salient action options.

In the third stage, small teams construct alternative action scenarios. The teams achieve a working consensus on which actions to include in each team's proposed scenario and present it to the group.

Again, a diagram is helpful in seeing how the group of participants moves from listing a wide variety of potential action options, to deepening their understanding of how these possible actions are similar to and different from each other, and finally choosing the most salient action options and assembling them into alternative action scenarios, as graphically shown in Figure 12.3.

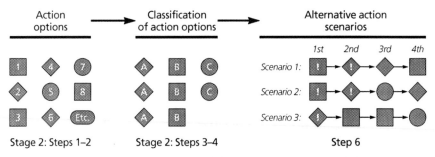

Figure 12.3.   Displaying the products of the steps of stages two and three.

Different groups will design alternative scenarios. Some groups will prioritize those action options that address very influential actions (designated by an ! in the diagram) as the first steps to be taken, whereas other groups might delay taking these actions until later. Having the groups explain their reasoning underlying their scenario provides another opportunity for stakeholder learning and advances the group towards making the wisest choices of what actions to pursue and how.

We now turn to the findings of the co-laboratory regarding potential solutions to the *Problematique* of improving CKD patient outcomes.

## Findings: The Action Options

On the second day of the co-laboratory, the stakeholders proposed and clarified ways to improve CKD patient outcomes. The stakeholders were divided into seven small groups. Each group then proposed action options in response to the following triggering question:

What are action options which, if adopted and implemented by the community of stakeholders, will help in addressing the roots of the tree of barriers shown in Figure 12.2?

Participants generated and clarified thirty-three action options. They were asked to vote individually and subjectively by selecting the five options that in their opinion are of higher relative importance in the context of the triggering question and Figure 12.2. The results of the voting on action options are shown in Table 12.1: Voting Results on Action Options for Improving Patient Outcomes in CKD. It is interesting to note that the top six actions received 46% of the total vote, and the top 12 received 70% of the total vote. These twelve dominant action options were determined as being high priority for improving patient outcomes in CKD and were used in the DELPHI study for finding out the commitment to collaborative leadership by the stakeholders who participated in the CKD workshop.

**Table 12.1.   Voting Results of Action Options for Improving CKD Patient Outcomes**

**Triggering Question:**
"What are action options which, if adopted and implemented by the community of stakeholders, will help in addressing the system of barriers?"

| | | # of Votes | Weighted count* |
|---|---|---|---|
| (2—Set B) | Build on and coordinate the activities of the many groups at this meeting who have been and who are working on this problem | 16 | 59 |
| (7—Set B) | Support the efforts of the National Kidney Disease Education Program to establish a laboratory group to coordinate the activities in laboratory standardization for GFR reporting | 12 | 42 |
| (4—Set B) | Develop and promulgate simple guidelines targeted to patients around screening CKD and the implications of CKD | 13 | 39 |
| (13—Set B) | Stage the effort to achieve acceptance of a uniform definition of CKD: 1) health providers and laboratories, 2) payers 3) public | 11 | 37 |
| (8—Set B) | Promotion of research into the effectiveness of disease management systems for CKD in multiple settings and stages of disease | 10 | 35 |
| (22—Set B) | Collaborate with accrediting organizations and regulatory bodies in developing CKD quality measures which would include GFR estimate equation reporting | 12 | 34 |
| (12—Set B) | Target at-risk socioeconomic and demographic population and representative organizations for public education campaigns | 7 | 26 |

**Table 12.1.　Voting Results of Action Options for Improving CKD Patient Outcomes (Cont.)**

**Triggering Question:**
"What are action options which, if adopted and implemented by the community of stakeholders, will help in addressing the system of barriers?"

| | | # of Votes | Weighted count* |
|---|---|---|---|
| (3—Set B) | Identify and classify the subgroups of CKD in which intervention have already been proven, are promising but questionable versus unknown and simultaneously developing and measuring patient outcomes of these interventions | 8 | 25 |
| (6—Set B) | Promote targeted clinical, basic and epidemiological research on relationship between CKD and CVD | 9 | 22 |
| (1—Set B) | Convene a stakeholder group to devise the needed research agenda | 6 | 21 |
| (24—Set B) | Encourage CMS demonstration projects on creative approaches to identifying and treating patients with CKD | 8 | 20 |
| (14—Set B) | Wide dissemination of available evidence linking CVD and CKD to non nephrologists and the lay community | 7 | 20 |
| (18—Set B) | Own NKDEP: participate in shaping/expanding its role | 6 | 18 |
| (32—Set B) | Integrate renal care into existing diabetes clinics | 5 | 17 |
| (5—Set B) | Simplify the definition of chronic kidney disease | 4 | 16 |
| (17—Set B) | Leverage research resources by studying extant CKD populations and coordinating prospective studies with high risk populations such as diabetes and heart patients | 6 | 13 |
| (25—Set B) | Establish a group for developing and sharing cost/benefit data | 5 | 13 |
| (31—Set B) | Patient education, especially across ethnic barriers is imperative to moving this process forward | 3 | 11 |
| (33—Set B) | Broaden the concept to include nurse practitioners, physician assistants, advanced practice nurses | 5 | 10 |
| (11—Set B) | Fund rigorous meta analysis and cost effectiveness analyses in the CKD population | 3 | 9 |
| (19—Set B) | Find inclusive partners to finance public education including as examples congress, NKDEP, industry, and advocacy organizations such as AARP, AAKP | 4 | 8 |
| (15—Set B) | Support the efforts of guideline development and implementation in chronic kidney disease | 4 | 7 |
| (10—Set B) | Encourage organizations, (non-profit, government, industry) to emphasize particular areas of expertise | 2 | 7 |
| (30—Set B) | Explicit and uniform guidance about integrated management and referral | 3 | 6 |

**Table 12.1.    Voting Results of Action Options for Improving CKD Patient Outcomes (Cont.)**

**Triggering Question:**
"What are action options which, if adopted and implemented by the community of stakeholders, will help in addressing the system of barriers?"

|  |  | # of Votes | Weighted count* |
|---|---|---|---|
| (16—Set B) | Support NKDOQI and RPA guidelines for outreach in patients with CKD | 3 | 5 |
| (9—Set B) | Organize a stakeholder CKD research body that can utilize funding from a variety of sources including public, industry and foundation in order to limit the overall costs of prospective CKD trials | 1 | 5 |
| (20—Set B) | Aggressive lobbying of and involvement of professional cardiologic community in education process | 1 | 4 |
| (21—Set B) | Creation of patient centered guidelines and care plans linked to computer/web/PDA based & other forms of communication for dissemination | 2 | 3 |
| (29—Set B) | Work hand in hand with other associations that have addressed successfully disease states and learn from them as we move forward | 2 | 3 |
| (27—Set B) | Promote a collaborative model and use of communication tools | 1 | 3 |
| (23—Set B) | Collaborate with accrediting organizations and regulatory bodies in developing CKD quality measures which would include GFR monitoring (*duplicate*) | 0 | 0 |
| (26—Set B) | Bring dipsticks to Congress | 0 | 0 |
| (28—Set B) | Financial restructuring for those that are under a cap versus fee for service | 0 | 0 |

* A vote of 1 corresponds to a weight of 5, while a vote of 5 corresponds to a weight of 1.

The twelve actions highlighted in Table 12.1 were confirmed through a post-workshop DELPHI survey, as the actions to focus on for the launch of Phase II of the initiative. Approximately ten of twenty respondents to the DELPHI have identified their interests to focus their effort on addressing these most widely endorsed, and important actions. This feedback from the DELPI further supports the participant's directive that the highest priority should be accorded to these twelve options. To effectively accomplish these high priority actions, the stakeholders should allocate resources in implementing the specific activities and roles identified explicitly by the DELPHI panel.

The sponsors of the CKD Initiative considered the application of the SDP paradigm to the CKD situation to be a breakthrough. It had major implications in terms of contributing to a paradigm shift by the various organizations interested in improving the CKD patient outcomes. It still, however, represents work in progress. Some findings and recommendations of the group work remain controversial to some stakeholder organizations because it implies changes to the status quo. Quoting again from the conclusions of the paper by Dr. Tom Parker (Parker et el, 2004):

> The primary purpose of the CKD Initiative was to bring together key CKD stakeholders who understand the issues, identify and aggregate barriers to improving outcomes for patient with CKD, provide a hierarchy of issues and a plan to solve them, and develop a concise and practical plan of action. These goals were accomplished. The next goal of CKDI was to forge a "chain of partnerships" to implement the change. Such a coalition is critical. It is the sincere wish of the stakeholders and Steering Committee that the societies will, in a timely manner, respond with a thoughtful and practical program to advance the care of patients with chronic kidney disease. It is important to note that this *CKD Initiative* was intended to synergize and help coordinate all of the work being done by all parties in this field: National Kidney Disease Education Program (NKDEP), CKD activities by the NKF, ASN, RPA, AAKP, marketing by pharmaceutical companies, and all others. The societies have requested that the task remain within their purview. It is they who are now accountable for advancing the cause of CKD and to form the partnership for a symphonic and timely solution.
>
> Patients with CKD have poor outcomes, are costly, and have documented poor quality of life. This must be changed. The *CKD Initiative* has taken the first major coordinated steps to achieve this change.

> *The world owes all its onward impulses to men and women ill at ease.*
> *The happy man inevitably confines himself within ancient limits.*
>
> —Nathaniel Hawthorne

CHAPTER 13

# DESIGNING A CAP FOR GOOD REVIEW PRACTICES

## CONTEXT

**A** team of experts from the Center for Drug Evaluation and Research (CDER) and the Center for Biological Evaluation and Research (CBER) of the Food and Drug Administration (FDA) employed SDP to design its Good Review Practices (GRP) Initiative for Clinical and Statistical Reviews of new drugs and medical devices. The project was completed within a three-month period in the spring of 1994 (Christakis, et al., 1994).

In the Discovery phase of the project, the SDP inquiry design team conducted interviews with a selected subset of the CDER and CBER staff and reviewed various relevant documents. Following the completion of the Discovery phase, and in consultation with a small design team from FDA, the goals of the Design phase of the project were agreed upon. These were:

- To enable the project team members to design a Collaborative Action Plan (CAP) for the accomplishment of the goals of the GRP Initiative;
- To heighten consensus in the design of the CAP;
- To enhance teamwork and commitment to the implementation of the CAP fostered by the learning and understanding that occur in applying the SDP paradigm.

In order to accomplish these goals, the Design phase included three two-day workshops and three rounds of DELPHI questionnaires. This work

*How People Harness Their Collective Wisdom and Power*, pages 87–92
Copyright © 2006 by Information Age Publishing
87

involved sixty FDA experts selected to represent a cross-section of skills, responsibilities, and experiences.

## CONTENT

The purpose of the triggering question selected for this project was to focus the dialogue on an area that needed a higher level of understanding and consensus. The triggering question was:

> "What should be the intent and the output of the Good Review Practices Initiative?"

By the conclusion of the third workshop the team had authored the CAP which was their answer to the question: "How will the FDA do what should be done to accomplish the *intent* of the GRP Initiative, in what sequence will the called-for actions be implemented, and who will implement those actions?" The CAP that resulted from the work of the team during the Design phase is presented in the Gantt chart, Figure 13.1, in terms of eleven distinct tracks of activities.

The Collaborative Action Plan, designed by the FDA team of participants, combines five essential themes necessary to meet the challenges posed by the GRP Initiative. In brief, they are:

## 1.  Individual Participation and Collective Learning and Wisdom

If the GRP Initiative is to succeed, it must be instituted not by fiat but by broad mutual assent. This requires the GRP Initiative, from its earliest stages, to involve members from all layers of "those who do the job." This broad participation offers two potential benefits. First, it will increase the likelihood that all members of the FDA will endorse the GRP Initiative and embrace its recommendations. Second, incorporating junior members of the FDA into the development of GRP and soliciting their input will enhance the learning of senior members regarding the daily realities and obstacles of doing quality reviews in the 1990s.

## 2.  Institutional Learning

To prepare to meet the challenges that the 21st century will present, it must develop new methods of review that utilize novel technologies and

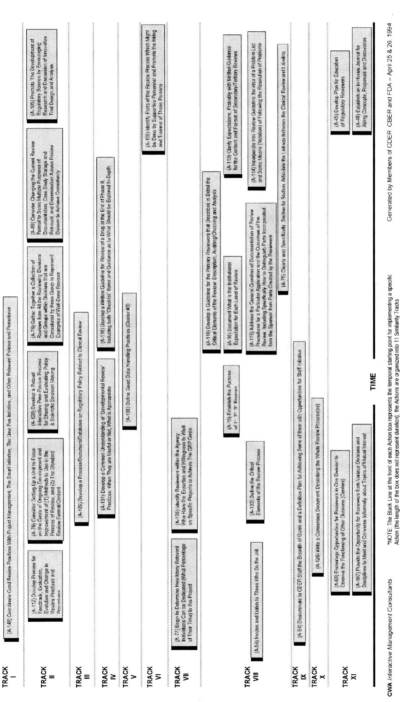

CWA *Interactive Management Consultants*

*NOTE: The Black Line at the front of each Action box represents the temporal starting point for implementing a specific Action (the length of the box does not represent duration); the Actions are organized into 11 Similarity Tracks

Generated by Members of CDER, CBER and FDA – April 25 & 26, 1994

Figure 13.1.    Collaborative Action Plan for achieving the intent of the GRP initiative.

techniques. In other words, the GRP Initiative must not merely *initiate* but rather seek to *perpetuate the continuous betterment* of "Good Review Practices." To do so, the FDA should consider establishing a unit of "Review Practices Development" that fosters ongoing redesign and refinement, innovation and improvement of review processes. If successful, one legacy of the GRP Initiative would then be an evolving, interactive, and flexible process of improving review practices and systematically developing a science of review.

## 3.   Institutional–Individual Learning and Cross-disciplinary Exchanges

The GRP Initiative should take advantage of the collective knowledge held by the wide array of FDA members, encouraging cross-fertilization of their knowledge and experience across traditional institutional boarders defined by divisions or disciplines. Heightened interaction and exchange would further the learning not only of individual members but of the institution as a whole.

## 4.   Individual–Institutional Learning and Continuously Revised Guideline Documents

One way in which the GRP Initiative can improve the learning of individual reviewers is to provide them with a guidebook that covers a variety of review practices, good and bad, and describes in detail the critical elements of the review. This guidebook could be accompanied by seminars and other opportunities to improve one's review techniques. As all members of the FDA realize, this guidebook must be flexible and would need frequent—almost constant—revision. These requirements offer an ancillary benefit to the FDA, namely they could foster ongoing institutional learning. Preparing successive editions of the guidebook could promote and then disseminate innovations and improvements in review practices.

## 5.   Organizational Coordination and Learning

Last, for the sake of efficiency and ultimate efficacy, the FDA should ensure that the GRP Initiative is coordinated with other related FDA initiatives. Not only should the work of one initiative neither duplicate nor contradict the work of another, but also the initiatives should attempt to integrate their efforts so as to learn from each other and eventually provide a synergistic set of improvements for the FDA.

These five themes emerged from the deliberations and planning of the FDA members who participated in this project, and reflect their consensus of what the GRP Initiative must do in order to succeed, not just next year, but for decades. These elements and their emphasis on learning provide the outlines of a long-term strategy for regulating a dynamic industry and even for offering leadership in the development of safe and effective pharmaceuticals and medical devices.

## CONCLUSIONS

### a.   Commitments

As a result of the deliberations that preceded the design of the Collaborative Action Plan, some significant *commitments* by the team emerged. These were:

- To engage in an open and inclusive process;
- To involve a wide range of people in the development of the GRP, in particular, primary and secondary reviewers;
- To build in flexibility, evaluation, and continuous improvement into the GRP guideline development as an ongoing process; and
- To focus on the entire review process (including relevant parts of the drug development process), not just documentation of the last steps of the process.

### b.   Two Fundamental Tracks

The team also recognized the significance of concurrently implementing two fundamental tracks of activities for achieving the intent of the GRP. The two tracks are:

1. A continuous learning and improvement process,
   (Track II in Figure 13.1)

2. Guideline development and documentation,
   (Track VIII in Figure 13.1.)

### c.   Feedback from GRP Leaders

Dr. Janet Woodcock, M.D., Director of the FDA's Center for Drug Evaluation and Research, after the completion of the project commented that:

This particular Interactive Management consultancy helped us develop a consensus and succeed in initiating meaningful internal process changes. The company has provided us with a road map to chart a new drug review course. Eighteen months later we still rely on the action plan that was created by our interaction with the Interactive Management consultancy.

Mary Jo Veverka, former FDA Deputy Commissioner for Management and Systems, stated that:

More than ever before the organization is working together to solve its problems with speed and efficiency.

After the completion of this project, CWA Ltd. (*www.CWALtd.com*) was retained for approximately five more years to work with other complex issues within the FDA, leading eventually to the building of internal capacity to apply the SDP paradigm with minimal support from the CWA consultancy.

## FDA AWARD OF EXCELLENCE

For efforts like this in fulfilling its primary goal: Speeding new drugs to Americans while preserving high standards for quality, efficacy, and safety, the Federal Drug Administration (FDA) won the 1999 Innovations in American Government Award given by the Council of Excellence in Government and sponsored by the Ford Foundation and Harvard University's JFK School of Government.

Using SDP, it adopted procedures for developing, reviewing, and approving drugs that bring new drugs for serious and life-threatening diseases (AIDS and cancer, for example) to market more quickly. It also developed a system linking the ranking of new drugs on their medical benefits to even faster review goals, thus insuring the greatest attention to breakthrough drugs for serious conditions. The agency cut new drug approval times in half, while doubling the new drugs approved in a year.

After another SDP co-laboratory in a medical setting, a physician wrote:

I wish to express our most sincere appreciation for you and your team's leadership in the recent workshop. The response was indeed more than I expected—much more. The results were outstanding and will significantly alter the direction of the initiative. I have thought of little else since the meeting and am astounded at the insights your process provided me. We were asking for direction. You provided direction. And prioritization. And confidence to proceed.

—letter from Tom F. Parker, III MD March 4, 2003

CHAPTER 14

# MASTER PLAN
# FOR A NEW PRODUCT

## CONTEXT FOR DRUG DEVELOPMENT

**A** very complex task facing pharmaceutical companies and the Food and Drug Administration (FDA) is to speed the development and commercialization of new drugs, which have the potential of significantly enhancing the quality of life of individuals with medical conditions ranging from minor ailments to life threatening diseases. It takes on the average 12 to 15 years and $350 million to $500 million for a significant new drug to move from discovery to pharmacy shelves. This time and cost are staggering and have an impact not only on the pharmaceutical company developing the product, but also on society as a whole. As an example, the financial rewards to a pharmaceutical company for shaving even six months off the process of a new drug development can be on the order of $100 million in profit. And this number may pale in comparison to the cost borne by society of treating the disease without access to a better therapeutic. Pharmaceutical companies, the FDA and other key stakeholders responsible for developing new drugs are working diligently to reduce the time to develop and commercialize new drugs while maintaining high standards for product safety and efficacy.

Effective Front-End Work is generally recognized as a critical success factor for the rapid development of any new product. An area for improvement, often overlooked in the pharmaceutical sector, but arguably the area of greatest leverage relative to the speed and quality of development, is in the Front-End Work. Much of the work in the Front-End stage involves

*How People Harness Their Collective Wisdom and Power*, pages 93–98
Copyright © 2006 by Information Age Publishing
All rights of reproduction in any form reserved.

planning and decision-making by a therapeutic team created to work on the project.

Most pharmaceutical companies manage the drug development process by forming interdisciplinary project teams to oversee the development of the "master plan." This plan guides the activity from the point of discovery, to the submission of an Investigative New Drug (IND) application to the FDA, to the submission of a New Drug Application (NDA), to the final production and manufacturing of the drug after NDA approval. Some examples of sub-processes in the Front-End stage include new product concept definition, technology and technical approach selection, requirements definition, and market positioning.

A typical interdisciplinary team is made-up of from five to fifteen members, representing the various departments involved in the development and commercialization process. This includes clinicians, pharmacologists, biologists, domestic and international marketing experts, manufacturing engineers, and the like. In the conventional approach, members of the project team work largely independently because of geographic, disciplinary, and organizational divisions. The conventional, and primary, mode of coordination is through a project manager.

Typically, a project manager assigns team members specific areas of responsibility and calls periodic meetings with participation by a subset of the team. Deadlines are set for collection of individuals' contributions, accommodating people's multiple, time-shared responsibilities. After individuals' contributions are assembled by the project manager, a draft of the team's output is circulated for individual team member review. After a suitable review period and a meeting to collectively discuss comments, individuals generate their additional contributions and, by another deadline, provide them to the project manager. Eventually, the team produces an output for wider review.

In the conventional approach, team interactions are often unstructured and absent of effective facilitation. As a result, the Front-End Work is time consuming. In addition, many project issues are never addressed because they are never raised, are discounted as non-important by an influential person on the team, or because there is no formal tracking of them. Many decisions are made without understanding implications on the overall project because of the partitioning of responsibilities, and the large degree of individual work. Very few team members achieve any overall understanding of the project, since they focus mainly on their specialties. The consequence is typically a Front-End Master Plan that is under-conceptualized and does not reflect the overall "wisdom of the team." This approach essentially corresponds to what has been described by Kahn (1996) as the "interaction without collaboration philosophy". This situation represents a perfect example of the need for further "democratization of science" and for processes to manage the inherent "escalation of complexity."

## The SDP Approach to Front-End Work

The SDP approach to front-end work enables collaboration among all key members of the project team in the planning and decision-making stages of a project. The principal benefits from the application of the SDP process in a drug development project are that it provides drug development teams:

- The capability to accomplish, in three to six days of dedicated workshops, work that would typically take place over several weeks or months;
- The capability of producing faster and better Front-End Master Plans that will ultimately reduce the time to develop, review, and commercialize a new drug entity, reduce development costs, and increase profitability by faster time to market;
- Faster termination of drug candidates that are not safe or effective; and
- Ability to provide useful clinical information for healthcare practitioners and patients earlier in the process.

## CONTENT FOR THE DEVELOPMENT OF XY234

XY234 was a novel compound being developed by the XYZ Pharmaceutical Company as a therapeutic for the symptomatic treatment of Alzheimer's dementia. At the time the compound was undergoing early Phase II clinical development in patients with mild-to-moderate Alzheimer's disease. Several key decisions needed to be made regarding process scale-up, formulation, dosing, and the Phase III clinical development program. SDP was employed to facilitate the inquiry process.

The following Target Product Profile defines the qualities that were deemed necessary for XY234 to be successful in the Alzheimer's Market:

- Effective in the short-term treatment of core symptoms of Alzheimer's dementia.
- Risk-benefit assessment equal to or preferably better than other developmental and marketed agents.
- Also desirable would be effectiveness in slowing the progression of Alzheimer's.

## Front-End Work for XY234

The first major goal of the application of the XY234 project was to engage the interdisciplinary team in creating a Front-End Master Plan, collaboratively. The project team was interdisciplinary, with representatives from pre-clinical pharmacology, drug safety, product development, marketing, pharmaceutical development, project management, clinical research, clinical pharmacology, drug regulatory affairs, chemical research and process development. Each team member was knowledgeable about XY234 with respect to his or her job function.

## Triggering Question

Throughout the project, the dialogue of the team members was focused on responding to the following triggering question:

"What should we do in order to achieve world-wide sales of XY234 of at least $60 million one year post-launch, while maximizing our preparedness for a Subpart E application?"[1]

## CONCLUSIONS

The tangible results obtained from the application of the SDP approach to designing a Front-End Master Plan for the development of XY234 were:

- A set of over 130 requirements for the achievement of worldwide sales of at least $60 million, one year post-launch.
- A system of requirements represented by (a) an affinity pattern, which draws distinctions between similar and different requirements, and (b) an enhancement tree-pattern, which draws distinctions between strong and weak leverage requirements.
- A set of 114 distinct options which, if implemented, would contribute to the achievement of the system of requirements.
- An organization of the set of options into an Options Field representation that facilitated making choices and designing Action Scenarios.
- A Consensus Action Scenario graphically represented by an Options Profile representation incorporating 65 distinct options.

---

1.   The "Subpart E" portion of the question refers to aspects of the regulatory review process that permit a speedy review process in the case of drugs which treat catastrophic illnesses, such as Alzheimer's.

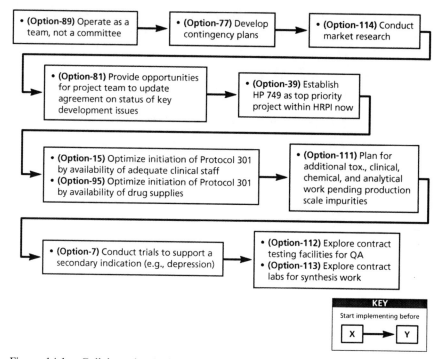

Figure 14.1.    Collaborative Action Plan for the development of XY234.

- A Front-End Master Plan representing the collective judgments of temporal sequencing of the options included in the Consensus Action Scenario (See Figure 14.1).

The intangible results, which are equally as important, were:

- The learning that took place among the members of the XY234 team.
- The integration of the diversity of observations into "team mental models" representing the collective wisdom of the team and the building of consensus and ownership of the Front-End Master Plan.
- The benefit of improving the collaboration and the quality of team-work among the members of the XY234 team.

The value of the intangible results is captured best through post-workshop comments by team members:

"There was a feeling of respect and acceptance by the group."

"The willingness to share both information and questions about unclear meanings or interpretations was most valuable."

"I am certain that all the knowledge and ideas that were shared and discussed during the process would never have come forth in a standard project team meeting."

"The product is more complete and more reflective of the total impact of the problem situation than the traditional committee process."

"This is a great alternative to waiting until a problem happens before we get together to discuss options."

"I think we all feel much more comfortable with each other. It's like opening doors to knowledge. It has also heightened our appreciation for the scope of responsibilities that each person has."

CHAPTER 15

# ANTICIPATING ALTERNATIVE FUTURES IN ENERGY EFFICIENCY

## CONTEXT

The last few years have seen a growing recognition of the importance of the efficient use of energy. The vision of the Northwest Energy Efficiency Alliance (Alliance) is to create a culture in the Pacific Northwest (PNW) in which the efficient use of energy is a core value among consumers and businesses. The rationale for this, as stated in the Alliance's strategic plan, is that energy savings, resulting from the marketplace embracing energy-efficient products and services, will lower the long-term cost and environmental impact of the region's electricity system, resulting in a healthier economy and a cleaner environment. Additional benefits resulting from the Alliance efforts, such as increased production or reduced waste, can help Northwest businesses become more competitive.

To address the challenge of improving energy efficiency in the Region, the Alliance initiated a project titled "Consumer Trends in the Pacific Northwest and the US." As part of the Discovery phase of the SDP, the project was launched with an electronic survey distributed among all the participants prior to a three-day co-laboratory. This was a modified version of the White Paper production and dissemination, so it represents an innovative approach of employing the Internet technology as a means to interact with the participants prior to the co-laboratory.

*How People Harness Their Collective Wisdom and Power*, pages 99–110
Copyright © 2006 by Information Age Publishing

The participants to the co-laboratory, scheduled on March 14-16, 2001, represented futurists, environmentalists, utility company executives, journalists, social and political scientists, administrators, regulators, and consumer advocates. At this event, stakeholders explored the long-term national and regional trends that will impact the adoption of energy efficiency in the PNW and chose specific actions to undertake in the near future. This case has been published in *World Futures* (Christakis et al., 2003).

## CONTENT

Thirty-five stakeholder representatives and six observers from thirty organizations interested in anticipating the adoption of energy efficiency for the Pacific Northwest identified and described one hundred and sixty-eight national and regional trends extending to the year 2015 impacting energy efficiency, and proposed more than ninety actions for addressing these trends at the regional level.

In the Definition Stage of the co-laboratory, participants described and clarified ninety-seven national trends and seventy-one regional trends. The participants identified the twenty trends they considered the most important to focus their dialogue. Through a robust investigation of plausibility influences among these trends, they decided by over fifty-eight strong majority opinions, four tracks of influence were agreed upon.

In the Design Stage, the participants generated and clarified more than ninety proposed actions for impacting the trends in a desirable way for the future of energy efficiency in the Pacific Northwest. Working methodically in four small teams, the participants identified the eight action options with the highest leverage. The combination of these action options represents a recommended desirable regional alternative future to be implemented by the Alliance and other Regional bodies participating in the event.

Prior to the co-laboratory, the participants responded to the Internet survey, which was designed as a means for identifying the most relevant trends in terms of their impact on progress in electric energy efficiency at the national/regional level, and hence establish a context for their deliberations at that level. In addition to selecting trends within 24 themes of trends at the national and regional contexts of the Internet survey, the participants were asked to propose new national/regional trends from their own perspective and experience, and to be prepared to explain their meaning to other participants at the co-laboratory.

After the explanations of the meanings of those trends proposed in response to the survey, the participants were engaged in generating additional trends by responding to a triggering question. The triggering question selected for the first two days of the group work was:

"What national/regional trends/events would you consider as having the greatest impact on electric energy efficiency over the next fifteen years?"

Stakeholders described sixty-seven national trends that were generated in response to the survey, and contributed another thirty trends in response to the triggering question, i.e., a total of 97 national trends. They clarified the meanings of all these trends during discussion with the entire group. They grouped these trends into affinity clusters based on distinctions and similarities between trends made by the stakeholders during the clarification dialogue. Each participant chose five trends, ranking them from 1 to 5 (most important to less important). Twelve national trends received at least five votes. These trends were used for the construction of a plausibility tree of influence among the most important national trends.

Stakeholders described sixty regional trends that were generated in response to the survey and contributed another eleven trends in response to the triggering question during the workshop (71 regional trends total). They clarified the meaning of these during discussion with the entire group. Each participant chose five trends, ranking them from 1 to 5 (most important to less important). Nine regional trends received at least six votes. Eight of these regional trends were also included in the construction of the plausibility tree of influence mentioned above in conjunction with the national trends.

## Pattern of Plausibility Enhancement among the National/Regional Trends/Events

Through a robust investigation of plausibility influences among the twenty most important trends, decided by over fifty-eight strong majority opinions, four tracks of influence were agreed upon, as shown graphically in Figure 15.1:

- Track 1: Energy Conservation, which includes six important trends (shaded in Dark Grey in Figure 15.1);
- Track 2: Energy Efficiency, including six important trends (shaded in Medium Dark Grey);
- Track 3: Lifestyles of the Future, including five trends (shaded in Medium Light Grey);
- Track 4: Energy-Supply, including three trends (shaded in Light Grey).

Employing SDP dialogue the participants made judgments of the relationships among the trends, and produced a pattern displaying how some trends impact others in the set of the twenty most important trends. The

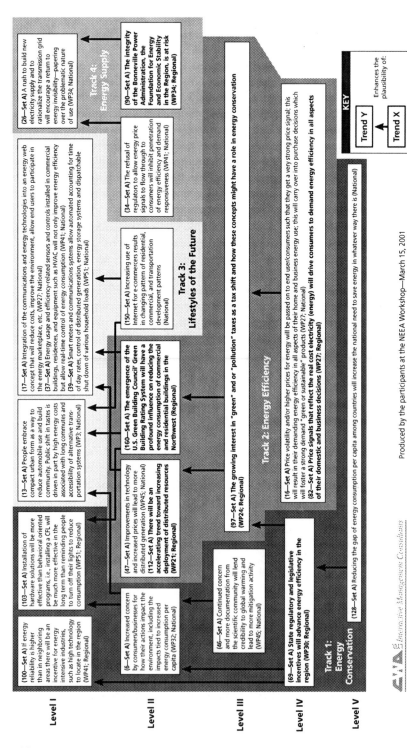

Figure 15.1. Plausibility pattern among most important national/regional trends/events.

most influential trends are positioned at the lower levels of the tree-like influence pattern shown in Figure 15.1, where the arrows indicate the propagation of plausibility among the trends, so that addressing trends at the lower levels of Figure 15.1 will help significantly in addressing trends at the higher levels, provided there are arrows connecting those trends.

In accordance with the judgments of the majority of stakeholders, three of the four dominant tracks are connected. The interpretation of the linkages among the first three tracks is: Reduced consumption of energy by consumers and their awareness of the need to protect the environment will enhance the plausibility of increases in energy efficiency through the adoption of "green" technologies and a more distributed generation of electricity, which in turn will have a significant impact in terms of consumer lifestyles around the year 2010. For example, people will start embracing compact urban form as a way to reduce automobile use and build community while integrating communications and energy technologies into an energy web concept.

Only one trend on the Plausibility Map is positioned at the deepest level. This is:

(Trend-128) Reducing the gap of energy consumption per capita among countries will increase the national need to save energy in whatever way there is.

The author of this trend stated during clarification:

I find "sustainable development" as the most important context for handling any thought about energy matters in the whole world, and that "sustainability" (leaving our descendants a livable planet to develop themselves with no imposed restrictions) is my main interest and the reason to be here as a participant.

Stakeholders judged this particular trend as the "deep driver," exerting leverage at the deepest level of the Plausibility Tree. According to their judgment Trend #128 will enhance the plausibility of directly influencing state regulatory and legislative bodies to provide incentives at the regional level that will promote the adoption of energy conservation and efficiency in the Pacific Northwest. Trend #128 impacts directly or indirectly twelve of the twenty trends appearing in Figure 15.1.

Because of the meaning the author ascribed to this trend it is assigned in the Energy Conservation Track (Track 1). However, its influence propagates along the pathways of the Plausibility Tree and enhances the plausibility of other trends belonging in the tracks of energy efficiency (Track 2), and lifestyles of the future (Track 3). The interpretation of the stakeholder judgments in terms of plausibility influences among the trends is that by reducing the gap of energy consumption per capita among all countries, it will impact ecological integrity and social sustainability. The ecological sustainability trend will manifest its impacts on consumer behavior in terms of lifestyles at the national and regional levels of analysis by the year 2010.

## Action Options

At the third day of the co-laboratory the participants initiated the implementation of the Design Stage of the SDP dialogue. To perform this task they were asked to study the Plausibility Tree of national and regional trends (Figure 15.1), and to respond to the following triggering question:

> "What are short-term action options which, if we adopt, will impact in a desirable way the anticipated effects of the national/regional trends as displayed in the Plausibility Map?"

A similar process for the generation and clarification of the option statements was employed as the one used for the generation and clarification of national and regional trends. Participants generated and clarified ninety-one action options.

A member of the facilitation team prepared a preliminary set of clusters for the action options according to perceived similarities by responding to questions according to the following format:

> "In the context of designing a regional alternative future for the adoption of energy efficiency, does:
> (Option-X)
> have *significant* characteristics in common with (is similar to):
> (Option-Y)?"

The resulting clusters form the basis for the categorical view of action options that was provided to the participants. The Options Field pattern was also displayed on the walls of the Collaborative facility. Participants were engaged in identifying names that would characterize the overall intent of each cluster.

Using the categorical view of stakeholder explanations, participants voted for the action options they judged to be most salient. Out of a total of more than ninety action options proposed by the participants, fifty-seven received one or more votes and only fourteen received three or more votes, indicating a significant convergence in terms of relative saliency among the participants. If there was 100% divergence in terms of voting preferences all 91 options could have received at least one vote, since the total number of votes was equal to 165. The measure of divergence of preference for this case is equal to 60%, which is 10% higher than the average divergence obtained from data gathered from 81 applications of SDP during the decade of the 1980s. The fourteen options that received three or more votes received over 30% of the total number of votes.

Four teams of stakeholders were then asked to consider how they would combine action options across all categories to impact in a desirable way the national and regional trends presented in the Plausibility Tree (Figure 15.1). They presented their selections as "alternative regional futures" to the group, also explaining how their alternative will address some specific trends of Figure 15.1.

Eight out of a total of ninety-one action options were selected by 3 or more teams. These eight are included in the Consensus Regional Future, and are shown in Table 15.1: Individual and Team Voting on Action Options Impacting the Plausibility Map in a Desirable Way. Note that all five of the most important options from the individual votes, have been selected by three or more teams in their team alternative. Two options that received less than two individual votes, namely Action #7 and Action #24, are included in the Consensus Regional Future because three of the four teams selected them in their team alternative. Six of the eight most preferred options are also presented in the context of four of the twelve affinity clusters identified by the stakeholders. These six are shown as Figure 15.2: Partial Options Field Representation of Consensus Regional Future Based on Small Teams. This Figure displays graphically six action options selected for the Consensus Regional Future, which are connected to the "TIE LINE." By studying Figure 15.2, which displays only a subset of the 91 action options proposed by the stakeholders, the reader will appreciate the number and diversity of options from which the participants made choices of inclusion and exclusion in constructing the consensus scenario.

## Scenario Construction

As mentioned earlier, the participants were arranged into four small teams based on the criterion of maximizing the diversity of perspectives within each team. The teams deliberated on selecting actions that they would include in a prospective Regional Alternative Future. The clusters of action options they had developed in the large group (see Figure 15.2), during the previous step were provided as a working template. The groups were instructed to first consider the inclusion of each of the one dozen action options that had received at least three individual votes (see Table 15.1). In this workshop nine of the options that received three or more votes were not selected by three or more teams and hence are not included in the Consensus Regional Future. On the other hand, three teams selected Option #15, which received two individual votes, and also selected Options #24 and #7, which did not receive any individual votes. This phenomenon happens frequently in SDP co-laboratories because SDP has been designed to promote evolutionary learning in terms of meaning and judgments of saliency among the observations made by the participants, as indicated by the principle of evolutionary learning discussed briefly in Chapter 9.

**Table 15.1.   Voting Results on Action Options for Impacting in a Desirable Way the Plausibility Map (Individual Votes and Team Scenario Votes)**

| Team Scenarios | Individual Votes | Action Option: |
|---|---|---|
| **All 4 Teams** | (4)* | **(1—Action Option)** Develop tiered rate proposals to encourage energy efficiency and/or distributed generation instead of growth in loads **(Cluster #1)**. |
| 2 Teams | (3) | **(3—Action Option)** Conduct or survey existing research regarding fundamental belief structures as they relate to energy and natural resource use **(Cluster #3)**. |
| 3 Teams | (7)* | **(4—Action Option)** Establish competitively neutral, equitable requirements for utility investment in energy efficiency **(Cluster #4)**. |
| 3 Teams | (0)* | **(7—Action Option)** Review barriers to distributed generation and try to reduce or eliminate **(Cluster #6)**. |
| 1 Team | (3) | **(8—Action Option)** Provide incentives to attract companies to the nw that make energy efficiency products/green products **(Cluster #7)**. |
| 0 Team | (3) | **(9—Action Option)** The NW is recognized as the "silicon valley" of revolutionary, distributed energy technology **(Cluster #7)**. |
| All 4 Teams | (5)* | **(12—Action Option)** Encourage state regulatory agencies to experiment with innovative pricing mechanisms and consumer signals **(Cluster #1)**. |
| 1 Team | (3) | **(13—Action Option)** Promote the formation of a regional forum to attract companies into the region who will provide energy efficiency products and services **(Cluster #7)**. |
| 3 Teams | (2)* | **(15—Action Option)** Use public credit to create a buying/purchase guarantee cooperative tool for regional hardware purchases **(Cluster #8)**. |
| 3 Teams | (0)* | **(24—Action Option)** Establish a standardize protocol for smart meter installation across the region **(Cluster #5)**. |
| All 4 Teams | (6)* | **(25—Action Option)** Encourage widespread installation of electric metering that allows alternative rate design **(Cluster #5)**. |
| 2 Teams | (3) | **(29—Action Option)** Provide an authoritative analysis of the transmission and distribution benefits and the energy cost benefits of distributed generation **(Cluster #6)**. |
| 2 Teams | (3) | **(46—Action Option)** Strongly encourage (with incentives) implementation of communication infrastructure for implementation of real time energy pricing principles **(Cluster #5)**. |

**Table 15.1.   Voting Results on Action Options for Impacting
in a Desirable Way the Plausibility Map
(Individual Votes and Team Scenario Votes)**

| Team Scenarios | Individual Votes | Action Option: |
|---|---|---|
| 3 Teams | (5)* | **(52—Action Option)** Adopt region wide DSM marketing strategy that has a common theme or logo **(Cluster #3)**. |
| 2 Teams | (3) | **(53—Action Option)** Develop collaboration between the alliance and the oregon energy trust **(Cluster #8)**. |
| 1 Team | (4) | **(64—Action Option)** Develop a regional energy efficiency/green product certification program (using John Pyrch's logo) **(Cluster #8)**. |
| 2 Teams | (4) | **(84—Action Option)** Develop web-based feedback tools for homes and businesses that report instantaneous energy use and cost rather than relying on monthly after the fact utility bills **(Cluster #5)**. |

* These eight action options are identified in Figure 15.2 as those selected for the Consensus Regional Future
Produced by the participants at the NEEA Workshop March 16, 2001

The teams were then coached in developing narrative descriptions of their Alternative Regional Futures. They presented their Futures to the full set of participants. The teams typically employ a narrator, two people using the wall displays of the Plausibility Tree and the Options Tree, and one person with a Laser Pointer guided the participants through the team scenario from display to display.

## Small Team Regional Futures

The Consensus Regional Future was developed as a composite of small group work by four interdisciplinary teams, and appears in Figure 15.2. The summary of their selected actions appears in Table 15.1. Eight actions were selected by three or more of the four teams. According to the tally of the team selections they were Actions #1 and #12 from Cluster #1: Price & Taxes, Action #52 from Cluster 3: Education and Marketing, Action #4 from Cluster #4: Regulatory Action, Actions #24 and #25 from Cluster #5: Metering, Action #7 from Cluster #6: DG Infrastructure, and Action #15 from Cluster #8: Tools. The overriding intent of the team action scenarios most directly targeted the theme of Energy Efficiency track (see Medium Dark Grey Area in the Plausibility Tree of Figure 15.1). On account of the location of the trends belonging to the Energy Efficiency track at Levels IV, III, and II, their influence will propagate along the arrows and enhance the plausibility of other trends located at Level I.

| Cluster #1: Price and Taxes (Financial Incentives) | Cluster #3: Education and Marketing | Cluster #4: Regulatory Action | Cluster #5: Metering | Cluster #6: Distributed Generation Infrastructure | Cluster #8: Tools |
|---|---|---|---|---|---|
| **(Action Option 1)** Develop tiered rate proposals to encourage energy efficiency and/or distributed generation instead of growth in loads ◆◆◆◆ | **(Action Option 52)** Adopt a region-wide DSM marketing strategy that has a common theme or logo ◆◆◆ | **(Action Option 4)** Establish competitively neutral, equitable requirements for utility investment in energy efficiency ◆◆◆ | **(Action Option 5)** Solicit proposals for a "smart wall plug" system to help households discover their energy sinks ◆ | **(Action Option 7)** Review barriers to distributed generation and try to reduce or eliminate ◆◆◆ | **(Action Option 10)** To create a robust financial model that building owners and managers can use to bridge initial capital costs with those costs associated with maintenance operations i.e., internal rates of return |
| **(Action Option 6)** Begin adoption of green taxes as a mechanism for increasing awareness of true costs and environmental impacts of energy use | **(Action Option 57)** Use market techniques such as "regional branding" to create and sustain a political and economic regional identity ◆ | **(Action Option 22)** Support legislation that will require both immediate and long-term conservation/ renewable programs | **(Action Option 24)** Establish a standardize protocol for smart meter installation across the region ◆◆◆ | **(Action Option 19)** Provide comprehensive development and deployment news and information on DER and DSM and DER–DSM linkage | **(Action Option 15)** Use public credit to create a buying/purchase guarantee cooperative tool for regional hardware purchases ◆◆◆ |
| **(Action Option 12)** Encourage state regulatory agencies to experiment with innovative pricing mechanisms and consumer signals ◆◆◆◆ | **(Action Option 58)** Launch essay and poster design contests for energy efficiency themes | **(Action Option 27)** Educate and encourage legislative members on benefits of incentives that will advance energy efficiency ◆ | **(Action Option 25)** Encourage widespread installation of electric metering that allows alternative rate design ◆◆◆◆ | **(Action Option 29)** Provide an authoritative analysis of the transmission and distribution benefits and the energy cost benefits of distributed generation | **(Action Option 38)** Promote and incent the integration of the U.S. Green Building Councils LEED program to building owners and design professionals ◆ |
| **(Action Option 16)** Fund incentives for energy saving buildings, equipment and vehicles with a tax on emissions of $CO_2$ and other pollutants | **(Action Option 59)** Include energy efficiency and sustainability tracks throughout the education system including sponsoring curriculum and faculty | **(Action Option 32)** Establish reasonable accountability mechanisms for utility investments in energy efficiency | **(Action Option 46)** Strongly encourage (with incentives) implementation of communication infrastructure for implementation of real-time energy pricing principles ◆ | **(Action Option 37)** Invest in small-scale, hyper-efficient energy machines | |
| **(Action Option 17)** Influence PNW energy regulators to allow/encourage RTP/TOD rates | **(Action Option 63)** Secure a high profile spokesperson for energy efficiency | | | | |

◆ = Team vote

*Produced by the participants at the NEEA Workshop—March 16, 2001*

TIE LINE

Figure 15.2.   Partial options field representation of consensus regional future based on small teams.

As can be seen by looking at the Plausibility Tree, some of these trends at Level I belong to the tracks of energy conservation (dark grey color) and life-styles of the future (medium light grey color). The interpretation of this finding is that by implementing the Consensus Regional Future the PNW is taking actions to have desirable impacts on the Energy Efficiency track of the Tree, but because of the linkages of this track with the other two tracks of the Tree, it is very plausible that the energy conservation and life-style trends of Figure 15.1 will come to pass in the region.

Actions #1, #12 and #25 received unanimous endorsement by the four teams (see Table 15.1). These three Actions also stood out in the presentation of the team scenarios. These actions appear to have the highest priority in the judgment of the majority of participants in terms of leveraging the adoption of energy efficiency in the PNW, which will in turn enhance the plausibility of life styles for the region that are compatible with the ethic of sustainability and energy conservation.

## CONCLUSIONS

The findings of the co-laboratory, in terms of the eight consensus action options included in the Consensus Regional Future (see Figure 15.2), are clearly supportive of the mission of the Alliance. Implementation of these actions will impact directly in a desirable way the trends that the stakeholders identified as belonging in the Energy Efficiency track (Track 2), and will consequently be supportive of the Alliance's mission. These same action options, because of the linkages between the Energy Efficiency track and the Lifestyles track, will also have indirect desirable impacts in terms of social sustainability as manifested by the lifestyles adopted by the consumers of the region.

Future collaborative regional action to promote the adoption of energy efficiency in the PNW should give serious consideration to the eight consensus actions belonging to the six categories identified above.

For more details about this application the readers are referred to the *World Futures* paper, which was published in collaboration with Dr. Ben Bronfman (Christakis et al, 2003). Ben was the staff member of the Northwest Energy Efficiency Alliance responsible for this particular application of the SDP paradigm.

\*    \*    \*

An extended and detailed description using the whole panoply of SDP consensus methods and covering all four SDP design stages is presented in Appendix A. Because of time constraints, the rigorous Trade-Off Analysis of Stages 3 and 4 is often replaced with more informal procedures, such as those described above in terms of the construction of the Consensus Action Scenario.

# CHAPTER 16

---

# WISDOM OF THE
# PEOPLE FORUM

## CONTEXT

**F**orty Indigenous leaders from the Americas and New Zealand and several non-Indigenous experts participated in a "Wisdom of the People Forum" held in Washington, DC from September 16–18, 2002. The challenge facing this Forum was to lay the groundwork for an expanding web of transnational, grassroots Indigenous cooperation that could integrate intangible traditional core cultural values into a contemporary reality. The group examined the current situation of transnational Indigenous leadership interactions and identified effective ways to enhance those interactions in the context of globalization.

The first purpose of the Forum was to create, through true dialogue, a shared understanding of the barriers that need to be addressed in the enhancement of liberating transnational interactions among emerging Indigenous leaders in the context of globalization.

The leaders opened their deliberations sitting in the traditional Comanche circle sharing their "medicine"—their sources of inner strength and personal power—principally based on respect for the Earth, ancestors, family, and peaceful co-existence.

## CONTENT

On the first day of the Forum, they considered the obstacles that stand in the way of worldwide cooperation and generated 79 barriers. In dialogue

*How People Harness Their Collective Wisdom and Power,* pages 111–113
Copyright © 2006 by Information Age Publishing
All rights of reproduction in any form reserved.

and in the spirit of participative democracy, they identified not only the barriers that they deemed most important but also those whose overcoming would exert the most leverage in overcoming the other barriers. The system of barriers they identified is presented in Figure 16.1.

On the second day of the co-laboratory, the stakeholder/participants proposed and clarified ways to overcome this system of barriers for effective transnational Indigenous interaction. They answered the following triggering question: "What are action options which, if adopted and implemented by the community of stakeholders, will help in meeting the system of barriers?" They generated and clarified 49 action options, which were posted on the wall. Then they grouped similar action options together by clustering them on the wall and giving them category labels i.e., creating an Options Field representation on the wall. In preparation for designing action profiles, each participant was given five sticky dots with which to vote by pasting the dots for their favorite five options. The number of dots on an option gave prima facie evidence of its importance.

On the third day, participants were broken into small teams and given printed copies of the Options Field they had created and the number of votes awarded to each option. Each table was instructed to create an action scenario by selecting a reasonable number of action options and to develop an explanation for their choices with reference to the Influence Tree (Figure 16.1) constructed on the first day.

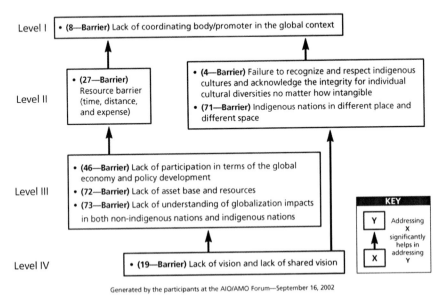

Figure 16.1.   Influence tree of barriers in the context of globalization.

Then a spokesperson from each team described their scenario while a representative from the team pasted large dots on their selected options. Six teams explained (or acted out) their scenarios and pasted their large dots, answering questions from other participants.

By this time, the participants understood the action options, the system of barriers, and their many interrelationships. In examining the results of their individual and group voting, they found that four or more teams had selected eight actions that fell into five categories. The 8 consensus actions that were included in the Consensus Action Scenario are:

- Identify generic core culture values, philosophies, principles of participants;
- Understand our own Indigeneity and culture before we begin studying others;
- Strengthen existing strategic alliances and form new ones;
- Research and develop a diagram of Indigenous organizations;
- Build network of Indigenous and non Indigenous contacts;
- Analyze the impact of globalization on the communities of the participants;
- Identify stakeholders and participants;
- Establish an Indigenous exchange organization of corporate entities, profit and non-profit (yin and yang).

## CONCLUSION

These eight action options are effective, practical means that embody Indigeneity. Using the SDP dialogue, the Indigenous leaders produced an action plan in less than three days, which sets the stage for sustained Indigenous involvement in the corridors of economic, political, and media power (Christakis and Harrris, 2004).

The Advancement of Global Indigeneity (AGI) and its two founding members, Americans for Indian Opportunity (AIO) and the Advancement of Maori Opportunity (AMO), have continued to make progress on these options. In 2003, they held a large Wisdom of the People Forum during an international conference in Crete (Harris and Wasilewski, 2004). In 2005, they jointly ran a Wisdom of the People Forum in Japan (reported in the next chapter).

CHAPTER 17

# INTERNATIONAL BOUNDARY-SPANNING DIALOGUES

## Project "Successful Cypriot Women"

### CONTEXT

**C**yprus is a divided island nation scarred by war and bloodshed. Since 1974, Cypriots have existed in two hostile enclaves, Turkish and Greek, separated by a buffer zone. There is not even direct telephone communication between them. The antagonism has many roots including the 400 year occupation of Greece and Cyprus by the Ottoman Empire, the occupation of the island by the British, and a war for self-determination of the island people in 1956–1964.

Marios Michaelides and Antigone Petropoulos are working to heal this rift. Using SDP, they hold bi-communal workshops in the neutral zone to build mutual understanding, respect, and cooperation. In late January and early February of 2003, they designed and conducted a workshop with Turkish and Greek Cypriot women professionals who "are interested in setting up a Non-Governmental Organization (NGO) that will offer services for the empowerment of women in their communities. The *'Successful Women'* Project is part of their efforts at realizing this vision." A significant part of this project will be a video "that will be used in workshops for young women on the theme of 'success.'"

*How People Harness Their Collective Wisdom and Power*, pages 115–119
Copyright © 2006 by Information Age Publishing
All rights of reproduction in any form reserved.

**CONTENT**

The objectives of this co-laboratory were:

- To provide the participants the opportunity to explore and obtain a deeper understanding of the concept of "success" for women in the two communities of Cyprus today.
- To identify a set of criteria, which will be used by a small committee, to select three women from each community to participate in the documentary film.
- To experience the consensus-building dialogue process.
- To develop a community of women with shared understanding and common language.

Using SDP, this group generated 106 qualities of success and selected 24 of these as being more important. They explored the influence relationships among these 24 and produced collaboratively the Influence Tree represented in Figure 17.1. Also, they organized the 106 qualities in 11 categories, also shown in Figure 17.1.

As can be readily seen, by reading the Influence Tree from bottom-up, the deepest drivers (Qualities #18, 2, and 60) at the root of the Tree influence everything above them. Thus, being an informed person (#18) helps a woman be aware of gender discrimination (#22), which in turn helps her have vision, which helps create opportunities (#88), etc. Similarly, having a balanced and independent personality helps a woman be aware of her choices and opportunities (#5) and bolsters her self-improvement efforts (#12), which helps her generate the abilities, qualities, and relationships identified in the large box in the middle of the Tree (see Figure 17.1). Finally energy, drive, and stamina (#60) greatly influence a woman's mastery of the qualities in the same larger box. Conversely, the big box at the top of the Tree contains many of the ideal qualities of a successful woman, but these qualities will not materialize unless the qualities lower on the Tree are achieved. In other words, the influence from the qualities located at the root of the Tree propagates upwards along the branches of the Tree and impacts many other qualities. Those qualities at the root of the Tree are the ones that require the highest level of attention for success.

**CONCLUSIONS**

This Tree has been used to design the "Successful Cypriot Women" video and also helped in the selection of the women who will exemplify alternate conceptions of success and different pathways to achievement. The whole effort is designed to build bridges between Turks and Greeks on Cyprus.

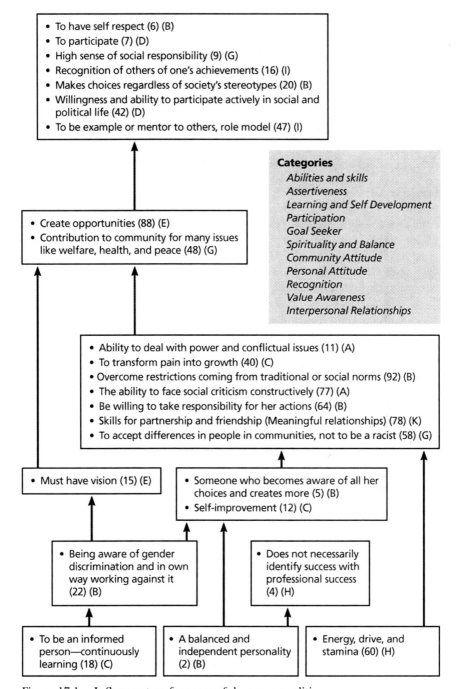

Figure 17.1.   Influence tree for successful women qualities.

A new young president, Tassos Papadopoulos, assumed office in Cyprus on March 1, 2003. It remains to be seen how he might use SDP to build areas of consensus in his divided nation. A team has been trained and has been using the scientific dialogue process for over five years on the island in a variety of settings. In the summer of 2004, I was asked to visit the island again for some advanced training in the theory of the science of dialogic design, which will be presented in Part IV.

## SPANNING BOUNDARIES IN NORTHEAST ASIA

### Context

In February 2005 twenty-five Japanese, Korean, Chinese and Russian students gathered at International Christian University (ICU) in Tokyo to engage in a Boundary-Spanning Dialogue founded on the SDP paradigm (Christakis and Brahms, 2003). The purpose of this dialogue was to identify obstacles to intercultural communication in the North East Asian Region. Participants in the dialogue also included indigenous people (Ainu and Evenki) from the North East Asian region. Simultaneous interpretation was provided between English and Japanese, but interpretation for other local languages were necessary because some participants spoke only one language, which was neither English nor Japanese. The facilitator team for this dialogue was composed of indigenous people, one Comanche and one Maori from the US and New Zealand, respectively. They were responsible for enforcing the SDP rules of engagement in focused and open dialogue. They were able to create a very inclusive and affirmative atmosphere throughout the co-laboratory, which according to a participant (Yupta, 2005) contributed to the success of the event.

### Content

The triggering question selected for the first day of the group work was:

"What are the barriers/obstacles to intercultural boundary-spanning dialogue in Northeast Asia?"

Seventy-eight obstacles were identified. They constructed the *Problematique* of the situation and discovered that the fundamental obstacle was/is the problem of the contested history of the region.

They subsequently constructed five alternative action scenarios to overcome these obstacles. Because of time limitations they were not able to construct a Consensus Action Scenario at this event.

## CONCLUSION

A second dialogue will be held in November this year (2005) to develop an implementation plan for dealing with the contested history. On June 12th of 2005, a subset of the participants gathered to integrate the five existing action scenarios and to decide the Triggering Question for the next dialogue in November. It is hoped that the ultimate outcome of this project will be an International Day of Reconciliation in the North East Asian Region.

CHAPTER 18

# COMMUNITY-BASED CO-LABORATORY OF DEMOCRACY

## CONTEXT

**O**n January 11, 2003, thirty-four residents of the Bryn Gweled intentional community in Bucks County, PA, applied the SDP to define intentions for the future of their community. The co-laboratory took place in the Bryn Gweled Community Center shown below as Figure 18.1.

Figure 18.1.

*How People Harness Their Collective Wisdom and Power*, pages 121–125
Copyright © 2006 by Information Age Publishing

## CONTENT

In a one day working session, the community stakeholders generated and clarified 42 distinct intentions, such as:

- Restore the intentional diversity of the community.
- Learn to have fun together as a community.
- Encourage members to act on the saying "It takes a village to raise a child."
- Develop effective ways of resolving disputes so that no one feels like a winner or a loser.

They subsequently voted individually and subjectively on the relative importance of the 42 intentions and selected those intentions that they thought were of higher relative importance (see Figure 18.2 for the pattern of voting in the Collaborative facility).

In the voting, 39 out of the 42 received one or more votes from the participants. This result corresponds to a divergence in terms of preference of 91%, which is very high when compared to the average divergence from a variety of applications of SDP. The 5 most important intentions were:

- Make the transition from our early stage of growth to one of stewardship.
- Identify better ways to improve our decision-making process.
- Re-explore ideas to allow elderly members to remain on the Bryn Gweled Homestead.
- Re-unite less active members of our community with an invitation to participate anew.
- Use our past knowledge to enlighten our future planning.

In the afternoon, the stakeholders engaged in a strategic dialogue exploring the influences among the 12 intentions that received the most votes. The resulting Influence Tree is displayed in Figure 18.3.

Figure 18.2.

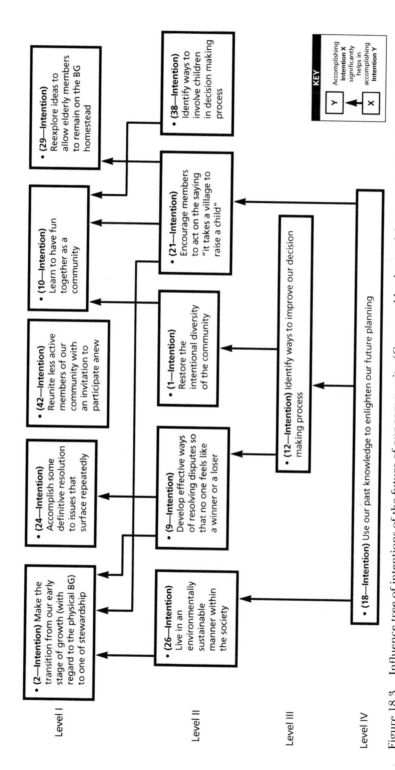

Figure 18.3. Influence tree of intentions of the future of our community. (Generated by the participants at the Bryn Gweled Community Center—January 11, 2003.

Figure 18.4.    Interpreting the influence pattern.

This Influence Tree-pattern is a "tree of meaning." Relevant to the community, the intentions at the base of the tree are the most influential ones. If those intentions at the base of the tree were neglected, the community would be greatly handicapped in its efforts to accomplish intentions higher on the tree. The stakeholders were intrigued by the discovery of the most influential intentions, shown in Figure 18.4, which were the following two:

- Use our past knowledge to enlighten our future planning.
- Identify ways to improve our decision-making process.

The implication of this discovery was that the Bryn Gweled community should focus its energy on meeting those two intentions. If it fulfills these two most influential intentions, it will be much easier for them to accomplish the other intentions higher on the tree. In looking at the Tree, it became clear to the participants that the intentions they voted most important were not the most effective for attaining the goal.

This is a recurrent phenomenon when stakeholders use the co-laboratory of Democracy process. It will be discussed in detail in Chapter 23.

The two other intentions that should be given serious consideration by the community, because of their positioning in the influence tree, are:

- Identify ways to involve children in the decision-making process.
- Reunite less active members of our community with an invitation to participate anew.

## CONCLUSIONS

By working on the four intentions discovered during SDP dialogue, the community has already made significant progress towards accomplishing all the other important intentions shown in the Influence Tree.

The commentary at the end of the session was very positive, including statements by the stakeholders that the Influence Tree made explicit and transparent their long tradition of decision making. The community has been using *Robert's Rules of Order* for many years, and they appreciated SDP dialogue, in the sense that it enables them to have a true dialogue instead of a debate.

In February 2005, the stakeholders revisited their earlier work by means of a dedicated "Day of Dialogue" focusing on ecosystemic issues confronting the community on account of the significant increase of the deer population. A task force is implementing the recommendations of the second co-laboratory of democracy for this community. One member of the community recently made the statement:

> Before using this dialogue process we were experiencing a serious breakdown in terms of our capacity to sustain our traditional intentional community values and construct our future. We are now clearly on the correct path.

Bryn Gweled Homesteads was created in 1940 to give 80 families enough land to raise their food. "Homesteading" is no longer practiced, and the community is now completely surrounded by Philadelphia suburbs. But Bryn Gweled has never lost sight of its founder's dedication to cooperation, to environmentalism, and to racial, economic, and religious diversity. This Co-Laboratory of Democracy was called to reinvigorate processes dedicated to those ideals.

# Part IV

## A SCIENCE OF DIALOGIC DESIGN

**O**ur understanding of social systems is changing in the 21st century. We are beginning to realize that the hierarchical view of social organization is a relic of an older age and that a self-organizing web model better expresses how social systems work. We are also realizing that this self-organizing has two parts: an automatic systemic process and a more difficult process that depends upon human consensus, which requires active listening and the formation of a consensual linguistic domain. It further requires disciplined dialogue and numerous aids such as those supplied in SDP.

Thirty years ago, in Paris, I had a strong feeling that the residents of Paris should design the future of Paris. Gerard de Zeeuw has since formulated that feeling in his description of Third Phase Science, which holds that the observer-independent data prized in classical physics are of secondary importance to the observer-dependent information of flesh and blood people in designing human systems. A valid people science, then, would surface the knowledge and wisdom of stakeholders and harness their power to construct the future. A Greek word for this people science is Demosophia (Wisdom of the People).

In trying to construct the science of Ekistics for Doxiadis, I came to a similar realization. The methods of physical science were inadequate for the task. Creating alternative methods has been the quest of John Warfield and me for the past 35 years. This quest has led not only to the SDP paradigm, but also to formulations of the science underlying it.

Warfield in *A Science of Generic Design* produced "a thorough discussion of the management of complexity through system design" (1994). From an epistemological viewpoint, he provided in exacting detail the justification, foundations, theory and methodology for any design science, be it social, mechanical, or cybernetic. In order to make the wisdom of this scholarly tome accessible, Warfield and Roxana Cardenas published *A Handbook of Interactive Management* (1994).

Part IV presents the foundations of "a science of dialogic design," casting it as an axiomatic science. This science rests on three axioms, six basic laws, and the methodological components of the architecture presented in Part II. The advantage of an axiomatic approach is simplicity in determining what belongs to the science: those constructs that fit all three axioms and enhance the practice of the axioms in the arena constitute the science.

# CHAPTER 19

# CONTEXT OF THE SCIENCE

**D**esign is done in context. In the 21st century, the context of social systems design is changing. The staid mechanical model of organization where slow changes were decreed from the top of a hierarchy is being questioned. In its place, a self-organizing web model has appeared, with every node and connection contributing to rapid systemic change. Some key concepts—communicative action, cognitive reasoning, conscious evolution, linguistic domains—clarify the workings of self-organization in the social context. It is in this new context that Dialogic Design finds its home.

## COMMUNICATIVE ACTION

Dialogic design requires dialogue: communication where we respect one another, listen to each other, and try to understand what we believe and what we ought to do. When we engage in dialogic design we are engaging in "communicative action," which Jurgen Habermas once portrayed as an "ideal speech situation" (Habermas, 1971). In this portrayal, participants express themselves freely, forthrightly, and truthfully; therefore, they put aside external power relationships and address each other on an equal footing. In such an ideal discussion, every viewpoint and argument is heard and decisions are made by the power of the better argument. Communicative action can be contrasted to "instrumental" and "strategic" action, but not in an exclusive sense. The people involved in communicative action

*How People Harness Their Collective Wisdom and Power*, pages 129–137
Copyright © 2006 by Information Age Publishing
129

over drug XY234 (chapter 14), for example, used instrumental action with their clinical trials and strategic action as they examined the marketability of that drug.

Instrumental action reduces problems to their simplest parts and strives for technical control. It is employed in mechanical systems and in operational systems management under names like operational research, systems research, and systems engineering. This approach was pioneered by Rene Descartes who said in his *Discourse on Method* (1637), "The second [rule] was to divide up each of the difficulties which I examined into as many parts as possible, and as seemed requisite in order that it might be resolved in the best manner possible" (Britannica translation). This method is commonly described as "reductionistic."

Strategic action works to maximize one's self-interest, and tries to control the activities of other actors. "The focus is on problem identification and understanding" (Ulrich 1991, p. 260). Salesmen, for example, identify a client's needs and motivations in order to make a sale. Impressive techniques like cybernetic modeling, game theory, and "key factors of success" are used to accomplish strategic action. Equally impressive "carrot and stick" techniques are used in the world of advertising, labor relations, globalization, and some manipulative techniques of social psychology.

| *Dialogic Design Works Well* | *Dialogic Design Is Ineffective* |
|---|---|
| As communicative action | As instrumental and strategic action |

## COGNITIVE THINKING

In school, we are taught to be "objective" and "rational" in our thinking, and that there is only one correct answer to a problem. This *rational* thinking leads us to believe that people should not understand things differently—if they do, one of them is wrong. Decision-making requires "consistent, value-maximizing choice within specified constraints" (Campanella, 1993, p. 243) and strategies of optimal choice and cost-benefit analysis in terms of a goals-means economy. It ignores certain limits to rationality: namely, actual actors are integrated people and not the mere economic actors of economic theory; no political actor acts in an organizational vacuum (Campanella, p. 243). It also ignores time constraints and fluid situations that render dispassionate and leisurely contemplation of rational alternatives impossible (Luhman 1971) and, therefore, require shorthand rules for decision-making.

The *cognitive* model of decision-making centers on the real-life strategies that we use to make our way in the world. It considers the human actor "not at rest but in action" (p. 242). It "emphasizes unexpected factors, pertaining to the subject and to the environment of the action, and these vanish from view when operating under the assumption of rationality and consistency" (p. 242). It assumes that people form a simplified cognitive map of their world in order to cope with the confusing complexity of their lives. They use this map to make choices that are not optimal but are nevertheless satisfying.

In the cognitive approach, individuals confront situations of high complexity and ambiguity with a simplified and flexible set of beliefs and information. They use these cognitive filters to overcome (or succumb to) the complexity, the ambiguity, the uncertainty, etc. of the surrounding world.

Campanella summarizes the applicability and effectiveness of these two paradigms:

> The cognitive paradigm considers more clearly the ever-changing situation of the actor-in-action, while the rational paradigm demands steady-state situations. If the rational paradigm is able to resolve problems under selected conditions of space and time, the cognitive paradigm copes with "fuzzy gamble situations" (p. 244).

| *Dialogic Design Works Well* | *Dialogic Design Is Ineffective* |
|---|---|
| In a combination of cognitive and rational paradigms | In an exclusively rational paradigm |

## SELF-ORGANIZING WEB

As the new insights of evolutionary biology, relativity, quantum mechanics, and thermodynamics sifted into the psyches of people during the 20th century, thinkers faced increased pressure to resolve the contradictions between competing paradigms. By mid-century the intellectual tensions had gone far-from-equilibrium. The stage was set for another paradigm leap in physics. Classical dynamics, quantum dynamics, and evolution finally came together in a new paradigm, non-linear thermodynamics, which was pioneered by such notable thinkers as Henri Poincare, Ilya Prigogine, and Stuart Kauffman.

In the world of non-linear dynamics, entities self-organize within a web structure. Notable manifestations of this self-organization are:

- The Benard effect, in which convection currents in liquids brought to a slow boil generate a honeycomb pattern (Prigogine and Stengers, 1984).

- The Belousov-Zhabotinski reaction popularized by Prigogine, in which chemical solutions gradually assume identical distinctive patterns (Prigogine and Stengers, 1984).
- The generation of amino acids by solutions of minerals (Eigen, 1992).
- The generation of cellular life ("compartmented hypercycles") from proteins and amino acids (Eigen, 1992).
- The generation of order through simple Boolean (+, −) operations (Kauffman, 1993).
- Cellular automata that evolve on computer monitors by following a few simple rules (Wolfram, 1982).
- The Mandlebrot set, which consists of a beautiful evolving visual set of infinite depth from a simple equation (Gleick, 1987).
- Connectivist artificial intelligence, in which webs of connected microprocessors learn complex behaviors (Varela, Thompson, and Roach, 1991).

In the mechanical worlds envisioned by Ptolemy, Copernicus, and Newton, domination of the lower by the higher was presupposed. Gods ruled angels; angels controlled humans; humans were to dominate the world. This dominator mentality also ruled human interactions. The combination of non-linear dynamics, globalization, and telecommunications, especially the World Wide Web, has generated a new cultural paradigm that is challenging this mechanical world view.

Sally Goerner (1999) contrasts the hierarchy and web paradigms in a very constructive way. The Clockwork/Hierarchy paradigm portrays reality as separate things to be manipulated for individual benefit. Human relationships are modeled upon nature, which is portrayed as impersonal, random, and ruthless. It is considered natural for the powerful to control the weak. Some of the qualities of this model are listed below (Goerner, pp. 448–451):

- Reality is separable, controllable, and merely material.
- The world has no direction. It is largely purposeless, random, and cruel.
- Life is about struggle and looking out for Number One.
- Being 'realistic' means accepting that the world is ruthless.
- The current scientific view is essentially fact and all but done.
- Coercive hierarchies are nature's natural order. Some elements are meant to rule and others to be ruled.
- Societies run best on command-and-control plus conformity.

This is a coherent belief system and one that is widely shared by the world's elites. It also lurks in the unconscious of many of us who are schooled in Western scientific and economic theory.

The Self-Organizing/Web model portrays reality as an energy-driven, universal, interactive, self-organizing process. As processes are pushed far-from-equilibrium or maintain themselves at the "edge of chaos," they can no longer maintain mere linear progress. An example might be an engine that becomes increasingly turbulent as it picks up speed and shakes so badly that we think it is coming apart. At this point, the engine faces a bifurcation. Under some alternatives, it will destroy itself. Under other alternatives, it will process energy more efficiently and run at a higher level of efficiency. An example from biology is the non-nucleated protozoan that could not go on living as it was used to because it was being attacked by bacteria. Many protozoa died as a result, but some protozoa and bacteria combined forces—the bacteria becoming nuclei of the protozoa—thus setting up a new stage of evolution (Margulis, 1970).

According to this paradigm, we live in a web world. This web world consists of nodes and connections. Individuals are the nodes; the communications between those nodes are society. In the web world, an individual is not part of society; nor is society a composite of individuals; even though they cannot exist independently of each other. They exist as (quasi) autopoietic (i.e., self-producing) systems structurally coupled that provide requisite noise for each other.

In web world, the activities of individuals set up ripples in the communication net as it adjusts to accommodate those activities. Conversely, the ripples of communication disturb the homeostasis of individuals who adapt to maintain their autopoiesis.

Linear clockwork thinking is not abandoned in the web, but it is seen as a special kind of cognition that is useful in straightforward mechanical situations. Web thinking is multidimensional, parallel, tangled, and all at once—self-organizing. It offers ways into the hearts of people and their situations that are unknown in the clockwork world of confrontational debate with its predetermined rules of acceptability. One comes on as a reasonable listener and honors the authenticity of all members in a dialogue. One honors disagreements and treasures the creative tension they create, letting intricacy build without needing to prematurely integrate it into one's cognitive map. One honors the interactive process in the faith that it will produce superior results. One works cooperatively and patiently with others when consensus does emerge.

| *Dialogic Design Works Well* | *Dialogic Design Is Ineffective* |
| --- | --- |
| In web-oriented organizations | In exclusively hierarchical organizations |

## CONSENSUAL LINGUISTIC DOMAINS

Humberto Maturana observes that cognitive activity is common to all organisms as they face the challenges of life. An organism does not exist in a vacuum; it interacts with its surrounding medium and co-evolves with it (Maturana and Varela, 1980, 1987). In other words, organisms live in an interactive world and cognition is the way they survive and create their future in that world.

Among the many sources of interaction for an organism are other organisms, some of the same species and some of different species. In their interactions, organisms sometimes couple their functions with the perturbations generated by the other, a process called structural coupling, and begin to act in consort. This mutual process can lead to interlocked patterns of behavior that become the medium in which those organisms live. In this case, their living domain becomes a *consensual domain.*

For example, non-nucleated protozoa were at one time on the forefront of evolution, but they were being attacked by bacteria. They surpassed this threat by coupling with the bacteria. The result was that the bacteria became nuclei of the attacked cells, thus creating living cells with nuclei, which are the foundation for later stages of evolution (Margulis, 1970). In this case, the attacker and the attacked constructed their future by joining forces.

Maturana refers to behavior in a consensual domain as "linguistic behavior." He extends the term "linguistic" to include *any* mutually generated domain of interactions. It thus includes all coordinated efforts among organisms. Clearly, human language (as a process) generates consensual domains and (as a product and a resource) *is itself* a consensual domain. A language exists among a community of individuals, and is continually regenerated through their linguistic activity and the structural couplings generated by that activity.

We are linguistically interacting human beings. We create consensual domains of behavior through our cooperative interactions. Across groups, however, we do not all create compatible consensual domains. Different people in different situations cooperatively develop different interpretations of realities, especially social realities.

In our efforts to understand social realities and design better futures, therefore, we must not assume commonly agreed upon linguistic domains. People come from different cultures and have different cultural sensitivities. They see things differently; have opposing ambitions; prize different values. The first priority, then, in a designing effort is to create a consensual linguistic domain among many diverse voices. Accordingly, the first step for successful design is for the stakeholders to respectfully listen to each other. It is in understanding each other in a jointly constructed consensual linguistic domain that we open the door for new evolutionary construction.

Problems always arise for human beings in situations where they live, as consequences of their "being-in-the-world." Problems should not be thought as having some kind of objective existence. They arise for a specific community of stakeholders within their particular praxis of living. Different stakeholders will observe and describe different aspects of a problem situation recommending different approaches, potential actions, and design solutions. In many cases, especially for the multidimensional problems of the Information Age, what is a problem for one stakeholder won't be a problem at all for another. When stakeholders who see "problems" in very different ways come together in a common linguistic domain, they are likely to uncover unexpected "solutions." In such situations, stakeholders use language to create new designs for their future. In that sense, language creates their world through the participative design process.

| *Dialogic Design Works Well* | *Dialogic Design Is Ineffective* |
| --- | --- |
| When people recognize and honor points of view differing from their own and work to build consensual linguistic domains | When people assume that everyone shares their points of view and understandings of key words and phrases |

## THE SYSTEMS DILEMMA

John Oliga identifies a systems dilemma: There is an inherent conflict in questing for comprehensiveness of thought (in antithesis to the orthodox scientific dogma of reductionism) when it is impossible to achieve such comprehensiveness (Oliga, 1996). This impossibility arises because "vast tracts of modern society...are uncoupled from communicatively shared experience in ordinary language, and coordinated instead, through the [steering] media of money and power" (Habermas, 1987). In other words, institutions like market forces and bureaucracy evolve on their own and do not respect (for the most part) the democratic decisions we might make. Even though these systemically controlled institutions cannot be controlled by dialogue, they have structural components (i.e., institutions, normative structures, and social practices) that make social reproduction possible (Oliga, 1996).

Two trends that appear to be dominant in all social systems create havoc for groups trying to do democratic design. The first is the demand for the *democratization* of knowledge generation and assimilation in designing social systems. The second is the *escalation of complexity*, which occurs in the process of democratizing interdisciplinary and cross-functional stakeholder teams. The result is that organizations increase the complexity of their situation in their very efforts to enhance the knowledge base through democratic means—and the designing gets bogged down.

## DESIGNING AROUND THE DILEMMA

The simplest response to the dilemma is to steer clear of democracy and let leaders or experts make designing decisions. This course of action works well in "hard," that is, engineering situations. It does not work very well, however, as social engineering that involves "soft" or human systems for several reasons:

- Such designs lack sufficient input.
- They provoke resistance because important stakeholders are excluded from the process and their ideas are ignored.
- They are generally technocratic and unconnected to realities on the ground.
- For these reasons, the do not produce substantial change.

This inadequacy is commonly recognized today and it became obvious to me as I was trying to formulate the science of Ekistics.

Most soft systems designers today employ a hybrid form of decision-making in which designers consult stakeholders regarding their perceptions of a situation, then they try to make sense of the situation and supply solutions. The Soft Systems Method (SSM) devised by Checkland (1981) adds the further step of requiring stakeholders to approve the expert-derived solutions and possibly requiring the experts to design different solutions. This hybrid works fairly well as it combines the special knowledge of involved stakeholders with the expertise of their consultants.

Different degrees of discipline are imposed on dialogues to make them work in certain situations. The free exchange of ideas between colleagues possessing professional discipline is often productive and sufficient for systems of limited complexity. Facilitator-aided dialogue can work with larger groups in not-too-complex situations. Very careful facilitation is required in cases of high situational complexity, where the lack of common viewpoint, language, and motivation are combined with a complicated social system. For these very complex situations, careful applications of SDP are ideal solutions.

| *Dialogic Design Works Well* | *Dialogic Design Is Ineffective* |
|---|---|
| When facing challenges and opportunities in new situations | When things are status quo and there is no desire for change |

## CONCLUSION

The ideas discussed in this chapter:

- Recognize the great importance of dialogue especially in the cognitive mode, but point to the need for disciplined dialogue.
- Show the necessity of creating consensual linguistic domains.
- Describe a web world whose parts are constantly influencing each other and self-organizing into increased complexity.
- Describe a world where collaboration is more successful than domination and where hierarchies of privilege are leveled.
- Describe a web world where people can consciously contribute to their evolution, especially when they employ disciplined dialogic design science.
- Describe the limits of dialogic design, those self-organizing systemic forces like money and bureaucracy that race ahead of our ability to control them and are even accelerated by our dialogues.

It is my contention that designs that ignore these forces of today's world are fundamentally flawed and will not efficiently produce progressive social change.

| Dialogic Design Works Well | Dialogic Design Is Ineffective |
|---|---|
| As communicative action | As instrumental and strategic action |
| In a combination of cognitive and rational paradigms | In an exclusively rational paradigm |
| In web-oriented organizations | In exclusively hierarchical organizations |
| When people recognize and honor points of view differing from their own and work to build consensual linguistic domains | When people assume that everyone shares their point of view and understanding of key words and phrases |
| When facing challenges and opportunities in new situations | When things are status quo and there is no desire for change |

# CHAPTER 20

# A PEOPLE SCIENCE

**W**e have an opportunity to reverse the dismal trends of decline and discontent prevalent in most societies and organizations today. Communities of stakeholders are demanding the opportunity to voice their opinion on issues confronting them. We can enable people from all walks of life to experience participative democracy in national, inter-national, organizational, and inter-organizational settings. We need to go about this in a scientific way.

## OBSERVER-INDEPENDENT AND OBSERVER-DEPENDENT DATA

Observer-independent data, such as apples falling from trees, are preferred and are relevant to the analysis and design of mechanical systems, such as nuclear power plants or airplanes. They have limited utility in complex social system situations.

For example, a tool called Root Cause Analysis (RCA) was developed in the '80s for investigating the root causes of nuclear power plants accidents, such as the Three Mile Island disaster of 1979. RCA assumes that data used to perform the analysis are observer-independent and also time and space invariant. This assumption is compatible with the clockwork/domination paradigm. It implies that a human observer seeing an apple falling from a tree in London in 1900 will report the same phenomenon with another

*How People Harness Their Collective Wisdom and Power*, pages 139–145

observer seeing an apple falling from a tree in Los Angeles in 2000. This Newtonian physics paradigm was constructed deliberately to enforce time and space invariance, in order to enhance our capacity to generalize from specific observations. Using observer-independent data to perform root cause analyses for a nuclear power plant or for the space shuttle is appropriate, because these are mechanical systems.

Using only observer-independent data to perform root cause analyses for social systems, however, is not appropriate. For example, discovering the root causes for high rates of student dropouts in a school located in a neighborhood in the center of the city of Detroit requires the engagement of the neighborhood stakeholders and the generation of observer-dependent data. The RCA tool used for mechanical systems is not transferable to the domain of social systems without appropriate adjustments in terms of data generation and utilization.

The emergence of the Information Age makes it desirable and possible to escape the intellectual bounds of a clockwork universe in which linear causality and command-control hierarchies held sway (Goerner, 1999). Our new intellectual model, web world, is reflected in the Internet and global interconnections that defy linear analyses and hierarchical control. This reality militates against exclusively top-down efforts to steer society's course, be those efforts aimed at maintaining the status quo or changing society's basic structure (Hubbard, 1998).

## THIRD PHASE SCIENCE

Gerard de Zeeuw (1996) advocates a distinction between "First Phase, Second Phase, and Third Phase Science." The definitions that he presents place the challenge of stakeholder participation in the forefront of contemporary thinking about second order cybernetics.

> "Observation" refers to any report of what people claim to have seen, or experience, which is intended to be used in the construction of a high quality observation (the most common form is a visual report, but other forms such as reports on emotions are possible).

> "Science" refers to all (research) actions that aim to construct high quality observations which make it possible to improve on action; science can be differentiated into different forms, each using alternative interpretations of the notion of observation presented above:

> "First phase science" refers to that form of science in which it is assumed that the construction of high quality observations can be *fully separated* from the actions that are to be improved by their use (e.g., astronomy);

"Second phase science" refers to that form of science in which it is assumed that the construction of high quality observations *fully depends* on the actions that are to be improved by their use (e.g., first order cybernetics);

"Third phase science" refers to that form of science in which it is assumed that the construction of high quality observations *fully includes* the actions that are to be improved by their use (e.g., second order cybernetics; this phase seeks the transfers that support the development into a "collective" such that the efforts of maintaining the transfers are minimal). (Emphasis ours)

"Linguistic structure" refers to the constraints on the words, signs, tokens, symbols that are needed to implement the transfer that is intended to improve on action. "Getting a voice in science" refers to the need for developing and using linguistic structures in the construction of high quality observations that are different from what the 'first phase of science' allows. (de Zeeuw, 1996)

I read de Zeeuw as offering the following definition of science. It is all research actions *that aim to construct high quality observations* and make possible improvements on action. There are three distinct phases of scientific evolution. "First Phase Science" assumes that the construction of high quality observations can be *fully separated* from actions that are to be improved by their use. "Second Phase Science" (e.g., first order cybernetics) assumes that constructing observations *fully depends* on those actions. Third Phase Science (e.g., second order cybernetics) *fully includes* the actions to be improved within the construction of high quality observations.

Classical mechanics is the epitome of First Phase Science. In this phase, scientists make deliberate efforts to construct theories so that observations are independent of the observer. In other words, as was mentioned before, someone observing an apple falling from a tree in England would have basically the same experience as someone else observing an apple falling from a tree in America.

In quantum mechanics, which was invented much later, Heisenberg stated the principle of Second Phase Science. Recognizing that an observer interacts with the object of observation and influences its behavior, he stated in the uncertainty principle that an observer couldn't simultaneously observe the velocity and position of a particle because of such an interaction.

Third Phase Science grounds its legitimacy in engaging stakeholders as "expert observers" of the situation in which they are embedded. They are the ones that should decide how to take action in their situation, since they are those most affected by the existing situation and its evolution. This grounding stands in contrast to first and second phase sciences, which assert that "academic experts" or authorities are more qualified to design the "systems" on behalf of the community of stakeholders.

Professor de Zeeuw takes the position that science can no longer be what it used to be during the last two or three centuries. It has to become more democratic and move into its Third Phase. It has to respond to the needs of the users of science who have an interest not only in *what* science studies, but also in *how* and *why* it studies a situation.

For example, HIV positive patients want to have a voice in the development and review of new antiviral drugs for the treatment and prevention of their disease. Recently, at an application of SDP dialogue focusing on designing an action plan for deploying the Internet for mental health reasons, patients found their voice. They declared, "nothing anymore about us without us." As a consequence of this kind of interest and insistence, the "new science" has to deal with a much wider collection of stakeholders and thus a wider array of viewpoints exchanged between them. This requires the invention of linguistic structures that help to improve on such exchanges. These exchanges require the shift to the Wisdom of the People (DEMOSOPHIA) paradigm and the practice of Third Phase Science.

In the societal arena, in contrast with the arena of physical science, it appears that models that are co-discovered with the engagement of stakeholders in structured dialogue are superior to those delivered by very respectable scholars/experts—certainly for the Information Age. For that reason, it is very hard to be an Einstein in the societal arena, even with the best intentions.

Third Phase Science regards the observations of every stakeholder as fully meaningful because they are the ones who experienced and will experience the birth as well as the aftermath of the situation; that is, they are responsible for it. This experience and responsibility ensures that their observations are not pointless rubbish. Although First and the Second Phase Sciences regarded the observations of "academic" experts as superior, Third Phase Science recognizes the stakeholders as so-called "lay experts" who have expertise about the situation for which they are responsible. Their observations are equally worthwhile to those of academic experts. Accordingly, the problem definitions, which come out of the participative dialogue of the stakeholders, are nothing other than legitimate and valuable. In a true participative democracy the definition and resolution of the global *Problematique* should not be the responsibility of scientific experts and politicians only, but also of people from all walks of life if real progress is to be made.

Most adult human beings love to learn from each other, but resent being taught what to learn. This behavior indicates that paradigm shifts toward inclusion and respect in the societal arena are by their very nature evolutionary. This evolution does not map onto the paradigms of physical science. It has progressed beyond First and Second Phase Sciences.

Third Phase Science has further advantages in an action scenario. It develops "linguistic structures" that provide a common understanding of the words, signs, tokens, and symbols that are needed to implement the proposed improvements. It also develops support among participants and their organizations for carrying out action plans and minimizes the effort needed to keep actions on track.

## PEOPLE SCIENCE

The development of a solid "people science" has been the subject matter of dedicated researchers for over thirty years, as described in this book. This people science is developed on the following premise: *externalizing the knowledge and wisdom of the people affected by a complex issue is necessary for the definition and resolution of the issue.* As the necessary and sufficient prerequisite for surfacing this wisdom, stakeholders must engage in disciplined dialogue. This simple premise is not so easy to practice when people are dealing with complex issues.

It is interesting to revisit the definition of the word "dialogue." As we mentioned in Chapter 1, it comes from the Greek *dialogos*, which is made up of the root words *dia* ("through") and *logos* (roughly translated as "the meaning"). Alex Pattakos, in an essay published in *Rediscovering the Soul of Business* (1995), finds that *logos* has deep spiritual roots. He writes:

> Viewing it [logos] as a manifestation of spirit or soul, carries with it significant implications, both conceptual and practical. Dialogue, as a concept, takes on a new and deeper meaning when it is perceived as a group's accessing a "larger pool of common spirit" through a distinctly spiritual connection between the members. This suggests more than "collective thinking," although dialogue certainly is a determinant of such a holistic process. Spirit flowing through the participants in dialogue leads to collective thinking which, in turn, facilitates a common understanding thereby resulting in "common education," or to use today's jargon, collective learning.

This spiritual explanation of logos resolved a dilemma that has been with me for many years. In 1987, Native American tribes started to apply SDP dialogue to the project of designing their future. They appreciated it because it supported their need to engage in dialogue. Nine years later, in February of 1996, the methodology was transferred to the Native Americans by training a small team of Comanche Indians, so that the tribes can use it on a continuous basis (Harris and Wasilewski, 2004). In this context it is appropriate to offer a quote from Reuben Snake, the Chief of the Winnebago tribe, regarding his perception of the similarity of SDP with the tra-ditional way the tribes were used to deliberate and make decisions.

# Testimonial

## by Chairman Ruben Snake, Winnebago

### THE WAY OF THE PIPE

Our grandfathers used to sit in the lodge with a clan representative from each clan of our nation. One of these grandfathers from my uncle's clan would light a pipe and the pipe would go around in a circle. And every one of those people would grab hold of that pipe, put their lips to it and blow on that pipe. They had a firm conviction in their minds that what they were doing was very meaningful, because each one in that circle understood that the tobacco they were using was a sacred, holy gift from the creator of all things. When they inhaled the smoke from this tobacco, it would clear their mind and they would have a clear conscience. And it would purify their tongue so when they'd say something it was going to be the truth. Everyone of these ancestors of ours who sat in that circle would have that understand-ing that that's the way it was going to be when they'd unitedly use that sacred gift from the Great Spirit. When they'd talk, what they were thinking was for the welfare of the people, and what they'd say was the truth. So each one of them in turn would talk about what they thought and what they felt would benefit the tribe, the people, and the nation. So that when all was said in the circle, they would each one understand the other very clearly, and then they could make a decision wherein the consensus would be to do a certain thing for the welfare of the people. They would go through their agenda, and when they were done, they would all be in agreement as to where they were going to go as a tribe and as a nation.

Now, we've come a long way from that time. I look around this table right here and I know that a lot of you, my relatives, don't have that understand-ing, and you don't have that feeling within you. If I was to bring my pipe over here, and I would ask my uncle to light that pipe and to say something, and then we were to touch that pipe and draw on that pipe, I know that the feel-ing and the thought within you would not be the same as that enjoyed by our ancestors. And therefore what we would want to happen would not take place. So last year, when I came across our friend over here [speaking about Dr. Aleco Christakis] and what he has going, I looked at and I thought, "This has some close relationships to the Indian way of developing a consensus." So that's why I was so anxious to bring it over here, so each one of you could experience this process and get that good feeling you've all expressed… When we get through all of this [process], it will in fact become a reality for our people. When we get through all of this, then each one of us is going to know what it means to use that pipe, and to have that common feeling, that common understanding again. And it's not going backwards. It is going onward to something better, something greater for our people to rekindle those kinds of thoughts and feelings deep within us.

—Chairman Reuben Snake of the Winnebago Tribe (1987)

## DEMOSOPHIA

DEMOSOPHIA, i.e. Wisdom of the People, grounds its legitimacy in the engagement of stakeholders as their own "expert observers" of the situation in which they are embedded. They are the ones that decide how to take action because they know the existing situation best and are most affected by its evolution. This grounding stands in contrast to traditional scientific approaches in which benevolent "academic experts" or authorities design "systems" for people, like the city of Paris as it was mentioned in the Prologue.

The new model for participative democracy through disciplined dialogue got its start in the '70s (Christakis, 1973). It has been called DEMOSOPHIA, which in Greek means the "wisdom of the people" (Christakis, 1993, 1996; Shapiro, 2002). The underlying premise of the new paradigm is that people must discover their wisdom in order to exercise their collective power. Because of the escalating complexity of the Information Age, it is much more difficult today to uncover the wisdom of the people than it was two thousand and five hundred years ago in the *Agora* of the Athenian Republic. As mentioned before, the complexity of the issues confronting Athenians in their Agoras was by at least one order of magnitude lower that the complexity of issues confronting stakeholders in the Information Age. I will elaborate on this insight in Chapter 25 after introducing the observer-dependent metric of the Situational Complexity Index (SCI).

In the complexity of the Information Age, we need assistance. We need a structured and efficient approach to deal with differences in values, disciplines, languages, and priorities. The absence of a good structured approach is painfully obvious in many interdisciplinary and contentious situations. As discussed in Chapter 2, I was privy to such a situation in the formative years of the Club of Rome, where differences in terminology and paradigms rendered dialogue across disciplinary boundaries impossible.

CHAPTER 21

# CONSCIOUS EVOLUTION

The movement for conscious evolution gathered force in the latter half of the 20th century (Hubbard, 1998; Christakis, 2005; Loye, 2003). Out of the devastation wrought by World War II, people sought ways to build a new and better society. Some of these initiatives were remarkably successful, witness the Marshal Plan that aided the rapid economic and political recovery of Europe. Other initiatives, such as those embodied in the United Nations, have endured and done well. Many other efforts were notable flops. The slum clearance projects of the 1950's that were implemented in many American cities are prime examples of this last category. These projects were among the root causes for the burning of Detroit and other cities in the '60s. The urban disasters of the '60s contributed to the emergence of the field of urbanology in the '70s, and also were the motivation for the research project discussed in Chapter 2 on designing a hypothetical city of 1 million people by an interdisciplinary team.

As was discussed in Chapter 2 in the context of the interdisciplinary team, the progress from good intentions to successful designs can be a tortuous one if one does not have a science of design. Over the last 50 years, numerous individuals and schools of thought have developed theories and employed them in the arena of practical application. Their efforts interweave with each other. Along the way, paradigms were scrapped, old ideas were re-discovered, laws were formulated, some techniques were borrowed and others were invented. This chapter extracts a thread dedicated to creating a science of human design from that tangle.

*How People Harness Their Collective Wisdom and Power*, pages 147–153
Copyright © 2006 by Information Age Publishing
All rights of reproduction in any form reserved.

## THE SCIENCE OF HUMAN SETTLEMENTS

Dinos Doxiadis, the world-renowned Greek architect and urban designer mentioned in the Prologue, was a keen observer of dysfunctional efforts of city planning and urban renewal. He yearned for a science that would increase the quality of design communication among urban planners, citizens, and decision-makers and bring success to well-intentioned efforts to improve the quality of life in human settlements. He eventually launched the science and movement of EKISTICS, the science of human settlements, establishing an Ekistics Research Center in Athens, Greece. In 1965, he hired me, a theoretical physicist fresh out of Yale University at that time, to help him invent the science of human settlements.

Doxiadis operated at a high-powered level. In the 1960's, he gathered some of the brightest minds of the age, Arnold Toynbee, Buckminster Fuller, Margaret Mead, Barbara Ward, and Hasan Ozbekhan among them, for weeklong symposia that took place on his yacht as it cruised the Aegean. At the end of the week, this group, which affectionately called itself "the ship of fools," docked at the isle of Delos and jointly issued declarations on what they had discussed regarding the future of human settlements. These gatherings took place for seven years and resulted in the seven famous "Delos proclamations."

As mentioned in the Prologue, I was very influenced by Doxiadis' commitment to the development of the science of human settlements and his vision of the Universal City (Ecumenopolis). I started introducing mathematical models and concepts of theoretical physics into the consultancy projects of the firm. In fact, the firm in the late '60s was involved in a very futuristic project of designing the Metropolitan Urban Detroit Area to the year 2000, sponsored by the Detroit Edison electric company. After doing this mathematical modeling work for a year and a half, I began to see the futility of trying to revamp urban design on the model of physics. I then began a 30-year quest to create a new scientific paradigm that would enable people from all walks of life to participate in planning their cities and take control of their social systems.

While I was working with Doxiadis, I was transferred to Washington DC and assigned the role of establishing a new venture between a leading edge information technology company, named the Systems Development Corporation (SDC) headquartered in Santa Monica, California, and the urban planning firm of Doxiadis, named Doxiadis Associates, headquartered in Athens, Greece. It was the beginning of the emergence of the Information Age, and Doxiadis wanted to be ready to address these new challenges by establishing a joint venture with a leading edge information technology firm such as the Systems Development Corporation (SDC).

With the help of Hasan Ozbekhan, who was Director of Planning of SDC, we established a new company called Doxiadis-System Development Corporation (D-SDC). The mission of D-SDC was to bring together the power of information technology of SDC with the knowledge of the science of human settlements of the Doxiadis firm. I became the Director of Research of D-SDC, reporting to Hasan Ozbekhan in California, USA, and to Dinos Doxiadis in Athens, Greece. As a result of this assignment Hasan and I became very good friends, as mentioned in the Prologue, to the astonishment of a lot of people because this was a friendship between a Turk and a Greek. We fueled each other's curiosity regarding social system design theory and methodology.

In 1969 Hasan had delivered a long paper in the Bellagio conference in Italy titled "The General Theory of Planning," which was later published in a book edited by Erich Jantsch (1969) titled *Perspectives on Planning.* When I read Hasan's chapter in the book by Erich, I thought it was the equivalent to Einstein's General Theory of Relativity in terms of depth of thinking and theory construction. I had studied the theory of relativity as an undergraduate at Princeton in the '50s with a very famous theoretical physicist named John Archibald Wheeler, who in his nineties wrote the most profound history of the evolution of physics in the 20th century (Wheeler, et al., 1998). The bond between Hasan and me became very strong.

During his participation in the Bellagio conference, Hasan had met Aurelio Peccei, an Italian industrialist and philanthropist. Aurelio had written a book titled *The Chasm Ahead,* in which he described the escalating technological chasm between the advanced industrialized countries and the third world countries (Peccei, 1969). Aurelio was very concerned and committed to working on closing this chasm.

Then in 1969 in New York City, Hasan and I sat down in a restaurant with Aurelio Peccei. Over drinks, we discussed ways to start an international initiative to address the global *Problematique,* namely the technology chasm as initially conceptualized in Aurelio's book. We decided to name this initiative The Club of Rome (CoR), primarily because Aurelio was very fascinated with the American concept of the "club." It was agreed to produce a proposal that would lay out in detail the work that would have to be done to create a more livable world for all the people of the planet Earth.

Subsequently, Aurelio, Hasan, and I, aided by Erich Jantsch, put together the first conceptualization of the global *Problematique* in the monumental first proposal of the Club of Rome titled "The Predicament of Mankind." With Peccei making the connections and paying the freight, I proceeded to trot the globe from Germany to Japan to Brazil and many points in between explaining the proposal and inviting world leaders to become members of the Club of Rome. By the end of 1971, approximately 60 people from countries such as the USA, France, Japan, Russia, Germany,

England, Italy, and many others, had accepted the invitation to become members of the Club.

## THE ORIGINAL PROPOSAL OF THE CLUB OF ROME

This proposal, (for a review of the proposal visit *www.cwaltd.com/pdf/clubrome .pdf*), was put together under the towering leadership of Hasan Ozbekhan, probably one of the best systems thinkers of the 20th century. It described very eloquently the predicament of mankind. It identified approximately 50 Continuous Critical Problems (CCPs), which on account of their strong interactions should not be addressed in a piecemeal fashion. Such problems as the "pollution problem," the "inner city problem," the "poverty problem" the "starvation problem" the "nuclear proliferation problem," the "population growth problem," and so on, are strongly interconnected contributing to the emergence of a new entity called in the proposal the global *Problematique* (Christakis, 2005). The concept and the name *Problematique* appeared for the first time in the Club of Rome (CoR) proposal. The proposal recognized and described the futility of addressing these problems in a piecemeal fashion, instead of addressing them as a system of problems. It proceeded to conceptualize and articulate very elegantly a philosophical, methodological, and institutional framework for penetrating and resolving the global *Problematique.*

Because no appropriate methodology was available in the early '70s for addressing the complexity and multidimensionality of the *Problematique,* the framework presented in the proposal was more like an architectural design than an engineering blueprint. Some readers of the proposal considered it an outstanding conceptual breakthrough, but others, especially the systems engineers of the '60s, found it lacking in methodological specificity and rigor.

The perceived lack of methodological rigor of the proposal contributed significantly in the decision of the Executive Committee of CoR to award, in the summer of 1971, a major grant to the systems dynamics group of MIT. This group, under the leadership of Jay Forester who was an electrical engineer by training and was a professor at the Sloan School of Management at MIT, had been working on developing the systems dynamics approach to the observation, explanation, and prediction of the dynamics of social systems. Forester had already applied the method to industrial and urban dynamics in the '60s, so it was easy for him to persuade the Executive Committee that it was appropriate to apply the method to world dynamics. The Executive Committee decided to sponsor the project on the development of the world dynamics model. The major outcome of this project was the production of the "world model" using the methodology of systems dynamics. The work and findings of this project culminated with the publication of the very popular book *Limits to Growth* in 1972 (Meadows, et al., 1972). The controversial nature of the findings reported in this book gave a lot of publicity and notoriety to the CoR.

When the Executive Committee made this grant award to MIT to develop the world model, Hasan and I resigned from the Club. We both felt that the systems dynamics methodology, which was used for deriving an extrapolated future for the world system to the year 2150, compromised the original intent of the CoR proposal which was to discover and use a methodology capable of engaging the stakeholders in a dialogical process with sensitivity to their cultural situation and the praxis of their lives. We felt that the system dynamics approach was perpetuating a paradigm of scientific elitism and social engineering in designing social systems, instead of legitimizing the wisdom of the people by engaging stakeholder in a dialogue for designing their futures. Hasan joined the Wharton School of the University of Pennsylvania, and I got involved with the establishment of the Academy for Contemporary Problems with the financial support of the Battelle Memorial Institute. Battelle was one of the founding sponsors of the CoR.

Working with many other colleagues, initially at the Academy for Contemporary Problems in Columbus, Ohio, and later in other academic institutions, it took approximately 20 years of research, development, and testing in the arena to invent and apply the model and methodology that rendered the original architecture of the Club of Rome proposal usable and applicable in the field of practice, as I will describe in the following chapters.

## INTERACTIVE MANAGEMENT

In the early '70s, the researchers at the Academy for Contemporary Problems, with the sponsorship of the Battelle Memorial Institute, began formal observation of the cognitive and behavioral limitations of interdisciplinary teams working on designing complex social systems, such as in large-scale urban planning. As was discussed in Chapter 2, a major finding of the researchers observing the dialogue of interdisciplinary teams was low productivity. Social psychiatrist James Taylor wrote, after observing the interdisciplinary dialogue of the urban planning team for over a year, (Taylor, 1976):

> "... there appears to be a pressing, well-recognized need for a kind of social invention: the interdisciplinary team which synthesizes knowledge in order to clarify complex problems. The promise of this social invention is clear, yet

in fact no workable model has emerged. The question becomes obvious: why not? What has gone wrong in existing efforts to develop 'meaningful syntheses of 'pertinent fields of knowledge'?"

After a thorough review of extant methods and conducting experiments on complex tasks, the researchers became convinced that a new scientific paradigm (Christakis, 1973) and a Domain of Science Model (Warfield, 1994) were needed to guide innovation and testing a process of social systems design inquiry. The U.S. National Science Foundation sponsored the launch of "Generic Design Science" (Christakis, Warfield, 1987, Christakis et al, 1988; Warfield, 1994). The codification of the methodology and its practice was named *Interactive Management* (Warfield, Christakis, 1987; Warfield, Cardenas, 1994).

As mentioned above, Hasan moved on to the University of Pennsylvania where he collaborated with Russell Ackoff in establishing the Social Systems Sciences group at the Wharton School of Business. John Warfield and I established centers for Interactive Management at the University of Virginia, 1982, and George Mason University, 1984. There, the practice and model were refined through applications in the arena in a large variety of diverse designing domains, subjecting the performance of the methodology to the peer review literature. In 1989, I decided to subject the emerging Structured Design Process, under the brand name CogniScope™, to the discipline of the market by establishing an Interactive Management consultancy called CWA (*www.CWALtd.com*).

Warfield organized his research and observations into a masterful work, *The Science of Generic Design* (1994), which develops some of the philosophical and theoretical principles needed for *scientific* design, and meticulously links them to the practice of design. This book is great science but it is not adapted to the needs of the practical social system designer. To remedy that situation, Warfield teamed up with Roxana Cardenas to publish the *Handbook of Interactive Management* (1994).

Over the past fifteen years, together with colleagues of the CWA consultancy, I have constantly fine-tuned the designing process so that more people could learn easily how to use it. I have been engaged in training more than one hundred people in the practice of SDP around the world (see Figure 21.1). At the same time, I have spent the last fifteen years constructing an axiomatic science of design dialogue in support of SDP.

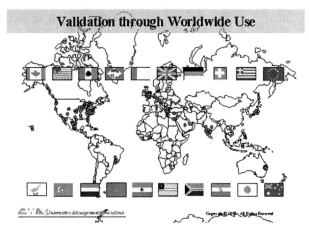

Figure 21.1.    Worldwide applications of co-laboratories of democracy.

# CHAPTER 22

---

# AXIOMS AND DEFINITIONS

$\mathbf{A}$fter the initial difficulties observed with unstructured dialogue in complex situations, especially as specified by psychiatrist Charles Taylor (see previous chapter), and building on the science of generic design (Warfield, 1994), my associates and I (hereinafter "researchers") set themselves to the challenge of creating a disciplined and effective process for the participative design of social systems in an effort to bring about the vision of DEMOSOPHIA for the Information Age. The decision was made to adopt an axiomatic approach in the development of the theory. In view of that, the first focus was on defining the axioms for a third-phase science of constructive design dialogue as exemplified by the SDP architecture presented in Part II.

## THREE AXIOMS OF SDP

From their observations and applications in the period of 1972 to 1992, the researchers eventually settled on the three axioms of the SDP paradigm regarding complexity, cognitive limitations, and relative saliency. The advantages of an axiomatic approach to theory construction is that by learning and understanding the three axioms of SDP, practitioners can deduce and internalize all the laws, principles, and rules of engagement in the arena, just as one can do after learning the five axioms postulated in the Euclidean geometry constructed by Euclid 2,500 years ago.

---

*How People Harness Their Collective Wisdom and Power*, pages 155–160

From the observation that complex design situations are multidimensional, the researchers derived the axiom of complexity:

> **Complexity Axiom**: Complex social-systems-designing situations are multidimensional. They require that observational variety should be respected in the dialogue among the observers, in an effort to strive for comprehensiveness. Comprehensiveness, however, is an objective not easily attainable by human observers, even through the application of the SDP.

This first axiom is stated in many different ways in the systems literature. Von Bertalanffy (1968) urges the need to see problems in a new light. Churchman (1979) asserts that the systems approach requires one to see the world through the eyes of another. Ulrich (1991) states that systems design should look beyond the horizons of systems science into social, ideological, and epistemological concerns. Flood (1990) urges us to mix metaphors in order to obtain a rounded appreciation of situations. Luhmann (1995) recommends that we welcome and channel the noise that generates social systems. This need for comprehensiveness is a constant theme in design literature.

Bausch (2001) explains this need for comprehensiveness in the following terms:

> In terms of operational practicality, comprehensiveness demands attention to the social, ideological, ontological, and epistemological parameters of the design situation. In terms of expression, it requires the employment of metaphors that fit the various parameters and explicit recognition of the biases involved in those metaphors. In terms of the orientation of the design situation, it requires an acceptance and adaptability to noise. This noise is generated by expressive stakeholders, divergent views and philosophies, and an awareness focused on the break-offs of any design.

> If comprehensiveness is neglected, important considerations may be ignored. Narrow interest can be thrust upon people unknowingly. Relationships can be warped by inappropriate metaphors. Emergent solutions will lack sufficient noise.

The researchers repeatedly observed that people involved in dialogue on complex designing situations experience cognitive overload. They also found ways to reduce and even to eliminate this overload. They concluded that any social-systems-designing dialogue addressing complex issues is undisciplined if it ignores the built-in limitations of human cognition. This axiom states:

> **Cognitive Limitations Axiom:** Observers are subjected to cognitive limitations during social-systems-designing dialogue, which must be explicitly recognized and avoided during the dialogue. Cognitive limitations demand that

designing teams: (a) control the pace of knowledge generation and assimilation, and (b) control the number of observations and relationships that observers must manage simultaneously during the dialogue.

The prime limitation of human intelligence lies in the limits of short-term (working) memory. This limitation is expressed in Miller's discovery (Miller, 1956), which states the limitations of human information processing capabilities in the famous formula of "7 ± 2." In other words, we can hold only about seven things in short-term memory at the same time. By employing basic set mathematics, Warfield (1988) reduced Miller's law to "3 ± 0" if there exist interactions among the members of a set. The Warfield "Law of Triadic Compatibility" will be discussed in more detail in Chapter 23.

Simon (1974) states the consequence of ignoring this axiom. His research indicated people tend to "satisfice" when they reach the limits of their bounded rationality. The implication of this axiom in the design of social systems with stakeholder participation is that stakeholders need methodological assistance to overcome the limitations of short-term memory. Without such assistance, and in light of the complexity of the issues they are confronting, they terminate their inquiry prematurely and make decisions on the basis of what appears to be satisfactory.

The limitations of short-term memory are exacerbated by the limitations of natural language, which is linear and expresses ideas only sequentially, i.e., one after another. When we try to express complex situations in natural language, we are forced to go on and on and on and thereby exceed the processing ability of our working memories. For this reason, unaided natural language is not sufficiently transparent and rigorous for communicating stakeholder observations and descriptions of complex problem situations confronting us in the Information Age. For example, Figure 17.1 shown in Chapter 17, depicts graphically and concisely in one page the characteristics of the successful Cypriot women. It will take many pages to translate into regular prose the essence of the meaning captured by the one-page graphic of Figure 17.1. The graphic language representation of meaning is clearly a major advantage of the SDP paradigm.

To overcome the shortcomings of natural language, the researchers devised several strategies:

- They constructed precise definitions specifying the relationships between various stages of activities that occur in stakeholder designing sessions.
- They employed the mathematics of set theory to produce software that improves the efficiency of making logical connections among observations and requirements that are encountered in designing social systems. The software shortens the decision-making process,

keeps track of logic and generates products for the examination of stakeholders.

- They worked out a smooth interface that integrates natural and graphic language producing efficiently graphic language patterns.

Employing these strategies, the researchers sought to overcome the dissonance emerging in design practice between the competing requirements of design comprehensiveness on the one hand, and the cognitive limitations of the observers on the other.

These strategies enable stakeholder/designers to produce collaboratively graphic structural models of social systems. These structural models represent group mental models describing the cognitive synthesis of individual mental models. They are expressed in a hybrid natural/graphic language that generates readily understood descriptions of complex situations. This graphic language, with computer support, can automatically produce graphics of the stakeholders' design dialogue depicting patterns of relationships among observations. For example, it produces multidimensional field representations displaying clusters of similar observations, namely Options Fields, and Options Profiles, which have been discussed in Chapter 4.

The third axiom about *relative saliency* emerged from observations by the researchers of the variance of relative importance that stakeholders assign to diverse viewpoints, problems, and solutions. Many times what is a problem for one observer would not be a problem at all for another. It was recognized from the outset that enhancing the capacity of the stakeholders to achieve convergence regarding the saliency of one observation relative to others was a desirable characteristic of theory construction work. This axiom states:

> **Saliency Axiom:** During social-systems-designing dialogue, understanding the relative saliency of observations can be brought into play only when the observers' authenticity, learning, and appreciation of variety are ensured so that the observers are able to construct categories of observations before assessing the relative saliency of individual observations.

In the Information Age, there is not an overall meta-narrative accepted across diverse groups of people concerning norms of rational action or values (Bausch, 2001). Numerous systems thinkers describe this lack of a compelling universal story and prescribe ways to deal with it. Churchman urges us to avoid the environmental fallacy of mistaking the part for the whole (Churchman, 1979, p. 6). Checkland urges the creation of several root definitions in accord with divergent worldviews (Checkland, 1981, pp. 166–169). Ulrich says that we should understand how metaphors build biases into systems thinking (Ulrich, 1991, p. 260). Luhmann urges us to incorporate as many conflicts as there are (Luhmann, 1995, p. 360–373).

The following four requirements, emerging from the three axioms, indicate ways to guard against a false presumption of consensus in social systems designing situations:

1. Groups of stakeholders should do the designing;
2. Group design should identify and articulate the dimensionality of the problem situation;
3. Design methodology should provide constructive group capabilities for generating, explaining, and structuring high quality observations, for designing action alternatives, and for selecting the preferred alternative; and
4. The group design work should be technically and behaviorally sound, i.e., it should not demand infeasible and undesirable behavior from the participating stakeholders.

These requirements cycle upon each other in the following way. When we do not presume consensus, we look for ways to manage disagreement. And vice versa, when we accommodate conflicts we are more likely to recognize a lack of consensus. The mindset required for dealing with a lack of consensus includes:

1. Alertness to the biases contained in the metaphors that lie behind any social systems design;
2. Awareness that social systems design cannot move forward without an agreement among the stakeholders coupled with understanding and consensus-formation;
3. Caution against presuming that any partial representation of the situation constitutes the whole of the situation; and
4. Openness to variety of viewpoints and dissonances, and the way that we accord them full consideration and representation in the design.

SDP gives direct attention to the inherent lack of consensus on values, priorities, norms of truth and behavior, expectations for the future, and the use of competing interpretations of complex situations.

## ELEVEN KEY DEFINITIONS

In light of the postulation of the three axioms of SDP, and before continuing on the theory development, it is desirable to offer some definitions of eleven key terms that will make the description of the espoused theory in practice more transparent. These terms are:

1. **Dialogue:** The participation of observers engaged in creating meaning, wisdom, and action through communicative and collaborative interaction.
2. **Culture**: A community of stakeholders founded on a consensual language built by a group of observers interacting in dialogue.
3. **Conscious Evolution:** Stakeholders engagement in the design of social systems for the purpose of creating their futures.
4. **Future:** The state of a social system that is more than a mere extrapolation of the past and present.
5. **Complexity:** The multi-dimensionality of the social-system-designing situations that engender confusion and uncertainty among observers.
6. **Triggering question:** A prompt framed carefully by a social system design team for the purpose of delineating the relevant context of a design situation.
7. **Elemental observation:** The succinct and content-specific response by an observer/stakeholder to a triggering question in the context of a co-laboratory.
8. **Science:** All research actions that aim to construct high quality observations and make possible improvements on action.
9. **Explanation:** An observer/author elaborates the meaning of his/her elemental observation for the purpose of making it transparent to other stakeholders participating in a co-laboratory dialogue.
10. **Problem:** The discrepancy for a particular social-system-designing situation between the belief by an observer of "what ought to be" and his/her observation of "what is."
11. **Issue:** An awareness of a problem coupled with an appreciation that pluralities of belief are integral components of the social-system-designing situation.

CHAPTER 23

# SIX DIALOGUE LAWS

The Structured Design Process paradigm is founded within Third Phase Science because it has recipient/victim/stakeholders design the systems that will affect them. It is built on the axioms and definitions just enunciated. Therefore, SDP is a new epistemology for enabling people from all walks of life to generate high quality observations in the context of the complex social system design situations in which they find themselves. This epistemology adheres to the following six laws identified by systems scientists over the last five decades. These laws are:

- Ashby's Law of *Requisite Variety* (Ashby, 1958);
- Miller's Law of *Requisite Parsimony* (Miller, 1956; Warfield, 1988);
- Boulding's Law of *Requisite Saliency* (Boulding, 1966);
- Peirce's Law of *Requisite Meaning* (Turrisi, 1997);
- Tsivacou's Law of *Requisite Autonomy* (Tsivacou, 1997);
- Dye's Law of the *Requisite Evolution of Observations* (Dye, 1999).

## Requisite Variety

Ashby's Law of *Requisite Variety* asserts that a design must possess an amount of variety that is at least equal to the variety in the problem situation. It implies that an individual or a group engaged in designing a solution to a complex problem situation can gain control over a design only by making appropriate specifications in all the dimensions of the design. One

*How People Harness Their Collective Wisdom and Power*, pages 161–173
Copyright © 2006 by Information Age Publishing

way to violate this law is to neglect some of the relevant perspectives and types of observers, and by not asking them to present their observations. Another way to violate the law is to disregard the cognitive limitations of the observers participating in a design.

## Requisite Parsimony

Miller's Law of *Requisite Parsimony* asserts that human beings can deal simultaneously with only five to nine observations at one time. As a consequence, in any social system design situation, however complex, the design should not require the designers to deal with more than nine items simultaneously, and usually should involve fewer. Parsimony should be invoked in design situations in order to make sure that the dialogue does not inherently try to force people to make judgments that exceed their short term cognitive capacities, or overburden their physiology.

The *Requisite Variety* Law pairs the inherent multidimensional nature of complex systems and the requirement for designers (working either in groups or alone) to conceptualize a variety of design options to match that complexity. The *Requisite Parsimony* Law corresponds to an observed physiological or psychological limitation of human beings.

Reflecting on the implications of these two laws in the context of design, one realizes that they impose contradictory requirements for the conduct of SDP. The First Law asserts the significance of espousing variety, even at the expense of parsimony. The Second Law asserts the significance of respecting parsimony, even at the expense of variety. SDP reconciles the contradictory nature of these two laws, so that the design will not violate either one of them.

## Requisite Saliency

Boulding's law of *Requisite Saliency* refers to the range of importance that people assign to observations relative to other observations. It requires that good designs (1) highlight the different ways that group members judge the saliency of design options, and (2) provide specific ways to reach consensual accommodation about relative saliency. The SDP paradigm meets these requirements in a variety of ways including:

- Having each observer clarify the meaning of his or her observation;
- Having participants consensually create categories (clusters) of similar observations;

- Having participants collectively rank observations within similarity clusters on the basis of their perceived saliency. This ranking is accompanied by focused and open dialogue during which every point of view is made clear to all the participants.

These procedures ensure that the stakeholder/designers understand each other's positions and why certain things are important to them, providing a rich background for judging saliency. They also provide orderly democratic methods for deciding saliency and evaluating options.

When dialogues ignore relative saliency, they produce sequences of choices that do not make maximum use of the knowledge available to the observers. They fail to achieve real consensus on the actions they propose. They often direct the resources of their participants into directions of low productivity.

## Requisite Meaning

Peirce's Law of *Requisite Meaning* expresses in explicit terms the objective of inquiry and design: to discover the essence of problem situations and to plan desirable futures for communities of stakeholders. It states:

> In addressing complex design situations collaboratively, the observations of the stakeholders must be excavated through disciplined inquiry in order to grasp their full meaning. Armed with this understanding, the community can: (a) construct authentic, anticipatory, and autonomous descriptions of those observations, (b) interpret their meaning, and (c) transfer these descriptions in accordance with the tenets of Third Phase Science; that is with full respect for the wording and autonomy of their authors.

It builds upon Maturana's definition of a consensual linguistic domain (Maturana 1970), C.S. Peirce's ideas of pragmatic meaning (Turrisi, 1997), and De Zeeuw's Third Phase Science (1996). The practice of SDP finds a comfortable home in the thought of these thinkers because they respect the autonomy of individual observers and the worth of their observations, descriptions, and descriptions-of-descriptions leading to consensual linguistic domains.

This law demands that the design process free its participants to express their ideas in their own words and symbols. It builds upon the ideas of Peirce that meaning arises as people conceive some kind of icon to explain a situation and develop it through continual reality testing. Peirce explains this in the following passage:

All necessary reasoning without exception is diagrammatic. That is, we construct an icon of our hypothetical state of things and proceed to observe it. This observation leads us to suspect that something is true, which we may or may not be able to formulate with precision, and we proceed to inquire whether it is true or not. For this purpose it is necessary to form a plan of investigation and this is the most difficult part of the whole operation. We not only have to select the features of the diagram which it will be pertinent to pay attention to, but it is also of great importance to return again and again to certain features. Otherwise, although our conclusions may be correct they will not be the particular conclusions at which we are aiming (Peirce, 1903 as quoted in Turrisi, 1997).

The kind of original and autonomous thinking that creates icons and continually revises them is the kind nourished in SDP. People are encouraged to grapple with the inchoate thoughts and feelings that well up within them because these thoughts are the seeds of originality and create design breakthroughs. In their stumbling descriptions of observations, they spark seeds of originality (iconic ideas) in other members of the designing team. As individuals and groups test and improve these icons, they communicate and share their meanings and create a shared mental model. In contested situations, people explain the meanings of their icons by interpreting what they have said. In interpreting what they have said, people describe their pictures and what they have come to mean for them.

John D. Collier (1999), relates the Peircean idea of "meaning" to anticipatory systems (such as group design sessions with the SDP) when he writes:

> The cognitive (intellectual) meaning of a representation is given by our expectations involving its object.... The content of a representation or idea is the information common to all these expectations... and this content provides the information needed to reason with the idea.

In design situations, our ideas are expectations about alternative futures and how our models will function in those futures. Our iconic models are interpreted on a background of pragmatic concerns and they are seldom exhausted by the ideas we impute to them. Creativity, spontaneity, self-organization, and reusability are hallmarks of open receptive dialogue. They are integral to the Peircean pragmatic concept of meaning.

Design co-laboratories that operate by the standards proposed by Peirce and Collier, operate in the realm of Third Phase Science. They develop high-quality observations that include the actions that are to be improved by their use. They induce naturally the kind of knowledge transfers that respect the integrity of observations and their authors, and provide the descriptions of description that build collective consciousness. They encourage the development of new linguistic structures, such as trees of meaning that are not hidebound in the language of First and Second Phase Science. In their practice, people from all walks of life get a voice in dialogue as authentic content experts of their situation in the praxis of their living.

## Requisite Autonomy of Distinction-Making

Tsivacou's Law of *Requisite Autonomy of Distinction-Making* asserts that power in the design situation derives to the person who makes the distinctions adopted by the group. It says:

> The actors that...have the chance to dictate the selection of the dominant explanatory path immediately put themselves into a position of power, reducing the others involved into a position of powerlessness. Independent of their social status and role, those who control the information distinctions in a given situation acquire power and restrict the autonomy of the others (Tsivacou, 1997).

One often thinks that good distinctions create the rationality of organizational culture. This law points out that communicative distinctions are responsible for the emergence of power as well. Usually, this power is wielded by the rich, the powerful, and the experts in a domain of knowledge. Seldom are the authentic voices heard of the stakeholders most affected by a social design initiative, such as those affected by the urban renewal projects of the late '60s, or those affected by the health care reform initiative of the '90s.

For good design, a corollary of this law demands that all participants must have an equal opportunity to explain their experience in the praxis of living. To allow this to happen, the autonomy of individual distinction-making must be ensured, and monopolies on distinction-making prohibited. Only then will the power of persuasion be equitably distributed among the observers. It is not unusual in SDP that the key observation that illuminates a situation is made by some otherwise obscure person who would not have been heard if special care had not been taken to protect individual autonomy and authenticity. Such a person was Victoria, a Lymphatic Filariasis (LF) patient from Ghana, who had a major impact on the final outcome of the LF Forum. As mentioned previously, this Forum, held in Geneva in 1998, was designed and conducted in collaboration with the World Health Organization (WHO) with the objective to eradicate LF by the year 2020. The participation and contributions of Victoria at this Forum changed the policy direction of the participants by 180 degrees.

The distinctions that people make represent selections from alternative explanatory paths. When a group hears and internalizes these observations and their clarifications, it can then iteratively converge on a plausible group interpretive linguistic model of the situation, which represents its consensual linguistic domain.

## Requisite Evolution of Observations

Dye's Law of *Requisite Evolution of Observations* was recently discovered and empirically substantiated. A group of researchers analyzed observer-dependent data from SDP dialogues that took place in 50 applications (Dye and Conaway, 1999), comparing the results of "importance voting" with the results of "influence voting."

Importance voting uses pair comparisons in which participants are asked questions such as: "Is elemental observation A more important than elemental observation B, in the context of XYZ?" The group's votes on these questions are tallied. When the individual and subjective voting is completed by the participants, the software generates an ordinal ranking of all the observations from most important to least important. Using this aggregate ranking, it generates a graph in which the numbered elemental observations are displayed on the x-axis and their importance rankings are indicated on the y-axis.

Influence voting, on the other hand, uses paired relationships and computer assistance. For influence voting, the questions to be addressed by the participants are similar to the following.

Suppose that in a co-laboratory dialogue the participants were able
to satisfy the requirement proposed in:
ELEMENTAL OBSERVATION #1
will this *significantly* enhance their capacity to satisfy the requirement
proposed in:
ELEMENTAL OBSERVATION #15
in the context of XYZ?

As in importance voting, votes are tallied, and the results are graphed in a similar manner.

The conclusions of this research are:

- Importance voting and influence voting produce radically different results.
- Dialogues must go beyond mere consensus on the "importance" of elemental observations (problems, objectives, options, etc.) if they are to effectively deal with complex social system designing situations.

- "Influence" voting identifies the key leverage elemental observations that must be addressed in order to effectively intervene and improve a situation.

In short, the law of *Requisite Evolution of Observations* asserts that the elemental observations offered in dialogues have not been properly processed until they find the key leverage points that can direct effective interventions. Its full text follows:

> Whenever the elemental observations made by stakeholders in the context of a complex design situation are interdependent, assigning priorities for action on the basis of aggregating individual stakeholder "importance voting" leads to erroneous priorities and ineffective action plans. The effective priorities for action emerge after an evolutionary search of interdependencies among the observations through a dialogue focusing on "influence voting."

To illustrate the difference between "importance" and "influence," we present the results of voting that took place in a goal-setting session with the Food and Drug Administration with the objective of designing a Collaborative Action Plan for its Good Review Practices Initiative (see Chapter 13).

As can be read from the graph of Figure 23.1 [in the fine print under the x-axis], goals #13, #27, #5, and #26 ranked highest in terms of *influence*. They each garnered more than twice the influence votes of any other goal. The ranking of this top four in the *importance* voting, however, was rather low. On the other hand, goal #1 stood on top of the importance voting, but its leverage (as revealed in the influence voting) is but one-third of that exercised by either of the "influence big four."

This illustration demonstrates the critical role that evolutionary learning plays in the identification of leverage points for effective intervention. If the design dialogue had terminated at the conclusion of importance voting, the regulatory agency would have concentrated on goal #1 and would have wasted its efforts. Going the extra step of systemic interconnections by means of influence voting, and the construction of an influence tree among the goals, identified important leverage points and was key to the success of the FDA Good Review Practices initiative.

An interesting observer-dependent metric emerged from this research. The results graphed above exemplify the *"Pareto Rule."* This rule essentially says that 20% of the elemental observations influence 80% of the situation. For example, in the case of the GRP, shown in Figure 23.1, there are 21 goals listed on the x-axis for which the influence was investigated. The total number of influences (# of times that one goal influenced others) among the 21 goals is equal to 374. The number of influences exerted by the four most influential goals, i.e., Goals #13, #27, #5, #26, is equal to 276. Simple arithmetic tells us that this number of influences, 276, is about 74% of the

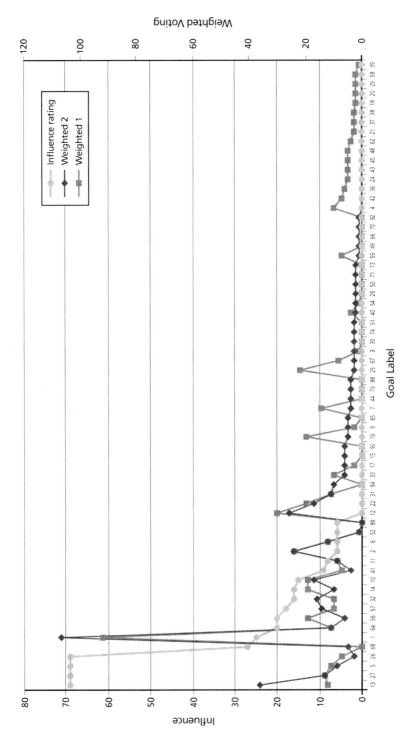

Figure 23.1.   Progressive evaluation of the voting results for the GRP.

168

total number of influences. Arithmetic also tells us that the top four goals are only about 20% of the total number of goals (21). The implication of this is that making progress on these four most influential goals (i.e., 20%) leverages 74% of the intent of the GRP case, while the other 17 goals only influence 26% of the intent.

## A HYPOTHETICAL DIALOGUE GAME

All of these six laws are essential to good social system design. Following their explanation, however, one might wonder about the relationships between these laws in terms of importance and influence. To explore those relationships, we invite you to participate in a hypothetical Dialogue Game. The six laws are displayed below in a simplified language.

    A. (_____) <u>APPRECIATION OF THE DIVERSITY</u> OF THE PERSPEC-
TIVES OF OBSERVERS IS ESSENTIAL IN MANAGING COMPLEX
SITUATIONS. (Ashby's Law of Requisite Variety).

    B. (_____) <u>STRUCTURED DIALOGUE</u> IS REQUIRED TO AVOID
THE COGNITIVE OVERLOAD OF OBSERVERS. (Miller's Law of
Requisite Parsimony).

    C. (_____) THE RELATIVE <u>SALIENCY</u> OF OBSERVATIONS CAN
ONLY BE UNDERSTOOD THROUGH COMPARISONS WITHIN A
SET. (Boulding's Law of Requisite Saliency).

    D. (_____) <u>MEANING AND WISDOM</u> ARE PRODUCED IN A DIA-
LOGUE ONLY WHEN THE OBSERVERS SEARCH FOR RELA-
TIONSHIPS OF SIMILARITY, PRIORITY, INFLUENCE, etc.
WITHIN A SET OF OBSERVATIONS. (Peirce's Law of Requisite
Meaning).

    E. (_____) DURING DIALOGUE IT IS NECESSARY TO PROTECT
THE <u>AUTONOMY</u> AND AUTHENTICITY OF EACH OBSERVER
IN DRAWING DISTINCTIONS. (Tsivacou's Law of Requisite Auton-
omy in Distinction-Making).

    F. (_____) <u>LEARNING</u> OCCURS IN A DIALOGUE AS THE OBSERV-
ERS SEARCH FOR INFLUENCE RELATIONSHIPS AMONG THE
MEMBERS OF A SET OF OBSERVATIONS. (Dye's Law of Requisite
Evolution of Observations).

You are asked to rank these principles. To do this exercise most effectively, ponder each principle and then rank the most *important* principle by
putting a "1" in the blank before the principle you think is most important,
a "2" in that blank for the next most important, etc.

When you have finished ranking the principles in terms of their importance, switch your mindset to consider the systemic influence these principles have on each other, i.e., explore their interactions. In order to do that you would have to ask yourself questions like the following:

Supposing that in a design dialogue the participants were able
to implement:
(PRINCIPLE # A: DIVERSITY OF PERSPECTIVES)
will this SIGNIFICANTLY enhance their capacity to implement:
(PRINCIPLE # B: STRUCTURED DIALOGUE)
in the context of conducting a co-laboratory to manage a complex issue?

Participants typically answer NO to this particular question. If you wish, you can continue this process by asking the follow-up question: "Would Principle #B significantly enhance the implementation of Principle #A?" You could then continue to ask similar questions of A and C, A and D, A and E, A and F, B and C, etc.

To methodically determine the influence relationships among the six dialogue principles in this manner, you would have to answer 30 pair-wise questions such as these. With the support of SDP computer software, groups answer only 15 questions instead of thirty to generate a tree of influence. This represents a factor-of-2 efficiency gain for six statements. As mentioned earlier, for a larger number of statements there might be an efficiency gain of 10 or more. This efficiency gain can reduce the work of months to that of just days when people need breaks from interminable meetings. The Good Review Practices initiative of the FDA was completed in six days of group work. Without the efficiency gains of the software it would have taken approximately sixty days of group work to converge to a Collaborative Action Plan. Also the likelihood of groupthink is reduced, which often occurs when busy people accept premature closure due to fatigue and other pressing needs.

Now at last out of this fascinating but often frustrating process of moving toward a goal that can at times be hard to keep in view, emerges the step that for most participants brings great satisfaction and a feeling of accomplishment. As a result of this pair-wise inquiry, a tree-like pattern emerges displaying graphically how the influences of the principle(s) located at the root of the tree work together to take the form of a "tree of meaning."

The tree displayed in Figure 23.2 represents the consistent result of this hypothetical Dialogue Game as it has been played by various groups of people.

The interpretation of the Tree implies that in order to produce meaning and wisdom through dialogue, namely Principle # D at the top, we must ensure that all the principles appearing along the trunk of the Tree

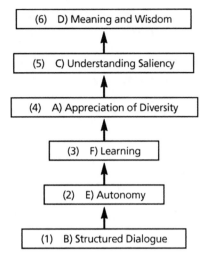

Figure 23.2.    A tree of meaning

are enforced. Principle # B, Structured Dialogue (i.e., Miller's Law of *Requisite Parsimony*), is the most influential principle because it is located at the root of the tree. On the other hand, Principle # D, Meaning and Wisdom (i.e., Peirce's Law of *Requisite Meaning*), is the least influential, even though it is the most important and desirable outcome from the conduct of any dialogue.

Reading Figure 23.2 from bottom-up, one sees that Structured Dialogue (1B) in this tree relieves participants of cognitive overload. If this basic step is taken, then the Authenticity and Autonomy (2E) of the participants and their observations are enhanced, thus demonstrating a spirit of Learning (3F) and appreciation of Diversity (4A). As the dialogue evolves, the basis of legitimacy shifts to the collective in their majority voting concerning relationships among observations that gradually leads to a determination of Saliency (5C) and ultimately Meaning and Wisdom (6D).

## WARFIELD'S LAW OF TRIADIC COMPATIBILITY

Warfield (1994) prescribes a large number of laws that lie behind the *science* of generic design. Many of those laws are omitted from the axiomatic formulation of a science of dialogic design, because I believe, on the basis of many years of practice in the arena, that understanding and internalizing: (a) the three axioms, (b) applying the architecture of SDP presented in Table 4.1, and (c) enforcing the six laws presented in this chapter, are sufficient conditions for managing the complexity and challenges inherent to designing social systems in the Information Age.

There is one law espoused by Warfield (1994), however, that is of special significance to the practice of SDP. In the Dialogue Game we noticed that structured dialogue, i.e., Principle B (Structured Dialogue), is located at the root of the Tree of Meaning, and hence is very fundamental in the application of the SDP process. Warfield's *Law of Triadic Compatibility* states:

> The human mind is compatible with the demand to explore interactions among a set of three elements, because it can recall and operate with seven concepts, these being the three elements and their four combinations; but capacity cannot be presumed for a set that both has four members and for which those members interact. (Warfield, 1998)

Combinatorial mathematics tells us something about how many different combinations may be formed from a given set of factors, such as observations about goals or problems for a particular design situation. For example, even if we have ten goals, the number of combinations involved is equal to 1,024.

In the FDA co-laboratory, discussed in Chapter 13, when the data were presented on the evolution of observations (see Figure 23.1), the number of combinations for the 21 goals proposed by the participants runs in the billions. Is it reasonable to suppose that the mind of a human being could simultaneously and systematically run through an analysis of such billions of observations, when it can only bring seven ideas into its sphere at a time?

The incapacity of the mind to work with more than a limited number of concepts simultaneously was discussed as Miller's Law of *Requisite Parsimony*. It has also been referred to in the literature as "bounded rationality" (Simon, 1974). This phenomenon is one of the driving forces behind the development and application of SDP. Because of human cognitive limitations, the idea of modularization of dialogue in ways that are compatible with this limitation is essential in dialogue addressing the complex issues of the Information Age.

Employing a historical analogy, it is worth noting that in the beginning of the 20th century it became necessary to replace Euclidean geometry and Newtonian mechanics, because of the incapacity of classical mechanics to explain certain physical phenomena, with Riemannian geometry and relativistic mechanics as discovered by Einstein. Both Euclidean and Riemannian geometries of space are axiomatic. However, the axioms of Riemannian geometry differ drastically from those of Euclidean geometry. It was this new axiomatic geometry of space proposed by the German mathematician Riemann in the 19th century that was instrumental in Einstein's discovery of relativistic mechanics.

In an analogous fashion, the discovery of the phenomenon of cognitive limitations of humans by Miller (1956), coupled to the escalating complexity of the Information Age, necessitates the adoption of a different geometry of languaging about social systems, so to speak. This is the "geometry" captured by the three axioms of SDP. In other words, SDP is the equivalent of a "new geometry" founded on the requirements of Third Phase Science. These requirements in the design situation demand that we discover and apply a new approach for constructing high quality observations by engaging stakeholders in a dialogue capable of surfacing their knowledge and wisdom (DEMOSOPHIA).

Warfield (1988), in his seminal paper *The Magical Number Three—Plus or Minus Zero*, has suggested that in situations where there exist interactions among the members of a set of observations, the magical number is three and not seven, as proposed by Miller (1956). It is critical for good design, therefore, to limit the velocity of information that is presented to stakeholder/designers. There are usually large numbers of factors, goals, issues, objects, or ideas involved in the designing process, but human beings cannot process interrelationships among them if more than three observations are involved simultaneously.

It follows that good design should apply a strategy that respects the impact of this limitation. The SDP paradigm meets this requirement. It systematically structures the set of observations involved, to work with no more than three, i.e., a pair of elemental observations and their relationship. As Warfield states:

> When we have developed patterns of interrelationships as documentation, we may work to develop the skill of reviewing and amending such patterns. Moreover, we may begin to see merit in group development of interrelationship patterns, since there is little in the capability to work with three items that suggests an overwhelming power of a single individual to construct patterns of interrelationships that are representative of actual conditions or systems, or of contemplated conditions or systems (Warfield, Staley, 1993).

CHAPTER 24

# A SCIENCE OF DIALOGIC DESIGN

**T**he Structured Design Process (SDP) is a scientific paradigm devised, tested, and refined over 30 years by a team of researchers to enable stakeholders:

- To surface and explain their observations on complex problem situations;
- To efficiently and collectively determine the roots (leverage points) of problems;
- To design a situation-specific Collaborative Action Plan to address those leverage points; in short,
- To constuct their own futures.

## SOME LESSONS LEARNED IN THE ARENA OF PRACTICE

The SDP paradigm was developed with the intent to test its applicability and reusability in the arena of practice. It is continually tested and refined by ongoing practice. In accordance with the Domain of Science Model (Warfield, 1994), any true science should conform with the cyclical relationship between theory, methodology and practice, i.e., the science should evolve in consonance with the findings and the lessons learned in the arena of applications. This section will describe some of the lessons

*How People Harness Their Collective Wisdom and Power*, pages 175–180

learned from the application of the SDP paradigm. More thorough descriptions of the applications in co-laboratories of democracy were presented in Part III. The description of the lessons learned offered in this section elaborates on the six laws presented in Chapter 23.

The respect for autonomy and its enactment in SDP are based on its commitment to rules of engagement and its context—content—process role distinctions that work within the solidarity of collective choice. In this process, legitimacy becomes aligned with parsimony. In their relational inquiry among observations stakeholders: (a) construct authentic, anticipatory and autonomous observations and graphic patterns (linguistic structures), and (b) interpret the meaning and the transfer of these patterns in accordance with the tenets of Third Phase Science.

As an example of the importance of enforcing *Requisite Autonomy*, I have experienced many cases in the arena of practice in which users of Information Technology (IT) systems were asked to participate in the design of IT systems for their organizations. The IT experts within the organization, as well as the IT contractors, were extremely reluctant to compromise their "technical expertise," and to listen to the autonomous and authentic voices of the potential users of these systems. I have had a number of experiences in which managers of IT programs had to be replaced by the leadership of the organization because of their reluctance to recognize and truly legitimize the authenticity of the IT user's voices.

As mentioned earlier, *Requisite Variety* corresponds to a phenomenological statement about the inherent multi-dimensional nature of designing social systems, and the need for groups to conceptualize and share a variety of observations. *Requisite Parsimony*, on the other hand, corresponds to the physiological or psychological limitations of human beings that constrain their capacity to communicate in groups. These two laws impose contradictory requirements for collaborative inquiry. *Requisite Variety* asserts the significance of espousing variety, even at the expense of cognitive overload. *Requisite Parsimony* asserts the significance of respecting human limitations, even at the expense of variety. The SDP paradigm has demonstrated in the arena of practice its capacity to reconcile the contradictory nature of these two laws. As shown graphically in The Tree of Meaning of Figure 23.2, the imposition of structured dialogue, as required by the Principle of *Requisite Parsimony*, enhances the autonomy of the participants, leading to an enhancement of their capacity to learn from each other, and hence to an intense and genuine appreciation of the variety of perspectives. So, variety is not compromised by parsimony because the two intervening principles of autonomy and learning enhance the search for and appreciation of variety.

Another interesting facet of the SDP is its capacity to normalize the role of power in drawing and communicating distinctions among the stakeholders. As was discussed in Chapter 19, the great German philosopher, Habermas (1971), from his analysis of "speech acts," proposes three forms of action orientation: (1) instrumental action in a nonsocial action situation, (2) strategic action in a social action situation, and (3) communicative action. The first two are oriented to achieving success, either through direct intervention (instrumental action), or through influencing decisions of opponents (strategic action). In either one of these two orientations, action is imposed by one party over the other. The SDP paradigm is most appropriate in those situations where communicative action is required because, by its very nature, it precludes such imposition since all stakeholders are interested to learn together and collaboratively converge on a mutual agreement. Examples of such communicative action orientation were previously presented in telling the stories of the "Successful Cypriot Women" and "Indigenous Opportunity" projects.

The normalization of power phenomenon manifested itself in a very visible way within a Federal Agency in an application focusing on the Agency's international position. One stakeholder, with considerable political power because of his contacts with the US White House, had been able in the past to dominate the distinction-making function in the international affairs arena. This individual became very antagonistic to the SDP paradigm and challenged its relevancy and utility in the formulation of international policy for the Agency. When this happened during the Design phase, the facilitation team offered to abandon the co-laboratory dialogue, and to let the group continue its deliberations without the discipline imposed by enforcing the six laws of the SDP paradigm. The leader of the Agency intervened immediately, and asked that the group work be continued in a disciplined and equitable manner, thus overruling the desire of this individual to dominate the discourse as he has done many times in the past.

Participants in co-laboratories describe the dialogical process as creating an atmosphere of serenity, equity, authenticity, and empathy. Most feel emancipated to make their observations without the fear of criticism or intimidation by other stakeholders. Some, however, consider it a humbling experience depicted in their feelings. One participant stated: "grieving the death of my worldview [was] followed by an expanded sense of the situation. I could only describe [it] as a new gestalt." Co-laboratories create a behavioral climate in which all stakeholders, independent of rank or authority, are able to legitimize their distinctions. This climate is a significant improvement over the conventional climate in most social-system-designing situations. In essence, the SDP paradigm promotes the power of persuasion through dialogue, as opposed to persuasion by power.

Because of this characteristic, those stakeholders who have been able to accumulate power and control within a social system are usually antagonistic to the deployment of the SDP paradigm. This phenomenon is manifested in applications in which the "leadership" of the organization does not clearly favor democracy and self-organization. It is becoming increasingly apparent, however, that the trend towards organizational democracy, in the face of escalating complexity, is not reversible. The SDP paradigm has demonstrated in the arena of practice its capacity to promote the emergence of a type of "transformational leadership" when stakeholders are engaged in learning together. The emergence of transformational leadership will be discussed in detail in Chapter 26.

In a paper I wrote in 1996 (Christakis, 1996), I identified the fundamental mechanism of how the SDP paradigm supports group learning of moral and spiritual consciousness. The necessity for coping with a complex designing situation forces the stakeholders to confront their weaknesses as observers of the multidimensional situation, and to come out from their self-referentiality by means of their interactions with other observers. They must transcend their self-referentiality and embed themselves in the role of observers and 'learners from each other'—and as learners, to draw distinctions. Each distinction is a choice made by the learner from among a great number of possible opportunities for learning. Through SDP dialogue, human beings are enabled to break the bonds of their self-referentiality as they repeatedly share observations and explanations with each other.

This phenomenon was observed in a number of instances in the arena. In the majority of cases, the participants were able to transcend their self-referentiality and construct collaborative action plans in harmony with the other members of the community. There were, however, some cases that the need for transcendence was very painful to some participants. For example, in one particular case, an MD who was a member of the therapeutic team designing a new drug for Alzheimer's dementia (see Chapter 14) had a difficult time. Subsequent to the co-laboratory, he had to undergo triple by-pass heart surgery. He confided later to other participants "that the scars and the pain from participating in the co-laboratory dialogue were more painful than the heart operation." It turns out that this individual after a few years has transformed himself into a humble and cooperative member of the community of learners.

Another lesson from the arena of practice is that the implementation of the Law of *Requisite Parsimony* slows down the pace of the dialogue process among the participants. My experience has been that some stakeholders, especially those that are accustomed to move with speed, find this characteristic of the dialogue problematic. On the other hand, my experience has also shown that speed in many cases causes cognitive overload. Also, some participants use high-speed dialogue as a means for dominating the distinction-making process. The cost of speed is the loss of autonomy and variety. There is substantial evidence in the literature that high speed in the pace of the design dialogue increases the risk of under-conceptualization, primarily because it violates both the Laws of *Requisite Variety* and *Requisite Parsimony* (Bausch, 2001).

In conclusion, my experience in the arena of practice has empirically verified that in addressing the complexity of large-scale social-system-designing situations it is imperative to accommodate the plurality and diversity of disciplinary and worldview perspectives of the stakeholders. The diversity and autonomy of stakeholders must hold pride of place over the objectivism and authority claimed by First and Second Phase Science paradigms, which have proven to be totally inadequate for the complex challenges of the Information Age.

## THE SCIENCE OF SDP

SDP is an axiomatic and pragmatic human science of design, similar to architecture or engineering that conforms to the requirements of the Domain of Science Model i.e., it is grounded in the arena of practice and the lessons learned from this arena. It details its philosophical foundations, its theory, and its methodology for designing solutions to complex social problems. Because social systems are so much more complex than cathedrals or airplanes, their design requires a deeper understanding of science; one that goes beyond that of physical science and its wonderful mathematical symbolism and models.

SDP's definition of science is "all research actions that aim to construct high quality observations and make possible improvements on action," (de Zeeuw, 1996). As explained in Chapter 20, SDP is a people science. It goes beyond the observer-independent observations of classical mechanics, i.e., First Phase Science. It also goes beyond first order cybernetics (Second Phase Science), which assumes that high quality observations fully depend on the actions that are improved by their use; for example, observing a wave or photon in quantum mechanics.

SDP is Third Phase Science or second order cybernetics. It insists that the subjects of a social system design must also be the designers of the system because only then will that design be based upon needed high quality, observer-dependent data. SDP rejects, therefore, expert-driven approaches to social-system-designing situations that do not directly involve the stakeholders and their observations in the construction of the future of the system.

SDP is, moreover, an axiomatic science similar to the model of Euclidean geometry. As discussed in Chapter 22, its three axioms are:

**Complexity Axiom**: Complex social-systems-designing situations are multidimensional. They require that observational variety should be respected in the dialogue among the observers, in an effort to strive for comprehensiveness. Comprehensiveness, however, is an objective not easily attainable by human observers, even through the application of the SDP paradigm.

**Cognitive Limitations Axiom:** Observers are subjected to cognitive limitations during social-systems-design dialogue, which must be explicitly recognized and honored during the dialogue. Cognitive limitations demand that designing teams: (a) control the pace of knowledge generation and assimilation, and (b) control the number of observations and relationships that observers must manage simultaneously during the dialogue.

**Saliency Axiom**: During social-systems-designing dialogue, understanding of relative saliency of observations can be brought into play only when the observers' authenticity, learning, and appreciation of variety are ensured so that the observers are able to construct categories of observations before assessing the relative saliency of individual observations.

These axioms form the basis of a deductive science on the model of Euclidean geometry for the successful practice of human science. The architecture of SDP spells out the implications of these axioms in terms of: consensus methods, application phases, role distinctions, interactive stages of inquiry, groupware components and collaborative facility, graphic language patterns, and dialogue laws. Because the architecture works when engaging stakeholders in designing their social systems in the arena of practice, the axioms of this human science are implicitly and indirectly validated. This is the essence of an axiomatic approach.

In physics, the progression to more adequate observations can be traced from Aristotle, to Galileo, to Newton, to Einstein, to Heisenberg, to Prigogine, etc. Similar progressions toward more pertinent observations can be traced in other natural sciences: chemistry, biology, medicine, even psychology and sociology. This essence of science, as the construction of observer-dependent high quality observations, is not as critical in the natural sciences because of the phenomenal success of the "scientific method" as manifested by First Phase and Second Phase sciences.

In the human sciences, attention to the quality of observations becomes increasingly important because the complexity of the human situation strains conventional scientific methodology to its limits. This complexity results from the multitudes of people who hold different insights into the nature of any social problem. In order to form good observations in any particular situation, those insights have to be heard and the stakeholder representatives have to organize and draw consensus conclusions from them in a systematic, systemic, and collaborative fashion.

CHAPTER 25

# MEASURING OBSERVER SPREADTHINK AND SITUATIONAL COMPLEXITY

In the SDP paradigm, complexity is defined as a confused and uncertain observer state of mind that incapacitates observer ability to understand and interpret the multidimensionality of the social-system-designing situation they confront. As a result of their confusion, they feel the need to interact with other observers in the hope that they can collectively capture all the various dimensions of the *Problematique*. As mentioned already, the practice of SDP has uncovered three distinct but interrelated sources of complexity. These are:

- **The Cognitive Burden**—This is measured by the numbers of discreet observations and insights regarding issues and action options which are focused on at a given stage during a co-laboratory.
- **The Diversity of Perspectives**—This is measured by the variety of viewpoints on what is salient to focus on at each stage of the co-laboratory.
- **The Systemic Interconnections**—This is measured by the number of influences/linkages mapped amongst the observations on the Definition stage of the co-laboratory.

By engaging observers in disciplined dialogue in the context of a *Problematique*, SDP enables the stakeholders to learn from each other in an

*How People Harness Their Collective Wisdom and Power*, pages 181–188

authentic way, without violating the Laws of *Variety* and *Parsimony*. Specifically, during application of the Nominal Group Technique (NGT), participants contribute their observations about the situation, clarify the meanings of their contributions, and finally vote individually and subjectively on the *five* relatively more important observations out of a total set of **N** discreet observations. When the participants vote, a subset of observations, say **V**, receives one or more votes. If every member of the set **N** receives at least one vote, it amounts to a 100% divergence of preferences among the stakeholders. On the other hand, if only five observations receive one or more votes, i.e., **V** = 5, then the divergence of the stakeholders in terms of relative importance is zero. We can capture this phenomenon by denoting the divergence measure by the symbol **D**, and devising an equation that reads:

$$D = (V\text{-}5)/(N\text{-}5),$$

so that, if **V** = **N**, then **D** = **1**, and if **V** = 5, then **D**= **0**. A divergence measure of **1** corresponds to a 100% disagreement among the co-laboratory participants in terms of relative importance of the observations. In the literature (Warfield, Staley, 1993), this measure has been referred to as the "spreadthink," because it is indicative of the spreading of the **V** votes of the participants within the set of the **N** distinct observations.

As stated in Chapter 4, the systemic interconnections amongst the observations are one of the sources of complexity. SDP explores the interconnections among the set of observations using Interpretive Structural Modeling (ISM). During the application of the ISM observers vote on the relational connections **R** among a subset of **N** discreet observations. In many co-laboratories, depending on time availability, **R** is the subset of observations that receives one or more votes in terms of relative importance, i.e., **R** = **V**. As a result of the voting on the relationships by means of ISM an Influence Tree is produced, such as those discussed in Part III, displaying the connections among the subset of **R** observations. We use the symbol **K** to denote the number of distinct interconnections resulting from the influence voting of the stakeholders.

For over 30 years, I have participated in studies targeted to managing complexity with many groups of stakeholders involving many systems. One outcome of these studies was the discovery of three definitive features, which are present in all instances:

- **A Plethora of component observations.** Through a variety of applications of SDP, many component observations relevant to the design task were identified and clarified, each observation being one facet of the system under study. As stated previously, the number of such observations is denoted by **N**. For example, in the case of an application for redesigning a department of a government agency, **N** was approximately equal to 80 component observations.

- **Widespread Difference of Belief Concerning Relative Importance (Spreadthink).** Individualized voting by the stakeholders displayed widespread difference of opinion among them on the relative importance of observations involved in the system being studied. As stated previously, the number of observations selected from the set of **N** that received stakeholder votes as one of the top five in terms of importance, is denoted by **V**. In the case of redesigning the government agency department, **V** was equal to 71 observations.

- **Large numbers of interconnections among the selected higher relative importance component observations.** By building tree patterns of influence relationships among the set of observations, it was discovered that there were large numbers of dependencies among them, which is characteristic of situations that induce complexity in the mind of the observers. The number of distinct paired dependencies **R** among the observations is denoted by **K**. In the case of the government agency department, **K** was over 357.

Using these three Definitive Features, and the associated designations of measures from a set **[N, V, K, R]** as described above, a Situational Complexity Index, which has been denoted as **SCI**, has been devised. The formula for calculating situational complexity is:

$$SCI = DK(N\text{-}7)/R(R\text{-}1),$$

where:

**N** = Total number of observations generated by the co-laboratory participants.

**V** = Number of observations that received one or more votes.

**K** = Number of distinct interconnections among the observations in the Problematique.

**R** = Number of observations included in the Problematique.

**D** = Divergence or "spreadthink" in terms of relative importance voting.

**7** = The Miller magic number of "**7 ± 2**."

**5** = The Warfield "spreadthink" number.

As stated previously, the formula for deriving **D** is:

$$D = (V\text{-}5)/(N\text{-}5).$$

Notice that when $V = N$, $D = 1$, and when $V = 5$, $D = 0$. In this manner, we have established that $SCI = 0$ for the minimum complexity system, with the maximum possible complexity being equal to $(N-7)$.

In applications extending over a period of 30 years with several hundred complex situations, typical values of $SCI$ lie between 15 and 55. The only case in which an index equal to 60 was obtained was in a project involving Native American Tribal leaders in 1987. One of the participants at that co-laboratory was the Chief of the Winnebago tribe, Reuben Snake, who was quoted in Chapter 20 regarding his experience with SDP co-laboratories.

Four interesting observations about the formula for calculating $SCI$ can be made:

1. If only five observations receive one or more votes during the individual voting for relative importance, i.e., $V =$ **the Warfield spreadthink number 5**, then $D = 0$, so that

$$SCI = 0$$

   The implication of this result is that the observers agree 100% on the relative importance of the $N$ observations, and as a result the situation is not complex and does not require the application of the SDP paradigm.

2. If $N = 7$, the Miller magic number, then $SCI = 0$, and again the situation is not complex to warrant the application of the SDP paradigm. With only seven observations there is no need to engage a group in an SDP co-laboratory.

3. If all the $N$ observations receive at least one vote, i.e., $V = N$, then according to the formula for calculating $SCI$:

$$SCI = K(N-7)/R(R-1).$$

   If $K = 0$, which means that there are no systemic interconnections among the $N$ observations, then $SCI = 0$. So even though the divergence measure is very high, there is no need to apply SDP for this situation because there are no interdependencies among the observations. In other words, the issues are independent of each other and can be addressed by individual investigators without engaging them in group-work.

4. If the number of interconnections $K$ in the *Problematique* is equal to all possible interactions among the observations, i.e., if the observations are in a cycle of mutual influence, then $K = R(R-1)$, and hence

$$SCI = (V-5)\ (N-7)/(N-5).$$

In the event that $V = N$ then $SCI = (N-7)$, which is the measure of maximum complexity because the divergence $D$ is 100%, and all the observations are related to every other observation in a cycle of mutual influences. The implication of this phenomenon is that the complexity index obtains the maximum value when the observers in their NGT voting select all the members of the set $N$, i.e., $V = N$, and subsequently in the ISM voting on the influences among the set of $R$ observations they discover that the observations are in a cycle of mutual influences. Using the average value of observations as determined from eighty-one co-laboratories conducted during the decade of the 1980s, which is $N = 64$, the maximum measure of $SCI$ corresponding to the average number of observations is **57.**

In Chapter 20, I discussed the distinction between observer-independent and observer-dependent data. Clearly the data used for calculating the **SCI** belong to the category of observer-dependent data. In recent applications of SDP in the arena of education, focusing on the issue of Adequate Yearly Progress (AYP) for students with disabilities as required by the No Child Left Behind (NCLB) Legislation passed by the US Congress in 2002, we have discovered that, employing the same triggering question with different sets of stakeholders corresponding to different school districts, the values of the Situational Complexity Index ranged from 8 to 15 (Ashworth, et al, 2005). There appears to exist a correlation between the measure of complexity obtained from the observer-dependent data of the stakeholders and the observer-independent data gathered during the Discovery phase for a particular school district. More specifically, higher measures of complexity are obtained from the stakeholders of schools experiencing higher levels of poverty and other socioeconomic variables associated with failing to attain Adequate Yearly Progress in mathematics by students with disabilities. However, no statistical correlation between the measure of SCI for these school districts and the observer-independent data for the same schools has yet been established.

## Measuring Situational Complexity for Drug Development

In the case of developing a Collaborative Front-End Master Plan for XY234, as reported earlier in Chapter 14, a therapeutic team composed of 15 individuals from different departments of the company represented a variety of disciplines. The number of requirements proposed by the team members, i.e., the **N** of the Situational Complexity Index, was equal to 123 ideas. The number of requirements selected from the set of **N**, which received stakeholder votes as one of the top 5 in terms of importance, i.e., the value of **V**, was equal to 36 requirements. The number of distinct paired dependencies among the **R** requirements, denoted by **K**, was equal to 249.

As one can see by studying Table 25.1, the Situational Complexity Index corresponding to the XY234 project is equal to 9, which classifies this case as relatively not very complex. Although the number of requirements **N** was large, **V** was equal to 36 indicating considerable agreement among the participants in terms of relative importance of the observations. As a result, the measure of divergence, **D**, was equal to 26%, which is about half the average measure of spreadthink from the projects reported in Table 25.1.

**Table 25.1.   Calculation of Situational Complexity Index in Selected SDP Projects**

| Project Title | Sponsor | Number of ideas (N) | Number of ideas that received a vote (V) | Number of ideas in relational pattern (R) | Relationship cardinality (K) | Situational complexity index (I) |
|---|---|---|---|---|---|---|
| 1) Strategic Plan for Office of Regulatory Affairs Cincinnati District | FDA[a] | 95 | 63 | 19 | 312 | 52 |
| 2) Action Plan for Turtle Exclusion Device (TED) Compliance Rules | NMFS[b] | 82 | 53 | 13 | 74 | 23 |
| 3) Redesigning the Office of Chief Counsel | FDA[a] | 80 | 71 | 21 | 357 | 55 |
| 4) Action Plan for a Drug Development Project | Schering-Plough Research Institute | 107 | 31 | 22 | 342 | 19 |
| 5) Action Plan for the Development of XY234 | HRPI[c] | 123 | 36 | 30 | 249 | 9 |
| 6) Achieving 1994 Performance for HRPI | HRPI[c] | 146 | 50 | 39 | 1,432 | 43 |
| 7) Administrative Management Files Project | FDA[a] | 110 | 39 | 25 | 594 | 33 |
| 8) Good Review Practices (GRP) Initiative | FDA[a] | 85 | 46 | 21 | 374 | 36 |
| Maximum | | 146 | 71 | 30 | 1,432 | 55 |
| Minimum | | 80 | 31 | 13 | 74 | 9 |
| Average | | 104 | 49 | 23 | 466 | 34 |

[a] Food and Drug Administration
[b] National Marine Fisheries Service
[c] Hoechst-Roussel Pharmaceuticals Inc.

The smaller the spreadthink, the more likely that **SCI** will be small, unless K measuring relationship cardinality is very high, which is not the case for the XY234 co-laboratory. The highest **K** reported in Table 25.1 is in the case of the project dedicated to achieving performance for a pharmaceutical company conducted in 1994, with a value for $K = 1,432$ (see entry 6 of Table 25.1).

On the basis of measures obtained from seven other applications of SDP, as shown in Table 25.1, the maximum index is equal to 55, the minimum is equal to 9, and the average is equal to 28. So the XY234 index is about 3 times below the average complexity index. It is interesting to notice that the value of complexity for another drug development project, reported in Table 25.1, involving a therapeutic team from another pharmaceutical company was equal to 19. As a result of the co-laboratory work, the development of both these drugs was terminated by consensus of the therapeutic teams before proceeding to the manufacturing phase, saving these two pharmaceutical companies from investing additional millions of dollars in the development of drugs with low efficacy and low marketability. Getting a team consensus for discontinuing the development of a drug product is not an easy task, as acknowledged by the CEO of one of these companies. The reason for the reluctance to discontinue development is that many members of the therapeutic discovery team are intellectually invested in seeing their chemical compound becoming a marketable drug in the field.

The highest situational complexity index reported in Table 25.1 corresponds to an effort to redesign the office of the Chief Counsel of the Food and Drug Administration. The participants to this co-laboratory were 70 lawyers working for the FDA.

## SCI for the Athenian Agoras

It will be interesting to conjecture what was the average complexity of the dialogues taking place in the Athenian Agoras over 2,500 years ago during the Golden Age of Athens. As I stated in Part I, the complexity of the issues confronting the Athenians were most probably one order of magnitude lower than contemporary stakeholders engaged in co-laboratories. I will try to make this assertion more transparent by employing the SCI formula.

Suppose we were to hypothesize the average values for the Athenian Agoras corresponding to the set **[N, V, K, R]** as being: $N = 15$, $V = 10$, and $R = 10$. The value of **N** for the Athenian Agoras corresponds to about 25% of the average **N** observed in contemporary co-laboratories. The value of the spreadthink chosen for Athens is 50%, which corresponds to the average value we have been observing in the Information Age co-laboratories. With these assumptions, we can calculate a minimum and a maximum **SCI** for a typical Athenian Agora dialogue. Substituting the above values for **N** and **V** in the formula for calculating SCI, we obtain a hypothetical SCI for the Athenian Agora, which reads:

$$SCI = 4K/R \ (R\text{-}1),$$

so that:

1. If **K** corresponds to the measure of interconnections for a linear Influence Tree with ten Levels of influence, then **K** = 45, and **SCI** = 2.
2. If **K** corresponds to the measure of interconnections for a cyclical Influence Tree, then **K** = 90, and SCI = 4

It appears with the assumptions made above about the average values for **N**, **V**, and **R** for the Athenian Agoras, that the range of the Situational Complexity Index for the Athenian dialogues was between 2 and 4, which is smaller by almost a factor of ten than the average value reported in Table 25.1 for contemporary co-laboratories, namely 34. These calculations, based on the **SCI** metric, represent a conjectural confirmation of the statements made in Part I of the need for a new paradigm for engaging stakeholders in a dialogue for addressing the complexity of the issues confronting them in the Information Age. It should be recognized, however, that these findings for the **SCI** are based on hypothetical observer-dependent data and not on actual data gathered from the dialogues taking place in Athens during the Golden Age.

# Part V

## CONSTRUCTING THE FUTURE

**T**his book proposes a structure of dialogic design. It argues that people can harness their collective wisdom and power to construct their future in co-laboratories of democracy. SDP supplies the reins that allow people to explore new ground. It also generates direction and leadership for making the most of new opportunities. In SDP, people create their own paths into their future.

As we have seen, SDP blends traditional respectful listening with open expression. Individuals generate their observations, clarify their ideas and have their actual expressions posted on the walls of their meeting rooms along with those of all the other stakeholders. In these generative dialogues, a group consciousness emerges that is reinforced and strengthened through stakeholder interaction. In contrast to many group encounters where an initial euphoria is drained away in linguistic Babel, SDP advances further dialogue that clarifies meaning, surfaces values, and generates relational graphic patterns. The results of this dialogue process are: 1) emancipation of the stakeholders; 2) individual and collective learning; 3) integration of diverse viewpoints; 4) discernment of salient priorities for design; 5) the emergence of a situation-specific consensual linguistic domain that enables agreement and understanding; 6) identification of key leverage points; and 7) a Collaborative Action Plan (CAP) that sets performance goals and mutual accountability.

Success in the web paradigm requires different methods than those used in the clockwork/hierarchy framework. Command and control—the preferred methods in hierarchies—are recognized as counterproductive in the web because they draw on too small a wisdom base and inevitably set up negative feedback in the very web they are trying to influence. Dialogue and teamwork are the preferred methods of influence in web-world.

The participants of a co-laboratory are collectively a **high-performance** design team. The cohesion they gain in SDP ideally equips them to generate teams to carry out their Collaborative Action Plans (CAPs). Teams are the most common characteristic of successful change efforts. They are the ideal vehicle for carrying out CAPs.

People enjoy what they do and who they are in SDP, and they love what they produce. They make things happen with coordinated effort. In this way, they produce transformational leadership that enables organizations to adapt to new situations and take advantage of the opportunities that they present. We will examine the meaning of this kind of leadership and how it is ideally suited to the rapid 21st century.

In Webworld, innovation self-organizes. SDP supplies ideal conditions for guiding the self-organization into beneficial channels. In an effort to supply non-profit organizations with the dynamism of transformational leadership, the authors of this book have formed the Institute for 21st Century Agoras, with a strategy of spreading effective participative democracy around the world.

The Epilogue of this book completes the journey begun in its Prologue.

CHAPTER 26

# TRANSFORMATIONAL LEADERSHIP

This chapter sketches the transformational leadership that propels progressive change. This kind of leadership outstrips the capacity of transactional management. It surpasses even the efforts of a charismatic leader. Transformational leadership has three components: Mutual purpose, real change, and a flourishing influence relationship. It involves group learning where stakeholders share design, decision-making, and executive responsibility according to their individual capabilities.

I discussed earlier the paradigm shift from the linear, hierarchical, industrial model to the non-linear, web-based, post-industrial model. In this chapter, I discuss the difference between leaders and leadership, and the leadership modes that are associated with those paradigms: the transactional leader, the transformative leader, and transformational leadership. The emphasis is on the transformational mode, which departs from the notion of the leader of the pack and posits leadership in the organization of the team. Finally, I present a framework for developing transformational leadership.

## THE OPERATIVE METAPHORS

As oversimplification, two metaphors express the essence of the industrial paradigm: The organization as machine and employees as workforce (or

*How People Harness Their Collective Wisdom and Power,* pages 191–201

plow horses). In organizations as machine metaphor, things need to be maintained, serviced, and tinkered with. They can become very complex and sophisticated. Workforces are managed by stick and carrot. They are whipped into shape or enticed into willing compliance.

The post-industrial metaphor is the worldwide web. Organizations are seen as self-organizing webs where people constantly relate to each other and to influences outside the organization. In the web metaphor, change is the constant; and successful organizations continually change in appropriate ways.

## EVOLUTION OF THE LEADERSHIP CONCEPT

Early leadership models equated leadership with management techniques. In his seminal work, *Leadership* (1978), James MacGregor Burns transcended this equation. He distinguished two major prototypes of leaders: the transactional leader and the transforming leader. The *transactional leader* manages resources, tasks, and followers to get a job done. The *transforming leader* enables others to perform to a higher standard. The manager who aspires to transform an organization must not only balance the concern for task with the concern for people, but also summon followers to higher ethical reasoning in conducting their work.

Burns establishes an interactive basis for leadership, which is closely related to the leadership model developed in this chapter. He states that transforming leadership "occurs when one or more persons engage with others in such a way that leaders and followers raise one another to higher levels of motivation and morality" (p. 20).

Transforming leaders go beyond the boundaries of the current organizational system toward new possibilities that are rooted in shared values. They mobilize followers by engaging these values and use empowerment to create possibilities of transforming experiences for them. By communicating shared values and visionary thinking, they partially transcend the structural barriers of manager/employee or political leader/citizen.

To some extent, Burns' work escapes the manager-employee dichotomy, but as Rost (1991) points out, that work is still rooted in the paradigm of the industrial organization. Within the conceptual boundaries of that paradigm, leaders and leadership are intertwined. Leadership is not defined separately from the role of leader; it would seem to be the effects of what leaders (the "Great Men") do.

Burns also uses a notion of "empowerment" that is a holdover from the industrial paradigm. In this concept, leadership is derived from positional authority. Power is exercised, formally and informally, through delegation whereby a subordinate individual or group is entitled to make decisions within prescribed parameters. This kind of empowerment is too weak for the tasks of interactive work.

Joseph Rost, in *Leadership for the 21st Century* (1991), reviews the definitions of leadership (and lack of them) in the research literature of the 20th century, and finds them lacking. He rejects the assumed identification of leaders with leadership and develops the concept of *transformational leadership* that emerges as an interactive process between leaders and followers. He makes the critical point that leadership is a true group phenomenon:

> Leadership is an influence relationship among leaders and followers who intend real changes that reflect their mutual purposes (p. 102).

This definition has three key elements:

- Mutual purpose,
- Real change, and
- A flourishing influence relationship.

In other words, real change arises when leaders and followers share mutual purposes and work together in a vigorous cooperative manner. Leaders and leadership should not be confused. Transformational leadership is a developmental, interactive process that is not derived merely from the effective attributes of great leaders. It is the joint production of a team having a multiplicity of leaders.

## POWER AND LEADERSHIP IN THE POSTINDUSTRIAL PARADIGM

There are many possible leaders in post-industrial organizations. New knowledge workers through their discourse now create power to shape and direct decisions. The same individual may simultaneously perform leader and follower roles in different tasks. In this way, the role of leader may be passed around the group; and the group itself assumes leadership. This group leadership is the key to success in situations of complexity and rapid change, such as designing social systems for the Information Age.

What happens to organizational managers in this developmental process? They become transforming leaders with important new systemic responsibilities. They combine the role of system designer with that of administrator. They become promoters of an organizational culture that initiates and sustains the transformational leadership process. In the words of Sylvia Odenwald (1996): "Transformational leaders encourage each worker as an individual to grasp and live the culture change" (p. 24).

To summarize, power in the post-industrial paradigm is incorporated in leadership through an "influence relationship" rather than through hierarchical delegation. The driving force of leadership is "intended real change" rather than simply the leader's vision. Finally, the motivations of leadership are jointly developed "mutual purposes" rather than a leader's exhortation calling followers to a higher moral ground.

If transformational leadership is an emergent property of group interactions, what is the nature of the transformative process? It is a process of group learning through meaningful dialogue. It is this process that presents formidable challenges to groups trying to reach the level of consensual decision-making.

## LEADERSHIP AS A GROUP PHENOMENON AND ITS BARRIERS

Groups that test their emergent leadership in designing social systems confront three major barriers to their work. These barriers impair each individual's ability to manage the cognitive and behavioral burdens of problem solving and design in a group setting.

The first barrier relates to a misunderstanding of "*scale*," where groups misjudge the complexity of a designing situation. Individuals often come to a group setting with a predetermined idea of what the solution ought to be. If these ideas are not challenged, the group may leap to proposing solutions before it understands a complex problem. Complex, multi-dimensional problems defy quick-fix solutions. They require a group's best collaborative effort to integrate the variety of perspectives about the problem situation before proceeding to solutions. An unintended effect of poorly scaled solutions on the group is a belief that the design challenge is a relatively simple one. This is not usually the case. The challenges of complex systemic design must be respected, and not dismissed as simple.

The act of forming a group creates the second barrier: *escalation of complexity.* I discussed briefly this phenomenon in Chapter 20. If the group embarks on a process of group learning to tackle a complex problem, the interactive behavior of the members of the group generates a plethora of ideas commensurate to the number of group members. These ideas soon overrun the capacity of individuals to comprehend them.

The third barrier is *under-conceptualization.* It occurs for a variety of reasons including misjudgments of scale, mismanagement of people, and insufficient idea processing support. When a group under-conceptualizes, it develops inadequate or inappropriate "solutions." It essentially violates the Law of *Requisite Variety.* It then fails to get the real change that it wants because of group confusion or fatigue.

Without substantial methodological assistance of the type provided by SDP, many groups will be unable to overcome these barriers. In the sections below, I offer theoretical grounding for an effective transformational leadership process.

## A FRAMEWORK OF TRANSFORMATIONAL LEADERSHIP

As already stated, the three key elements of transformational leadership are: mutual purpose, real changes, and a flourishing influence relationship. In SDP, these elements are matched with the three phases of context, content, and process in the following ways:

- The *context* of mutual purpose invites commitment;
- The *content* of intended real change is generated and interrelated by the stakeholders; and
- The *process* of SDP enables democratic influence relations in which leadership is shared and consolidated among the stakeholders.

As discussed previously, the barriers to leadership are formidable. Many groups flounder in unexamined assumptions and the conflicts that surface when assumptions are not made explicit. Unless the context, content, and process distinctions of the roles to be played by the various actors are managed well, the likelihood of transformational leadership emerging through a group's work is not high.

It is my belief that the transformational leadership process is an emergent phenomenon of group learning. It is a spiritual connection that emerges within groups when we realize that "as human beings we have only the world which we create with others–whether we like them or not" (Maturana & Varela, 1987, p. 246). Transformational leadership emerges only when group participants spontaneously develop a sense of commitment and shared responsibility. I have witnessed this emergence in a variety of situations with various groups—in large part because of proper management of context, content, and process, as described in Chapter 6. These three concepts are explored in the following sections as they relate to transformational leadership.

## The Context of Mutual Purpose Invites Commitment

For transformational leadership to emerge in a group's work, a mutual purpose must be present in its early stages. Purpose is an overarching factor that links the group's work with the organization and its external environment. Purpose differs from goals, which constrain purpose to predefined channels. Purpose frees the group to pursue its own ideals within a context of mutually shared intention.

Even if a group begins its work with a "charge" or mission statement through some executive person or body, the individuals in the group must connect their understanding of the purpose to the stated purpose of the mission statement. Purposes imposed by an executive may be studied with consideration, but mutual purposes must be accepted at an individual level for them to become sources of group motivation. The foundation for learning and focus that mutual purpose provides must always be laid.

Nadler and Hibino (1994) claim that "purposing" may be the most essential step in any problem solving or design work. They identify three "red flags" that should warn us that purposing is not going well:

- A directive, including measures, is presented as the only solution;
- Functional fixedness—ideas, objections, and quick-fix solutions reflect the narrow scope of a particular function; and
- Impatience—"We don't have time. Let's solve this problem and get on with it" (p. 154).

The importance of heeding these red flags is expressed in the often-quoted aphorism: "There always seems to be enough time to fix a mistake, but never enough time to do it right the first time." Mutual purpose sets the scope, boundaries, and focus of the group's efforts.

## The Content of Intended Real Change Is Produced by Stakeholder Dialogue

Stakeholders possess the requisite knowledge for defining and resolving systemic organizational problems. Often executives and executive bodies do not realize this until they are overcome by the severity of the design situation. This is particularly true in cases where other "solutions" have already failed. For example, I know from many years of practicing SDP in the arena that the best opportunity for its application in a social system design situation is when all other efforts have failed.

Experience has shown that stakeholders are programmed to see situations in terms of the workforce metaphor. They have a good deal of skepticism in early group engagement about the intentions of management in convening a group to work on a social system designing situation. Their typical remarks include suspicions about what management really wants, e.g., "hidden agendas". If they judge that real change is not to be the focus of their deliberations or see that implementation difficulties are minimized, their cynicism escalates and their engagement is minimal. Rost

(1991) puts it succinctly, "Only when leaders and followers actually intend real change is a leadership relationship possible" (p. 115).

Stakeholders working as a group must perceive that the intended change is real and the content of that change is their contribution and responsibility. That is, they must draw upon their own experiences and wisdom to decide the content of the change. They must also be prepared to learn from others.

Effective group learning means that stakeholders will generate, understand, and interrelate their observations. In complex situations, they may generate hundreds of ideas. The generation of ideas is comparatively easy. Relating the ideas to each other is exceedingly complex and individual capacity for processing the relationships is limited. As discussed in the previous chapters, without methodological assistance, group members are tempted to select a number of related ideas (starting with their own) and to move quickly to solutions. This haste does not allow the necessary diversity of ideas to surface, nor does it identify the crucial leverage points at which to assert action.

In SDP, stakeholders provide the building blocks to group learning. With computer support to categorize and interrelate ideas, they manage all of their ideas in "real time." They can always view large visual displays of the variety of observations and their interrelationships. They have easy reference to the extensive documentation that is maintained of the explanations of meanings provided by each participant/author. The content they generate is accessible and transparent throughout the dialogue process.

## SDP Enables Democratic Influence Relations among the Stakeholders

Group learning is the core of transformational leadership. It can happen any time a group of individuals meets as a community of stakeholders to confront the design challenges of the Information Age.

It is not unusual, however, to have little or no learning in many group processes. The individual members simply do not learn from each other. They may come to the group situation primarily to voice their beliefs about a problem situation or to persuade others to their point of view. The assumption about influence relations in such situations is that someone wins and someone loses through debate. Debate may help distinguish differences in beliefs about an issue; it rarely builds group learning on design challenges.

Given human nature and our almost universal experience of debate in group meetings, one might ask: "Is it possible for groups to construct relational patterns of influence that supersede the influence of authority, personality, "expertness," or even conflicting beliefs in confronting change? How is group leadership possible?" This question makes perfect sense if one holds onto the presupposition that power is exercised by elected or designated authorities. In that context, the question is unanswerable.

There is, however, a concept of power that can explain transformational leadership as possible and natural. Michel Foucault (*Power/Knowledge*, 1980) calls it "Power as influence relationship." He distinguishes this form of power from the power exercised by constituted authorities. As mentioned earlier, he describes it as "capillary" because it is exercised in the minute interactions of everyday life.

At one extreme, this capillary power can be very manipulative, as in the minute discipline used to teach dressage to horses. In the field of marketing, the choices (distinctions) that are offered manipulate consumer behavior. In group decision-making sessions, people often fight to get their distinctions accepted by the group because they will then have power over the implementation of the decisions, as described earlier in Chapter 23 in discussing the *Law of Requisite Autonomy in Distinction-Making*.

So how can this kind of power emerge within a group as a constructive, positive force? By democratizing the distinction-making process as required by the *Law of Autonomy in Distinction-Making*. A group can give all of its stakeholders an equal opportunity to make distinctions. When they do, the power of leadership is distributed as well. Then, as the group proceeds to construct a common vocabulary of accepted distinctions, it collectively assumes the leadership role. In this way, democratic distinction making produces social reality by constructing a consensual linguistic domain.

In group situations, influence relations always occur. When they are developed in the context of a disciplined dialogue, in a democratic manner, they open paths to group learning. They also provide normative examples to group members:

- to understand before trying to be understood;
- to abandon narrow self-interest without losing self-esteem; and
- to build upon the ideas of others as others will build upon theirs.

Experience has shown that leadership is emergent when group members are engaged in the SDP paradigm. As the relationships among generated ideas are explored, learning begins to occur, particularly if the assumptions and beliefs behind an individual author's ideas are made explicit and transparent.

Practice in the arena suggests that individuals join a group believing that they have the answers to the problem and that other members of the group have ideas similar to their own. For group leadership through shared learning, this belief must, of course, be corrected. But this belief can rarely be corrected directly. Indeed, there is usually no need for open correction.

Early experiences within the group challenge this mistaken belief. When individual stakeholders contribute ideas, for example, they are invited to explain the meaning of their statements, which is recorded. Invariably, a stakeholder will indicate that the statement needs no explanation. As mentioned before, other stakeholders quickly challenge that assertion. Then the true diversity of beliefs within the group emerges. The individual stakeholders gradually transcend their self-referentiality and become immersed in the emerging consensual reality of the group. In most cases they become very enthusiastic with the superiority of the collective wisdom of the group.

To trust personal understandings and to feel confident to voice them requires an unusual group context. Unstructured conversation is too unfocused and undisciplined to provide the proper context for productive group interaction. Debate does not work either. Complex systemic issues and the bounded rationality of humans to deal with them require us to learn together through disciplined dialogue rather than debate.

A good forum for this learning together is provided in SDP where people voice their observations, meanings, and connections of ideas. The process is "focused" because mutually agreed-upon questions—a "triggering question" and a "generic question"—direct the generation and structuring of ideas. It is "open" because every person's ideas are listened to and the entire group respects the language of the person.

In SDP, the power that emerges among the stakeholders is that of mutual persuasion and respect. Often the experience of this power is a revelation to stakeholders. It is radically different than the power often experienced in other types of group work, where the power relation is based on authority (positional or expertise) or personality (the person who dominates). This power generates consensual linguistic domains and collaborative action plans with roles and responsibilities of every stakeholder.

This kind of leadership does not have to be sold to stakeholders because they are it. They are prepared to fulfill the designs they have constructed. Their designs meet little opposition and gain large majority acceptance. The future they construct has real meaning for them and has a likelihood of evolutionary change. The power generated in a co-laboratory is transformational leadership at its best.

## TEAMS

Collectively, the participants in a co-laboratory are a high-performance design team that exercises transformational leadership. That is what high-performance teams do. One might wonder whether the team's Collaborative Action Plan (CAP) has to be carried out by teams. Do they have to be implemented in web-world? Can they work in hierarchies?

Clear definitions will help us answer these questions. According to Jon Katzenbach and Douglas Smith, authors of *The Wisdom of Teams* (1993):

- A working group has "no significant incremental performance need or opportunity that would require it to become a team. The members interact primarily to share information, best practices, or perspectives and to make decisions to help each individual perform within his or her area of responsibility. Beyond that, there is no realistic or truly desired "small group" common purpose, incremental performance goals, or joint work products that call for either a team approach or mutual accountability" (p. 91).
- "A team is a small number of people with complementary skills who are committed to a common purpose, performance goals, and approach for which they hold themselves mutually accountable" (p. 45).

## Teams and Hierarchies

Working groups can function very well in hierarchical situations where there is no pressing challenge, either threat or opportunity, to be faced. In such situations, working groups can be just as effective as teams and require a lot less effort. Nevertheless, teams can be very valuable in hierarchical structures.

> Hierarchical structures and basic processes are essential to large organizations and need not be threatened by teams. Teams, in fact, are the best way to integrate across structural boundaries and to both design and energize core processes. Those who see teams as a replacement for hierarchy are missing the true potential of teams (p. 5).

The value of a CAP is achieved in its implementation, which will, of necessity, often be enacted within hierarchical structures. In those structures, either work groups or teams may be appropriate. Where teams are employed, they will contribute to the health of the overall organization and help it to bridge the "silos" that make up its structure. Even in hierarchies, CAPs offer the potential for generating teams.

## Co-Laboratories and Teams

Katzenbach and Smith describe the need for teams—"real teams not just groups that management calls 'teams'"—in terms similar to those used to describe the need for co-laboratories. "In any situation requiring the real-time combination of multiple skills, experiences, and judgments, a team inevitably gets better results than a collection of individuals operating within confined job roles and responsibilities" (p. 15). They believe that teams "should be the basic unit of performance for most organizations, regardless of size" (p. 15). Real teams are the most common characteristic of successful change efforts at all levels (liner notes). They are becoming "the primary unit of performance for increasing numbers of organizations" (p. 5). "Most models of the 'organization of the future' that we have heard about—'networked,' 'clustered,' 'nonhierarchical,' 'horizontal,' and so forth—are premised on *teams surpassing individuals as the primary performance unit in the company*" (p. 19). Teams are, therefore, the ideal vehicle for carrying out the plans created in co-laboratories.

"Groups become teams through *disciplined action*. They *shape* a common purpose, *agree* on performance goals, *define* a common working approach, *develop* high levels of complementary skills, and *hold* themselves mutually accountable for results." These five activities are largely accomplished in co-laboratories. As previously explained, purpose is *shaped* in the context phase of SDP. Participants in the workshops accept a *defined* working approach—structured and open dialogue. They *develop* skills of observation and listening, making use of each other's experiences and perspectives in their decision-making. They *agree* on a CAP that defines their performance goals and holds them mutually responsible for its results.

In these ways, a co-laboratory painlessly compresses the otherwise tedious process for forming teams into a two-day workshop. Follow-up on a CAP, of course, requires continued discipline, but the joy developed in SDP can rather seamlessly be transported to action teams.

CHAPTER 27

# BEING SUCCESSFUL
# IN WEB-WORLD

Transformational leadership of the style generated in dialogical design works best in the context of web-world. Combining as it does the genius of all members of the designing team, it generates effective consensus through focused and open dialogue. The harmony created in the small SDP web resonates in the larger web. Efficacious organizing in web-world is best accomplished through successful dialogue. Efforts to spread humane and sustainable practices using methods of the hierarchical model have only limited effectiveness because they generate negative feedback in the very web they are trying to influence.

## THINKING WITHIN THE WEB PARADIGM

Life is more humane in web-world than in the clockwork universe. Dialogue and interpersonal communication are as important in the web as they are in traditional societies, where linear clockwork thinking is not abandoned, but is seen as a special kind of cognition that is useful in straightforward mechanical situations. Web thinking is multidimensional, parallel, tangled, and all at once—self-organizing.

This kind of thinking and interacting offers ways into the hearts of people and their situations unknown in the clockwork world of confrontational debate with its predetermined rules of acceptability. One comes on

*How People Harness Their Collective Wisdom and Power,* pages 203–207
Copyright © 2006 by Information Age Publishing
All rights of reproduction in any form reserved.

as a reasonable listener and honors the authenticity of all members in a dialogue. One honors disagreements and treasures the creative tension they create, letting intricacy build without needing to prematurely integrate it into one's cognitive map. One honors the interactive process in the faith that it will produce superior results. One works cooperatively and patiently with others when consensus does emerge.

In order to make such interactions possible in a complex and fast-paced world, computer assistance can be employed to do the clockwork, linear, complex logical operations that usually consume our intellectual energy and overload our cognitive limitations. Computers do mechanical operations better than we do. Using computer assistance with considered discretion, we free ourselves to deal with the real thinking and interaction on complex issues for which we humans are well designed.

Approaching people respectfully, we come to understand their points of view and rise together with them to conceptions that transcend our previous ideas. We find that we share values beyond the paradigms we dwell in. We find that clockwork people and traditional/religious ones share web concerns for values, families, justice, environment, etc.

Many of us hang on to the clockwork/hierarchy paradigm because it provides the only coherent secular structure that we know. When we work and think within that structure, we are blocked from making a reasonable case for most of our humane impulses. Some of us develop a split personality in which cynical mental ruthlessness exists alongside a religious sentimentality that allows us to be warm and generous in the praxis of our lives.

In web world, the grounds of what is considered "rational" and "real" shift. The unfortunate consequences of the hierarchical model, manifested as racism, sexism, and elitism are exposed as frauds. Values of respect for family, community, autonomy, and integrity become essential and practical. Sustainable global development becomes a self-evident goal in everyone's eyes. Dreams of a free people in a just society are no longer seen as antithetical to evolutionary reality, but as a culmination of it.

The connections provided by the Internet hasten the advent of web world. They provide the sub-structures of possible intricacy and transparency that are necessary for self-organization in the Information Age. The billions of data that flood our terminals do not, however, guarantee emergent understanding and consensus action plans for designing social systems unless the stakeholders are engaged in dialogue. The data merely stress our ability to cope, thus pushing us far-from-equilibrium where we are faced with a bifurcation: Cope better or surrender our independent judgment.

The question arises: How can we share this web world vision and popularize it? Obviously, good publicity is a desirable thing. Education about the new paradigm in schools and universities would prepare new generations to live as full citizens in the participative democracy of the Information Age. The mass communications media, however, have so thoroughly bought into the clockwork model that they seems unlikely to lead the way into this new Age. Personal interaction and the Internet are the more likely media because they are more compatible with the way things are achieved in a web. Working in these media we can generate outstanding results that can later be broadcast through other media.

The motto: Think Globally, Act Locally, makes sense in web-world. If we build a local web that works, we can communicate that web to others who can implement it in their locality. The Internet and its spread during the last 15 years indicate the speed at which change can occur in the Information Age.

The converse motto: Think Locally, Act Globally, also makes sense in web world because things that happen in the web are not the result of linear causality. Ideas and action agendas move across the web as undulating waves, structurally coupling with other ideas and action agendas in orgies of self-organization.

## EFFORTS TOWARD CONSCIOUS EVOLUTION

Corresponding to the two paradigms, attempts to control our destiny can be roughly categorized as hierarchical or web-like. Hierarchical efforts work on the command-and-control model in which official policy dictates what happens. Such understanding and control can be simple or complex. Extreme examples of simple [minded] attempts to improve our lot were the slum clearance and public housing projects of post World War II that destroyed slum neighborhoods and erected slums of sterile barracks in urban America.

Far more sophisticated efforts to understand our history are exemplified in the first (1972) report of the Club of Rome, *Limits to Growth*, which identified five major interacting global variables that limit our ability to continue growing as a consumption society. They advocated experiments in alternative growth possibilities including birth control, recycling, pollution control, and contingency planning. Their point of view has strong advocates and has helped raise ecological awareness around the globe.

Their advocacy raised a storm of controversy in the '70s, raising hackles among adherents of the established clockwork/domination paradigm. Eventually, the findings of the Club were discredited partially because the computer models were too simple, partially because the predictions did not come to pass in the timeframes predicted, and partially because of establishment-media-machine ridicule.

Strong movements, many of them with the backing of the United Nations, are lobbying today to control destructive systemic variables by advocating sustainable development, environmental protection, population control, human rights, economic democracy, etc. These efforts try to turn the tables on hierarchy. It remains to be seen if these forms of "communicative action" (Habermas) will shape our destiny. These initiatives do spark widespread debate, but also trigger concerted opposition from entrenched power structures.

The opposition aroused by advocacy efforts such as that of the Club of Rome, Planned Parenthood, Green Movements, World Court, constraining Global Warming, even banning land mines, shows an inherent weakness of advocacy. Advocacy breeds debate in which winning is the objective and consensus is denied. Debate relies on linear thinking, oppositional logic, and deafness to the opponent's point of view. Debate is the prized methodology of the clockwork/dominator model. The use of debating tricks in complicated social situations muddies conceptual waters to the point where people do not trust their reason and rely on their emotions, which can often be manipulated to produce a numb conformity.

All of the movements mentioned above probably deserve our support; and they all share, to some extent, common strengths and weaknesses. The strengths are the rightness of their causes and their educational effectiveness. The fundamental weaknesses are an assumption of the clockwork/domination paradigm and an overdependence on tools that were adapted for use in that age.

## ORGANIZING IN THE WEB PARADIGM

The best way to overthrow the clockwork/hierarchy model is to make the self-organization/web model work brilliantly. Nature does this very well, witness evolution. Researchers in artificial intelligence, working with parallel processors, are beginning to show dramatic results. The very idea of democracy sparked in Athens and a staple of many indigenous cultures has grown in a self-organizing manner.

Modern reform movements have to move fast. Most of them begin democratically, but many morph into bureaucratic, clockwork modalities in order to process pressing business. In their clockwork orientation, organizations function well in routine operations, but they are insensitive to innovation. They atrophy without periodic revolution. When faced with a bifurcation, they barely register the danger they are in and face death unaware. They are obsolete in situations of rapid change. A global example of this kind of insensitivity is found in the foreign policy of the United States at the beginning of the 21st century, which tries to maintain its clockwork hegemonic organization in an era of rapid structural change. The policy is obsolete, but some politicians are oblivious.

There is no lack of anecdotal evidence that web approaches work. This approach used to be called "enlightened self-interest" as in the Marshall Plan, which continues to serve Europe and the USA to this day. Companies such as Hewlett-Packard and Herman Miller are icons of enlightened management of this model. Management gurus (Senge, 1990, and Wheatley, 1992, for example) trumpet the need for learning organizations, flat hierarchies, and sensitivity to change.

Non-profit organizations and citizen's movements generally need to school themselves in methodologies that work in the new paradigm if they wish to have a lasting impact. They need to move beyond educating themselves about the new paradigm. They need to concentrate on local relationships. Webs require local connections.

The atomization of our social lives deprives us of connections necessary for creating our own consensual reality. Our social isolation plays into the hands of dominators by making us easier to manipulate and more conformist. The speed of our lives also weakens our social solidarity. Our rushing about robs us of the leisurely dialogue that leads to consensus about important issues. We try at times to revive processes resembling town hall democracy and Quaker prayer circles, but few of us have the patience required to stick with them. We clearly need new forms of interaction that generate transformational leadership and make participative democracy work.

# CHAPTER 28

---

# CONSTRUCTING AGORAS
# OF THE GLOBAL VILLAGE

**S**ome of the best, most intelligent, motivated, and committed people are the backbone of the world's non-profit and community organizations. They put in hard hours to advance their goals, having some success, but often fail to produce the impact they desire.

These organizations are dedicated to bettering their parts of the world or making the world a more livable place. In our shorthand expression, they are "constructing agoras of the global village," which refers to the democracy initiated in the markets (agoras) of ancient Greece. These organizations generally lack funds. They need to concentrate their efforts on key leverage points and build working coalitions with similar-minded groups. Unfortunately, they often lack time for strategic reflection. As a result, scarce resources are often expended on activities that lack long-term impact.

The 47th annual conference of the International Society for the Systems Sciences (ISSS) in 2003 examined reasons why well-meaning and committed people have difficulty building livable, democratic, life-enhancing communities on the planet. They did so under the theme "Constructing Agoras of the Global Village," and they identified four basic activities that would vastly improve the agora-building success rate:

1. Provide methodology and facilities to continuously support the construction and sustainability of global agoras;
2. Organize planetary networks;

*How People Harness Their Collective Wisdom and Power*, pages 209–210
Copyright © 2006 by Information Age Publishing
All rights of reproduction in any form reserved.

3. Identify stakeholders who may not identify themselves as stakeholders; and

4. Link to an established entity that has the capacity to initiate agora construction activity (Hays and Michaelides, 2004).

The Institute for 21st Century Agoras is equipped to serve those needs, to aggressively "initiate agora construction activity." It exists to assist progressive non-profit organizations in their efforts to construct livable communities on the planet. To begin the process, we have identified dozens of organizations that would welcome Co-Laboratory assistance. These organizations recognize their need for internal cohesion and cooperation with like-minded people and organizations. They believe they can meet those needs by utilizing SDP.

Now is a great opportunity for growing global agoras:

- There is a need for sustainable strategies in the face of rampant depletion of world resources.
- There is a need to maintain local honor and living standards in the face of Westernizing globalization.
- There are numerous well-intentioned groups whose fragmentation and isolation prevent their making an effective difference.
- There is a lack of broad-based and inclusive progressive effort.

People who participate in the Structured Design Process are usually enthusiastic about the workshop and even more enthusiastic about the results they achieve on their action plans. We anticipate that the participants and observers of these co-laboratories will be interested in using them in other communities and organizations. We propose to make them available to parties that could not otherwise afford to invigorate themselves in this way. We aim over the next *four years* to conduct *100 demonstration projects* around the world with the potential for spreading agoras like crabgrass.

See Appendix C for a summary proposal designed to construct agoras of the global village.

# EPILOGUE

**P**eople from all walks of life had the opportunity to shape the issues of governance pertinent to them 2,500 years ago in the Golden Age of Athens. In their ancient agoras, Greeks introduced a revolutionary democracy that tapped their communal wisdom and unleashed their cultural energy.

Their style of participative democracy had drawbacks, however, even in an era of simpler issues and a more leisurely pace. It denied citizenship to women and members of the slave class. It was manipulated by political and self-serving oratory. It fell out of favor even in Greece.

Today, we have not lost our desires to be free and in control. We are not, either, relieved of our responsibilities to make our worlds better places for ourselves and future generations. We cannot be daunted by the complexity of globalization and the speed of information that strain our abilities to cope.

For us to be truly free and responsible, we must dialogue with each other in the practice of participative democracy. To that end, we can turn to the principles exemplified in SDP that tap our best wisdom, technology, and experience. SDP supplies a pragmatic science that enables such dialogue in complex social situations. It and similar methodologies can again allow us to tap our collective wisdom and unleash our creativity.

Western people yearn for the core values of democracy. I experience this yearning every summer when I am living in the village of Archanes in Crete. The villagers are desperate to have their voices heard by the representatives of different countries in the European Union (EU) Congress. Interestingly enough, the Mayor of Archanes was recently elected to represent Greece in the EU Congress, which is a great honor for the villagers. Even though they are proud to have their local mayor represent Greece, they still do not feel that they are included in the governance of their lives.

*How People Harness Their Collective Wisdom and Power*, pages 211–212

The public discourse on democracy must be extended so that it again becomes a living system of ideas and not something of the past to be sanctimoniously worshipped. Above all, democracy must grant power beyond the circle of scientific and public policy experts. It must return ownership for designing social systems to stakeholders and the common person. Democratic dialogue must return to people's neighborhoods, communities, and other social systems that are important in their lives.

For the past thirty years, the SDP paradigm has been developed to facilitate design that can bring democracy back to the common person. With focused and open dialogue that avoids cognitive overload, it encourages respectful listening, open expression, and opportunities for participants to explain the meaning of their contributions, thus creating a linguistic consensual web among stakeholders. The technological support of SDP also has the advantage of allowing participants to effectively deal with the complexity of the confounding issues of the Information Age, without being burdened with details of recording and interrelating ideas.

The advantages of the SDP are many. It is solidly grounded in systems science; it encourages individual as well as group learning; and it allows for focused and open dialogue that converges to Collaborative Action Plans. The SDP axioms are not specific to any particular culture, and apply to multitudes of cultural arenas, as demonstrated already from many applications with indigenous people. SDP provides equanimity for participants and has been proven effective in many years of application successes. The SDP paradigm is formidable in sustaining democracy, cultural dignity, and autonomy for all people. It can be foundational in realizing the ideal of a just and humane world.

# REFERENCES

Abu-Nimer, M. (1996). Conflict resolution in an Islamic context. *Peace & Change, 21,* (1), pp. 22–41.

Alexander, G. C. (2002). Interactive Management: An Emancipatory Methodology, *Systems Practice and Action Research, 15,* No. 2, pp. 111–122.

Americans for Indian Opportunity (AIO). (1989). *Tribal Issues Management System (TIMS),* AIO Report, Bernalillo, New Mexico.

Apel, K. (1981). *Charles S. Peirce: From Pragmatism to Pragmaticism,* University of Massachusetts Press, Amherst.

Arnstein, S. and Christakis, A. N. (1976). *Perspectives on Technology Assessment,* Science and Technology Publishers, Jerusalem, Israel.

Argyris, C. (1982). *Reasoning, Learning, and Action,* San Francisco: Jossey-Bass.

Ashby, R. (1958). Requisite Variety and Its Implications for the Control of Complex Systems, *Cybernetica,* 1(2), pp.1–17.

Ashworth, J. E., Christakis, A, N., and Conaway, D. S. (2005). *Addressing the Dropout Rate for Students with Disabilities in the Flint Community Schools,* Final Report by the Michigan Department of Education, Lansing, Michigan.

Banathy, B. H. (1996). *Designing Social Systems in a Changing World,* Plenum, N.Y.

Banathy, B. H. (2000). *Guided Evolution of Society: A Systems View,* Plenum, N.Y.

Banathy, B. A. (1999). An Information Typology for the Understanding of Social Systems, *Systems Research and Behavioral Sciences, 16,* No. 6, pp, 479–494.

Bales, R. F. (1951). *Interaction Process Analysis,* Addison-Wesley: Cambridge

Barber, B. (1995). *Jihad vs. McWorld,* Ballantine

Bausch, K. (2000). The Practice and Ethics of Design, *Systems Research and Behavioral Science,* 17, No 1, pp. 23–51.

Bausch, K. (2001). *The Emerging Consensus in Social System Theory,* Plenum, N.Y.

Bausch, K., Christakis, A.N. (2003). Technology to Liberate Rather Than Imprison Consciousness, in Loye, David (ed.), *The Great Adventure: Toward a Fully Human Theory of Evolution,* SUNY Press.

Bausch, K. (2004). *Constructing Agoras of the Global Village,* (ed.). Special Edition of *World Futures: The Journal of General Evolution, Volume 60, Numbers 1–2.*

*How People Harness Their Collective Wisdom and Power,* pages 213–219
Copyright © 2006 by Information Age Publishing
All rights of reproduction in any form reserved.

Belay, V. H., Christakis, A, N., and Conaway, D. S. (2005). *Increasing the Rate Students with Disabilities Meet AYP Goals in Mathematics for the Hilbert Middle School,* Final Report by the Michigan Department of Education, Lansing, Michigan.

Boulding, K. (1966). *The Impact of Social Sciences,* New Brunswick: Rutgers University Press.

Broome, B. J., Christakis, A. N. (1988). A Culturally-Sensitive Approach to Tribal Governance Issue Management. *International Journal of Intercultural Relations 12,* pp. 108–123.

Burns, J. M. (1978). *Leadership.* Harper & Row, New York.

Campanella, M. L. (1993). The cognitive mapping approach to the globalization of world politics, in: Laszlo and Masulli (eds) *The evolution of cognitive maps,* Philadelphia, Gordon and Breach.

Cardenas, R & Moreno C. (2004). A critical Reflection on Participative Planning for Regional Development. *World Futures, 60, Nos. 1–2.* January–March, pp. 147–160.

Checkland, P. (1981). *Systems Thinking, Systems Practice.* New York: John Wiley & Sons.

Christakis, A. N. (1973). A New Policy Science Paradigm, *Futures,* 5(6), pp. 543–558.

Christakis, A. N. (1987). High Technology Participative Design: The Space-Based Laser, in: *General Systems.* John A. Dillon Jr. (ed.), International Society for the Systems Sciences, *Vol. XXX,* pp. 69–75, New York.

Christakis, A. N. (1988). The Club of Rome revisited in: *General Systems.* W. J. Reckmeyer (ed.), International Society for the Systems Sciences, *Vol. XXXI,* pp. 35–38, New York.

Christakis, A. N. (1993). The Inevitability of Demosophia, in: *A Challenge for Systems Thinking: The Aegean Seminar,* Ioanna Tsivacou (ed.), University of the Aegean Press, pp. 187–197, Athens, Greece.

Christakis, A. N. (1996). A People Science: The CogniScope System Approach, *Systems: Journal of Transdisciplinary Systems Sciences,* Vol. 1, No. 1, pp. 18–25.

Christakis, A. N. (2004). Wisdom of the People, *Systems Research and Behavioral Science,* Vol. 21, pp. 479–489.

Christakis, A. N. (2005). A Retrospective Structural Inquiry of the Predicament of Mankind Prospectus of the Club of Rome, in *C. West Churchman Legacy and Related Works. Volume 1: Rescuing the Enlightenment from Itself,* Janet McIntyre-Mills (ed). Kluwer-Springer Academic Publishers.

Christakis, A. N. (2005). Dialogue for Conscious Evolution, in *C. West Churchman Legacy and Related Works. Volume 2: Wisdom. Knowledge and Management,* John P. van Gogch and Janet McIntyre-Mills (eds). Kluwer-Springer Academic Publishers.

Christakis, A. N., Warfield, J. N. (1987). NSF DTM, Ohio State University, Columbus, Ohio.

Christakis, A. N., Warfield, J. N., and Keever, D. (1988). Systems Design: Generic Design Theory and Methodology, in: *Systems Governance,* Michael Decleris, (ed.), Publisher Ant. N. Sakkoylas, Athens-Komotini, Greece, pp. 143–210.

Christakis, A.N., Christakis, N.A., Conaway, D., Feudtner, C., Geranmayeh, A., and Whitehouse, R.J. (1994). *Designing the Good Review Practices,* CWA Report FDA-694-1, Interactive Management Consultants, Paoli, Pennsylvania.

Christakis, A.N., Christakis, N.A., Conaway, D., Feudtner, C., and Whitehouse, R.J. (1995a). *Application of the* CogniScope *System for the Conceptual Design of the AMF*

*Project Plan,* CWA Report FDA-195-2, Interactive Management Consultants, Paoli, Pennsylvania.

Christakis A.N., Conaway, D. (1995b). *Designing the Development of Regulatory Science,* CWA Report FDA-395-4, Interactive Management Consultants, Paoli, Pennsylvania.

Christakis, A.N., Christakis, N.A., Conaway, D., Geranmayeh, A., and Snow R.M. (1996). *Designing Office of Chief Counsel,* CWA Report FDA-895-6, Interactive Management Consultants, Paoli, Pennsylvania.

Christakis, A. N., and Dye, K. M. (1999). Collaboration through Communicative Action: Resolving the Systems Dilemma through the CogniScope, *Systems: Journal of Transdisciplinary Systems Sciences,* Volume 4, Number 1 pp. 45–55.

Christakis, A. N. and Bausch, K. (2002). Technologue: Technology-Supported Disciplined Dialogue, in Roberts, Nancy (ed.), *Transformative Power of Dialogue,* Elsevier Publishing Co.

Christakis, A. N., Conaway, D., and Bronfman B. (2003a). Anticipating Alternative National and Regional futures, *World Futures, 59,* pp. 335–360.

Christakis, A. N., and Brahms, S. (2003b). Boundary-Spanning Dialogue for 21st-Century Agoras, *Systems Research and Behavioral Sciences, 20,* pp. 371–382.

Christakis, A. N., and Harris, L. (2004). Designing a Transnational Indigenous Leaders Interaction in the Context of Globalization: A Wisdom of the People Forum, *Systems Research and Behavioral Sciences, 21,* pp. 251–261.

Churchman, C.W. (1979). *The Systems Approach,* Delta: New York.

Cisneros, R.T. (2004). Latin American Agoras—Some Free Interpretations of the Results Given in the Dynamics of the Latin-American Group. *Systems Research and Behavioral Science,* 21, pp. 555–562.

Collier, J.D. (1999). Autonomy in Anticipatory Systems: Significance for Functionality, Intentionality and Meaning, in Daniel M. Dubois (ed) *Proceedings of CASY'98, The Second International Conference on Computing Anticipatory Systems.* New York: Springer-Verlag.

Delbecq. A. L., Van de Ven, A. H., Gustafson, D. H. (1975). *Group Techniques for Program Planning: A Guide to Nominal Group and DELPHI Processes,* Glenview, IL: Scott, Foresman.

Descartes, R. (1952). *Discourse on Method, Vol. 31* in *Great Books of the Western World.* Chicago: Encyclopedia Brittanica. Originally published 1637.

de Zeeuw, G. (1996). Second Order Organizational Research, *Working Papers in Systems and Information Sciences,* University of Humberside, Hull, England.

Doxiadis. C. A., (1968). *Ekistics: An Introduction to the Science of Human Settlements,* Hutchinson of London.

Dye, K. M. (1997). Collaborative Design Process Science, *Working Papers at MIT,* Boston.

Dye, K. M., Feudtner, C., Post, D., and Vogt, E. M. (1999). *Developing Collaborative Leadership to Reframe the Safe Use of Pharmaceuticals as a National Health Priority,* CWA Report, Interactive Management Consultants, Paoli, Pennsylvania.

Dye, K. M. and Conaway D. S. (1999). *Lessons Learned from Five Years of Application of the* CogniScope™ *Approach to the Food and Drug Administration,* CWA Report, Interactive Management Consultants, Paoli, Pennsylvania.

Eigen, M. (1992). *Steps toward life.* New York: Oxford University Press.

Eisler R. (1987). *The chalice and the blade: Our history our future*, San Francisco, Harper and Row.

Flood R. L. (1990). *Liberating systems theory*. New York: Plenum Press.

Foucault, M. (1980). *Power Knowledge: Selected Interviews and Other Writings, 1972–1977* (translated by C. Gordon). Pantheon Books, New York.

Friedman, T. L. (2000). *The Lexus and the Olive Tree*, Anchor Books, New York.

Gleick, J. (1987). *Chaos: Making a new science*. New York: Viking.

Goerner, S. (1999). *After the clockwork universe: The emerging science and culture of integral society*. Edinburgh: Flories Publishers.

Gutman, A,. and Thompson, D. (1996). *Democracy and Disagreement*. Cambridge, MA: Belknap Harvard.

Habermas, J. (1971). *Knowledge and Human Interests* (J. Shapiro, Trans.). Boston: Beacon Press. (Original work published 1968).

Habermas, J. (1984). *The Theory of Communicative Action*. Vols. I and II. Polity Press

Habermas, J. (1987). *The philosophical discourse of modernity*. (F. G. Laurence, Trans.), Cambridge: The MIT Press. (Original Work published 1985).

Habermas, J. (1987). *The Theory of Communicative Action: Lifeworld and System: a Critique of Functionalist Reason*, (Vol. 2, trans. by McCarthy, T.), Beacon Press, Boston, Mass.

Habermas, J. and Luhmann, N. (1971). *Theorie de Gesellschaft oder Socialtechnologie: Was leistetdie Systemforschung?* [Theory of society or social technology: What does systems research accomplish?]. Frankfurt: Suhrkamp.

Harris, L.D. and Wasilewski, J. (2004). Indigeneity, an Alternative Worldview—Four R's (Relationship, Responsibility, Reciprocity, Redistribution) versus Two P's (Power and Profit): Sharing the Journey Towards Conscious Evolution. *Systems Research and Behavioral Science, 21,* pp. 489–504.

Harris, L. and Wasilewski, J. (2004). Indigenous Wisdom of the People Forum: Strategies for Expanding a Web of Transnational Indigenous Interactions. *Systems Research and Behavioral Science, 21,* pp. 505–514.

Hayes, P. and Michaelides, M. (2004). Constructing Agoras of the Global Village: A Co-Laboratory of Democracy on the Conscious Evolution of Humanity. *Systems Research and Behavioral Science, 21,* pp. 539–545.

Hubbard B. M. (1998). *Conscious Evolution: Awakening the Power of our Social Potential*, New World Library: Novato, CA.

Irani, G. E. & Funk, N. C. (1998). Rituals of reconciliation: Arab-Islamic perspectives, *Arab Studies Quarterly, 20,* pp. 53–74.

International Monetary Fund (IMF). (2000/2001). *Globalization: Threat or Opportunity?* IMF: Washington, D.C.

Jackson, M. (1995). Beyond the Fads: Systems Thinking for Managers, *Systems Research 12,* pp. 25–42.

Jantsch E. (1969). *Perspectives of Planning*, OECD: Paris.

Kahn, K. B., (1996). Interdepartmental Integration: A Definition with Implications for Product Development Performance, *Journal of Product Innovation Management, 13,* pp. 137–151.

Kapelouzos, I.B. (1989). The Impact of Structural Modeling on the Creation of New Perspectives in Problem-Solving Situations, *Proceedings of the 1989 European Congress on Systems Science*, Lausanne, Switzerland, AFCET, October, pp. 915–932.

Katzenbach, J. R., and Smith, D. K., (1992). *The Wisdom of Teams,* Harvard Business School Press, Boston, Massachusetts.

Kauffman, S.A. (1993). *The origins of order: Self-organization and selection in evolution.* New York: Oxford University Press

Kemeny, J. G. (1980). Saving American Democracy: The Lessons of Three Mile Island. *Technology Review,* June/July, pp. 65–75.

Kuhn T. (1970). *The Structure of Scientific Revolutions,* (2nd ed.) Chicago: University of Chicago Press.

Laouris, Y. (2004). Information Technology in the Service of Peacebuilding: The Case of Cyprus. *World Futures, 60,* Nos. 1–2. January–March, pp. 67–89.

La Pointe, G. (1999)(Doc # 99141). A Socio-Psychological View of Social Systems and Design; *Proceedings of the 43rd Annual Conference of the International Society for the Systems Sciences,* Edited by J.K. Allen, M.L.W. Hall, J Wilby, ISBN 09664183-2-8.

Lopez-Garay, H. (2001). Dialogue Among Civilizations: What For?, *International Journal of World Peace, XVIII,* 15–33.

Loye, David (ed.) (2003). *The Great Adventure: Toward a Fully Human Theory of Evolution,* SUNY Press.

Luhman N. (1995). *Social systems,* Stanford: Stanford University Press.

Maturama H. R. (1970*). Biology of cognition.* Reprinted in Matrurana and Varela (1980), 2–62.

Maturana H. R., and Varela F. (1980). *Autopoiesis and Cognition: The Realization of the Living.* Dordrecht: Reidel.

Maturana, H. R. and Varela F. J. (1987). *The Tree of Knowledge: The Biological Roots of Human Understanding,* (Revised Edition). Shambhala, Boston, MA.

Magliocca, L. A., and Christakis A. N. (2001). Creating a Framework for Sustainable Organizational Leadership: The CogniScope System Approach, *Systems Research and Behavioral Science, 18,* pp. 259–279.

Magliocca, L. A., and Minati G. (2001). Transforming Leadership Through Coalitions: Building: The Ethics of Sustainable Development in Globalization, *Proceedings of the Associazione Italiana per la Ricerca sui Sistemi (AIRS).*

Margulis, L. (1998), *Symbiotic planet: A new look at evolution.*

Mason, G. H. (1995). Some implications of postmodernism for the field of peace studies. *Peace & Change, 20,* pp.120–132.

McIntyre, J. J. (2003). Participatory Democracy: Drawing on C. West Churchman's Thinking when Making Public Policy, *Systems Research and Behavioral Science, 20,* pp. 489–499.

Meadows D. H., Meadows D., and Randers J. (1972). *The Limits to Growth.* New York: Universe Books.

Miller, G. A. (1956). The Magical Number Seven, Plus or Minus Two: Some Limitations on Our Capacity for Processing Information, *Psychology Review 63,* pp. 81–97.

Mingers, J.C. (1992). Technical, practical, and critical OR—past, present, future? *J. Operat. Res. Society 42,* pp. 375–382.

Murthy, P. N. (2000). Complex Societal Problem Solving: A Possible Set of Methodological Criteria, *Systems Research and Behavioral Science, 17,* pp. 73–101.

Nadler, G. and Hibino, S. (1994). *Breakthrough Thinking.* Prima Publishing, Rocklin, CA.

Oliga, J.C. (1996). *Power, Ideology, and Control,* Plenum Press, NewYork.

Parker T. et al. (2004). The Chronic Kidney Disease Initiative, *Journal of the American Society of Nephrology, 15,* pp. 708–716.

Pattakos, A., (1995). Searching for the Soul. of Government, in *Rediscovering the Soul of Business,* Sterling & Stone, Inc., San Francisco, pp. 313–326.

Peccei A. (1969 ). *The Chasm Ahead,* Toronto: The Macmillan Company.

Prigogine, I. and Stengers, I. (1984). *Order out of chaos.* New York: Bantam Books.

Pusey, M. (1987), *Jurgen Habermas,* Ellis Horwood, Chichester, UK.

Roberts N. C. (2002*). The Transformative Power of Dialogue.* Elsevier, New York.

Rost, J.C. (1991). *Leadership for the Twenty-First Century.* Praeger, New York.

Sabet, A. G. E. (1998). The peace process and the politics of conflict resolution. *Journal of Palestine Studies, 26,* pp. 5–19.

Senge P. M. (1990). *The Fifth Discipline: The Art and Practice of The Learning Organization,* Doubleday, NY.

Shapiro, M. A. (2003). Facilitating a Global Conversation Through the Universal Demosophia Facility, in *Dialogue as a Means of Collective Communication,* edited by Banathy B, and Jenlick P., Kluwer Academic/Plenum Publishers.

Slater, P., and Bennis, W. (1990). Democracy is Inevitable, *Harvard Business Review,* Sept.–Oct.

Simon, H.A. (1974). How Big is a Chunk, *Science, 183,* pp. 482–488.

Suzuki, Yuta. (2005). *Demosophia—Dialogue and New Democracy in the 21st Century,* A thesis presented to the Faculty of the International Christian University, Tokyo, Japan.

Taylor, J.B., (1976). Building an Interdisciplinary Team. In Arnstein, S.R., and Christakis, A.N., (ed.) *Perspectives on Technology Assessment,* Science and Technology Publishers, Jerusalem, Israel, pp. 45–63.

Tsivacou, I. (1997). The Rationality of Distinctions and the Emergence of Power: A Critical Systems Perspective of Power in Organizations, *Systems Research and Behavioral Science, 14,* pp. 21–34.

Toffler, A. (1980). *The Third Wave,* Bantam Books, New York.

Tuckman, B. W., (1965). Developmental Sequences in Small Groups, *Psychology Bulletin, 63,* pp. 384–399.

Turrisi, P.A., (Ed.) (1997). *Pragmatism as a Principle and Method of Right Thinking,* State University of New York Press.

Ulrich, W. (1983), *Critical Heuristics of Social Planning: A New Approach to Practical Philosophy,* Paul Haupt, Berne, Switzerland.

Ulrich, W. (1991). Critical heuristics of social systems design; & Systems thinking, systems practice, and practical philosophy: A program of research, in: Flood and Jackson (1991), pp. 103–116.

Varela, F.J., Thompson, E., and Rosch, E. (1991). *The embodied mind: Cognitive science and human experience.* Cambridge: The MIT Press.

Von Beralanffy(1968). *General Systems Theory: Foundations, Development, Applications.* New York, N.Y., George Braziller, Inc.

Warfield, J, N. (1976). *Societal Systems,* Wiley & Sons, New York, N.Y.

Warfield, J.N. (1988). The Magical Number Three, Plus or Minus Zero, *Cybernetics and Systems, 19,* pp. 339–358.

Warfield, J. N. (1994). *A Science of Generic Design: Managing Complexity Through Systems Design,* Iowa State University Press, Ames, Iowa.

Warfield, J. N. (1999). The Problematique: Evolution of an Idea. *Systems Research,* *16,* pp. 221–226.

Warfield, J. N., and Christakis, A. N. (1987). Dimensionality. *Systems Research, 4,* pp. 127–137.

Warfield, J. N., and Cardenas, A. R. (1994). *A Handbook of Interactive Management,* Iowa State University Press, Ames, 1994.

Warfield, J.N., and Staley, S. M., (1996) Structural Thinking: Organizing Complexity through Disciplined Activity, *Systems Research, 13,* pp. 47–67.

Wheatley, M. J. (1992). *Leadership and the new science,* San Francisco: Berrett-Koehler.

Winograd and Flores (1986). *Understanding Computers and Cognition: A New Formulation for Design,* Ablex Publishing Corporation.

Wolfram, S. (1982). Cellular automata as simple self-organizing systems. Caltech preprint CALT-68-938.

APPENDIX A

# A HYPOTHETICAL CASE OF STRATEGIC MANAGEMENT

**I**n this Appendix we will provide an example of an application of the SDP to a hypothetical case of an organization attempting to implement its strategic vision. We assume that an implementation team consisting of representatives of the community of stakeholders has been assigned the task of designing an action plan for overcoming the inhibitors/issues related to the accomplishment of the strategic vision of the organization. The assumption is made that the organization has completed the phase of designing a Collaborative Action Plan for bringing to fruition its strategic vision, and is prepared to initiate the phase of implementation of the vision.

This example will provide an opportunity for learning in some detail the four generic stages of application of the SDP paradigm. In the discussion, we will present some hypothetical materials relevant to the case. These materials are illustrative of the type of elemental observations, explanations, graphic language patterns, and interpretations, which could be produced in an actual co-laboratory, such as those described in Part III.

In the discussion we will present each stage as depicted graphically in Figure 11.1, and the steps included in each stage as distinct. It should be pointed out, however, that there are linkages among the four interactive stages. The linkages are implicit and experiential within the context of a specific linguistic domain, and can never be made totally explicit through documentation.

*How People Harness Their Collective Wisdom and Power*, pages 221–237
Copyright © 2006 by Information Age Publishing
All rights of reproduction in any form reserved.

## STAGE ONE: DEFINITION

The intent of the definition stage is to enable the stakeholders to generate a consensual domain on the task being studied for design or redesign purposes. In my experience, based on over 400 applications of SDP, the definition stage is extremely critical because it delineates a boundary of relevancy and builds a consensus on the problem situation to be addressed collectively by the stakeholders. As shown graphically in Figure 11.1, this stage entails the implementation of three steps.

### Step One: Generation and Clarification of Issues

During this step the stakeholders generate and clarify ideas in response to a triggering question. The framing of the triggering question requires a lot of preparation and thoughtfulness by the Inquiry Design team, which usually includes a representative of the client organization.

In the hypothetical example presented here, the triggering question was framed to read as follows:

"What are critical current and anticipated issues to be addressed in order to achieve our strategic vision?"

In response to this question for this hypothetical co-laboratory the stakeholders generated a set of issues, a small subset of which are shown in Table A.1. Following the generation and recording of the observations in a computer file, the social system designing team members engaged in clarification of the meaning of the issues. An example of the discussion for clarification of meaning of three illustrative issues is shown in Table A.1A.

**Table A.1. Example of List of Unstructured Issues to be Addressed for Achieving the Strategic Vision**

| Triggering Question: |
|---|
| *What are critical current and anticipated issues to be address in order to achieve our strategic vision?* |
| (1—Issue)  Inability to break the functional and organizational silos |
| (2—Issue)  Lack of clarity of roles and responsibilities of many of the teams |
| (3—Issue)  Inadequate information management tools to meet external customers' needs |
| (4—Issue)  Refusal to face new market realities |
| (5—Issue)  Need to build two or more customer-driven products/projects |
| (6—Issue)  Conflict between regional and international efforts |
| (7—Issue)  Need for improved R&D productivity |

**Table A.1.    Example of List of Unstructured Issues to be Addressed for Achieving the Strategic Vision (Cont.)**

**Triggering Question:**
*What are critical current and anticipated issues to be address in order to achieve our strategic vision?*

(8—Issue)    Lack of feeling in the organization that we all have the same mission

(9—Issue)    Lack of a clear priority-setting process in product development and commercialization

(10—Issue)    Need for restructuring field sales force

(11—Issue)    Employee confusion about roles and responsibilities

(12—Issue)    Territorial nature of entire organization

**Table A.1A.    Example of Clarification of Issues to be Addressed for Achieving the Strategic Vision**

**Triggering Question:**
*What are critical current and anticipated issues to be address in order to achieve our strategic vision?*

(1—Issue)    Inability to break the functional and organizational silos

Our organization has been historically compartmentalized. As a result, one function does not inform or explain their mission to other functions. Sometimes, I feel that the very silos are reluctant to pass information to other parts of the organization because they are not secure to do so. We need to do something about the silos, especially if we want to become more competitive in the global marketplace.

(2—Issue)    Lack of clarity of roles and responsibilities of many of the teams

What I mean by that is that many people in our organization are unable to explain their roles and responsibilities, especially since we reorganized to a team-based organization. I know of cases that people have been assigned to a product development team and yet, their reporting responsibilities are not with the responsibility of the team but more with their function of their particular department.

(3—Issue)    Inadequate information management tools to meet external customers' needs

Our ability to serve our customers is diminished because when we make customer calls we don't have information with regard to their needs. I think we should try to design an information system that our salespeople can use for storing and retrieving customer related information.

I know of other companies who have been able to develop something called "Sales Force Automation System" and as a result, whenever a salesperson calls a customer he has advanced information about the customer, in fact sometimes a customer profile.

And so on . . .

## Step Two: Affinity Clustering Representation

In step two the stakeholders begin to explore relationships among observations and to produce "relational patterns" through focused and open dialogue. In order not to violate the Law of Triadic Compatibility, the dialogue focuses on two ideas and their relationship, i.e., an "information chunk" that respects every individual's short-term brain activity. The aim in producing relational patterns is to allow enough time for sequentially presented information to be interpreted in terms of the relationships among the observations, and to allow enough learning time during the dialogue to help ensure that the information is understood and remembered.

The *generic question* used in this hypothetical case for implementing step two is:

"In the context of the strategic vision for our organization, does:
(Issue-X)
have significant attributes in common with:
(Issue-Y)?"

As a result of the dialogue the stakeholders produced a pattern showing the classification of the issues into four affinity clusters. This illustrative pattern is shown graphically in Table A.2: Classification of Strategic Issues into Affinity Clusters.

### Table A.2.   Illustration of the Classification of Issues into Affinity Clusters

**Cluster #1: Silos**

(1—Issue)    Inability to break the functional and organizational silos

(6—Issue)    Conflict between regional and international efforts

(8—Issue)    Lack of feeling in the organization that we all have the same missions

(12—Issue)  Territorial nature of entire organization

**Cluster #2: Role Confusion**

(2—Issue)    Lack of clarity of roles and responsibilities of many of the teams

(7—Issue)    Need for improved R&D productivity

(9—Issue)    Lack of a clear priority setting-process in product development and commercialization

(11—Issue)  Employee confusion about roles and responsibilities

**Cluster #3: Information Technology**

(3—Issue)    Inadequate information management tools to meet external customers' needs

**Table A.2.   Illustration of the Classification of Issues
into Affinity Clusters**

---

**Cluster #4: Franchises**

(4—Issue)     Refusal to face new market realities

(5—Issue)     Need to build two or more customer-driven products/projects

(10—Issue)   Need for restructuring field sales force

---

After the clustering of the issues the participants are asked to vote on an individual and subjective basis by selecting the top five most important ideas from the representation shown in Table A.2. The results of the hypothetical voting are tabulated as shown in Table A.3.

**Table A.3.   Example of Voting Results on Issues of Higher Relative
Importance for a Hypothetical Case with a Number of Observation
Larger than 12**

---

**3 or more votes = 17**

   Issues:     1, 9, 13, 14, 22, 24, 25, 29, 34, 35, 42, 52, 59, 74, 75, 76

**2 votes = 15**

   Issues:     3, 7, 8, 12, 20, 21, 26, 41, 42, 45, 46, 51, 66, 68, 72

**1 vote = 21**

   Issues:     2, 4, 6, 10, 11, 17, 18, 27, 31, 32, 37, 40, 47, 48, 50, 54, 56, 61, 65, 67, 71

---

The number of observations that received one or more votes $V$ for this hypothetical case is **53**. Assuming that the number of distinct observations for this hypothetical case is equal to the average number, i.e., $N = 64$, the spreadthink measure is equal to 81%, which is significantly higher that the average.

## Step Three: Influence Representation (Problematique)

In step three the relational work continues by focusing the dialogue on a different generic question, namely:

> "Supposing that we were able to make progress in resolving:
> (Issue-X)
> will this progress help us *significantly* in the resolution of:
> (Issue -Y)
> in the context of the strategic vision for our company?"

The relational pattern produced as a result of the focused and open dialogue among the stakeholders is shown in Figure A.1: Preliminary Structuring of Strategic Management Issues into a Problematique. It is interesting to notice that in the representation shown in Figure A.1, the three deep-rooted issues, which happen to be in a cycle of mutual dependence, are:

- (Issue-1): Inability to break the functional and organizational silos;
- (Issue-6): Conflict between regional and international efforts;
- (Issue-12): Territorial nature of entire organization.

Enabling the stakeholders to understand and interpret the Problematique representation produced as a result of the step three dialogue is very crucial for the quality of the design work, which follows the completion of the definition stage. Because enhancement propagates along the pathways shown in Figure A.1, the ability to resolve issues that exert strong leverage, i.e. deep-rooted issues, is crucial to the achievement of the vision. The relationship cardinality corresponding to Figure A.1, $K = 39$, so that the Situational Complexity Index for the hypothetical case is equal to 14.

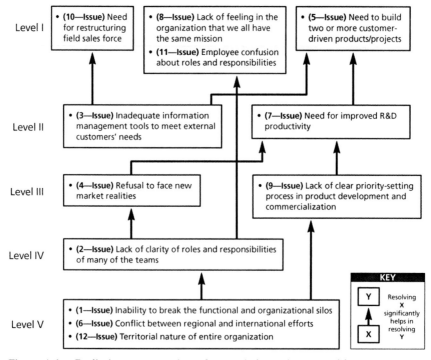

Figure A.1.    Preliminary structuring of strategic issues into a problematique. (Produced by CWA for training and installation of the *CogniScope*™ system)

## STAGE TWO: DESIGNING ALTERNATIVES

The purpose of the design stage is to enable the stakeholders to design alternative scenarios for the resolution of the Problematique.

### Step One: Generation and Clarification of Options

In the hypothetical case being presented in this Appendix the *triggering question* for focusing the dialogue was:

"What are options which, if implemented, will contribute to the resolution of the system of issues (i.e., the Problematique)?"

The action options proposed by the stakeholders and the discussion for clarification of the meanings of the individual observations are shown in Tables A.4 and A.4A.

**Table A.4.   Example of List of Unstructured of Options for Resolving the Strategic Vision Problematique**

| | |
|---|---|
| **Triggering Question:** | |
| *What are options which, if implemented, will contribute significantly to the resolution of the system of issues?* | |
| (1—Option) | Adopt a transparent process of project selection and prioritization |
| (2—Option) | Develop a clear understanding of roles, responsibilities, and accountability |
| (3—Option) | Develop milestones and a sense of urgency for meeting the milestones |
| (4—Option) | Simplify the organization to make it functional |
| (5—Option) | Maximize productivity in areas such as R&D |
| (6—Option) | Develop two new business opportunities that are a strategic fit and generate new revenue |
| (7—Option) | Emphasize everyone's role as a stakeholder in the achievement of strategic objectives |
| (8—Option) | Train, motivate and mobilize field sales force |
| (9—Option) | Redesign product development and commercialization process |
| (10—Option) | Consolidate certain functions to reduce or eliminate redundancy |
| (11—Option) | Adopt a team-based organization paradigm |
| (12—Option) | Merge with Company XYZ |
| (13—Option) | Reduce sales force by 20% |
| (14—Option) | Design an "idealized" sales force automation system |
| (15—Option) | Discontinue R&D in medical instrumentation |
| (B—Option) | Apply new problem-solving and design approaches |

### Table A.4A.   Example of Preliminary Clarification of Options for Resolving the Strategic Vision Problematique

**Triggering Question:**

*What are options which, if implemented, will contribute significantly to the resolution of the system of issues?*

(1—Option)   Adopt a transparent process for project selection and prioritization

Whenever we try to make decisions about product development we usually do not understand the underlying rationale for those decisions. Our ability to prioritize projects especially when it involves different perspectives has been marginal, as indicated by the problems identified in our problematique, and unless we adopt a rigorous and clear process for making those decision we will not be able to sustain our profitability.

(2—Option)   Develop a clear understanding of roles, responsibilities, and accountability

Well this idea follows the previous identification of barrier. We need to make everyone understand their roles, their responsibilities and hold them accountable for their commitments and performance.

One way to do that is to create a common vision for the organization and to make sure this vision is owned by every staff member.

(3—Option)   Develop milestones and a sense of urgency for meeting the milestones

This is self-explanatory.

(4—Option)   Simplify the organization to make it functional

The current organizational structure is so overlapping and confusing hat most of our people are not clear about their report responsibilities. I know that there exists alternative organizational designs that we might like to study and implement in order to improve the capacity of the organization to accomplish our mission and increase our profitability.

And so on . . .

## Step Two: Options Field Representation

In step two the dialogue is focused on the *generic question:*

"In the context of designing alternatives for resolving the Problematique, does:
(Option-X)
have *significant* attributes in common with:
(Option-Y)?"

The output of this disciplined dialogue is the Options Field representation shown in Figure A.2: Preliminary Options Field for Resolving the Strategic Management Problematique. This representation is also sometimes

| Cluster #1— Redesign | Cluster #2— Priority | Cluster #3— Productivity | Cluster #4— New Business | Cluster #5— Sales Force |
|---|---|---|---|---|
| • **(Option 2)** Develop a clear understanding of roles, responsibilities, and accountability | • **(Option 1)** Adopt a transparent process for project selection and prioritization | • **(Option 5)** Maximize productivity in areas such as R&D | • **(Option 6)** Develop two new business opportunities that are a strategic fit and generate new revenue | • **(Option 8)** Train, motivate, and mobilize field sales force |
| • **(Option 4)** Simplify the organization to make it functional | • **(Option 3)** Develop milestones and a sense of urgency for meeting the milestones | • **(Option 9)** Redesign product development and commercialization and process | • **(Option 12)** Merge with Company XYZ | • **(Option 13)** Reduce sales force by 20% |
| • **(Option 7)** Emphasize everyone's role as a stakeholder in the achievement of strategic objectives | • **(Option 16)** Apply new problem-solving approaches | • **(Option 15)** Discontinue R&D in medical instrumentation | | • **(Option 14)** Design an "idealized" sales force automation system |
| • **(Option 10)** Consolidate certain functions to reduce or eliminate redundancy | | | | |
| • **(Option 11)** Adopt a team-based organization paradigm | | | | |

*TIE LINE*

Figure A.2.   Preliminary classification of options for resolving the strategic planning Problematique.

referred as an "Options Field Representation," because the option clusters are presented in a column format and a "Tie Line" for connecting the options is introduced in the graphic. The role of the Tie Line will become more apparent when we discuss Step Four.

## Step Three: Superposition Representation

Prior to the design of alternative scenarios for the resolution of the Problematique, it is a desirable to engage the stakeholders in a dialogue focused on the *generic question*:

"Supposing we are able to implement:
(Option-X)
will it help us significantly in the resolution of:
(Issue-Y)
in the context of designing alternatives for resolving the Problematique?"

The output of this deliberation is shown in the representation of Figure A.3: Superposition of Options onto the Strategic Management Problematique.

The significance of this representation is that it makes transparent to the stakeholders those options with the maximum leverage in terms of the

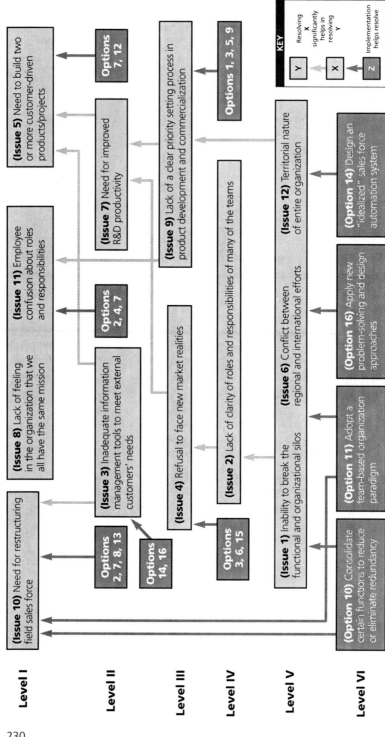

Figure A.3. Superposition of options onto the strategic Problematique.

resolution of the Problematique. Because of the propagation of the resolution power of a particular option, as displayed graphically by the arrows in Figure A.3, those options that penetrate the Problematique deeply are the ones with the maximum leverage. In this particular hypothetical example, four options are located at Level VI, i.e., the deepest level of the representation, and hence they exert the maximum leverage in terms of resolution of the Problematique. These options are:

- (Option-10): Consolidate certain functions to reduce or eliminate redundancy;
- (Option-11): Adopt a team-based organizational paradigm;
- (Option-14): Design an "idealized" Sales Force Automation System; and
- (Option-16): Apply new problem-solving and design approaches.

## Step Four: Options Profile Representation

In this step the stakeholders are engaged in a dialogue for designing alternative scenarios. Usually, this dialogue is carried out by small teams of two to five individuals. The small teams are asked to revisit the Options Field representation presented in Figure A.2, and to select options from each of the affinity clusters presented in Figure A.2. The selected options are connected to the "Tie Line" as shown in the Options Profile representations presented in Figures A.4 and A.5. The Alternative presented in Figure A.4 is called *"Interactive,"* and the one presented in Figure A.5 is called *"Reactive."*

In the hypothetical case, Figure A.4 could be the alternative proposed by one small team, and Figure A.5 the alternative proposed by another small team. A third small team might have proposed another alternative, which in this example we assume it has been captured by the two surviving alternatives presented in Figures A.4 and A.5.

It is interesting to note that, as shown explicitly at the bottom of the two Figures, it is easy to translate the selection of options made by the team into a continuous prose scenario.

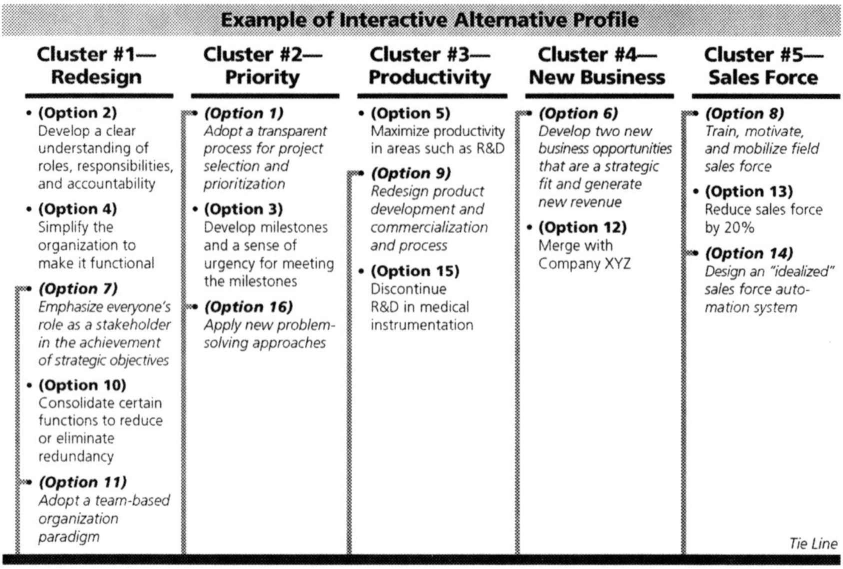

## Example of Interactive Alternative Profile

| Cluster #1— Redesign | Cluster #2— Priority | Cluster #3— Productivity | Cluster #4— New Business | Cluster #5— Sales Force |
|---|---|---|---|---|
| • **(Option 2)** Develop a clear understanding of roles, responsibilities, and accountability | • *(Option 1)* Adopt a transparent process for project selection and prioritization | • **(Option 5)** Maximize productivity in areas such as R&D | • *(Option 6)* Develop two new business opportunities that are a strategic fit and generate new revenue | • *(Option 8)* Train, motivate, and mobilize field sales force |
| • **(Option 4)** Simplify the organization to make it functional | • **(Option 3)** Develop milestones and a sense of urgency for meeting the milestones | • *(Option 9)* Redesign product development and commercialization and process | • **(Option 12)** Merge with Company XYZ | • **(Option 13)** Reduce sales force by 20% |
| • *(Option 7)* Emphasize everyone's role as a stakeholder in the achievement of strategic objectives | • *(Option 16)* Apply new problem-solving approaches | • **(Option 15)** Discontinue R&D in medical instrumentation | | • *(Option 14)* Design an "idealized" sales force automation system |
| • **(Option 10)** Consolidate certain functions to reduce or eliminate redundancy | | | | |
| • *(Option 11)* Adopt a team-based organization paradigm | | | | Tie Line |

**Alternative A:** *Emphasize everyone's role as a stakeholder in the achievement of strategic objectives while adopting a team-based organization paradigm. Adopt a transparent process for project selection and prioritization and apply new problem-solving and design approaches. Redesign product development and commercialization process. Develop two new business opportunities that are a strategic fit and generate new revenue. Train, motivate and mobilize field sales force and design an "idealized" Sales Force Automation System.*

Figure A.4.   Interactive alternative profile.

## Example of Reactive Alternative Profile

| Cluster #1— Redesign | Cluster #2— Priority | Cluster #3— Productivity | Cluster #4— New Business | Cluster #5— Sales Force |
|---|---|---|---|---|
| • **(Option 2)** Develop a clear understanding of roles, responsibilities, and accountability | • **(Option 1)** Adopt a transparent process for project selection and prioritization | • **(Option 5)** Maximize productivity in areas such as R&D | • **(Option 6)** Develop two new business opportunities that are a strategic fit and generate new revenue | • **(Option 8)** Train, motivate, and mobilize field sales force |
| • **(Option 4)** Simplify the organization to make it functional | • *(Option 3)* Develop milestones and a sense of urgency for meeting the milestones | • **(Option 9)** Redesign product development and commercialization and process | • *(Option 12)* Merge with Company XYZ | • *(Option 13)* Reduce sales force by 20% |
| • **(Option 7)** Emphasize everyone's role as a stakeholder in the achievement of strategic objectives | • **(Option 16)** Apply new problem-solving approaches | • *(Option 15)* Discontinue R&D in medical instrumentation | | • **(Option 14)** Design an "idealized" sales force automation system |
| • *(Option 10)* Consolidate certain functions to reduce or eliminate redundancy | | | | |
| • **(Option 11)** Adopt a team-based organization paradigm | | | | Tie Line |

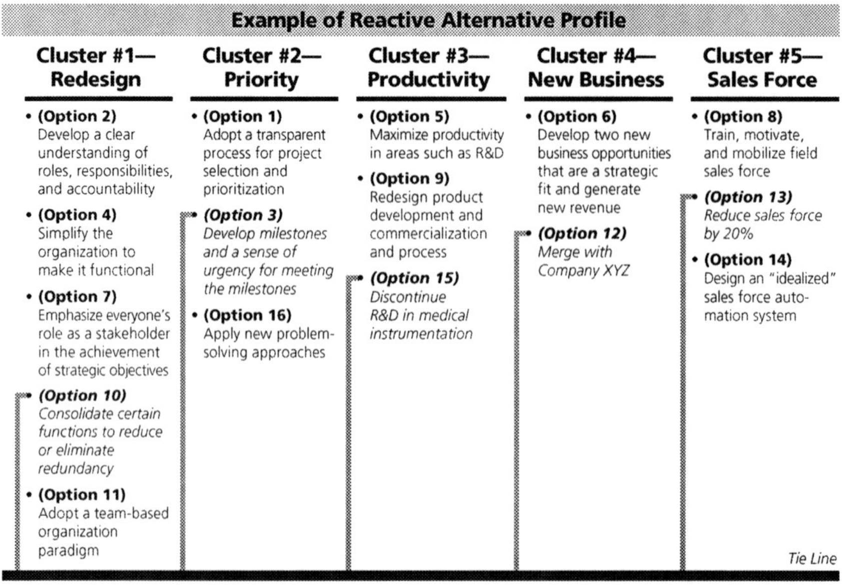

**Alternative A:** *Consolidate certain functions to reduce or eliminate redundancy while developing milestones and a sense of urgency for meeting the milestones. Discontinue R&D in medical instrumentation. Merge with Company XYZ and reduce sales force by 20%.*

Figure A.5.   Reactive alternative profile.

## STAGE THREE: DECISION

During this stage the dialogue is focused on evaluating the proposed alternatives. There exist different approaches for evaluating complex alternatives. The approach that has been adopted by the SDP paradigm is called the Trade-Off Evaluation procedure.

### Step One: Trade-Off Representation

The stakeholders are asked to propose criteria relevant to the evaluation of the alternatives presented in Figures A.4 and A.5. It is interesting to note that, up to this point, namely when the two alternative scenarios were designed and discussed, there was no explicit mention of a criterion set for evaluating the options for resolving the problematique proposed by the stakeholders. Avoiding the explicit mention of criteria until the emergence of the scenarios is intentional. The premature identification of criteria for evaluating ideas inhibits the creativity of the participants, leading to what sometimes is referred to in the literature as "premature closure."

The criteria proposed by the stakeholders and the qualitative or quantitative performance measures for each of the two alternatives are shown in the Trade-Off representation shown as Figure A.6: Relative Data of Alternatives for the Strategic Management Problematique.

| Relative Data of Alternatives | | | | | | | |
|---|---|---|---|---|---|---|---|
| Criteria/ Alternative | Stakeholder involvement | Implementation cost (2 years) | Productivity gain | Stakeholder satisfaction | Competitive advantage | Savings (downsizing) | Long-term pay-off |
| A: Interactive | High | $0.4M | Medium | High | Medium | $2.0M | High |
| B: Reactive (Reengineering) | High | $3.0M | High | Low | High | $6.0M | Low |

Figure A.6.   Relative data of alternatives for the Strategic Management Problematique

### Step Two: Priority Representation

During the implementation of this step the stakeholders focus the dialogue on the generic question:

"In the context of strategic management and Alternatives A and B,
is the difference in:
(Criterion-X)
more important (heavier weight) than the difference in:
(Criterion-Y)?"

Notice that the dialogue focuses on two alternatives at a time and on the *differences between the criteria for these two specific alternatives,* as shown in the matrix representation of Figure A.7: Comparison of Alternatives A and B.

| **Comparison of A and B** | | | | | | | |
|---|---|---|---|---|---|---|---|
| Criteria/ Alternative | Stakeholder involvement | Implementation cost (2 years) | Productivity gain | Stakeholder satisfaction | Competitive advantage | Savings (downsizing) | Long-term pay-off |
| A: Interactive | High | $0.4M | Medium | High | Medium | $2.0M | High |
| B: Reactive (Reengineering) | High | $3.0M | High | Low | High | $6.0M | Low |
| Difference | | $2.6M | | | | $4.0M | |
| Better | Equal | A | B | A | B | B | A |

Figure A.7.   Comparison of alternatives A and B for the Strategic Management Problematique.

The outcome of the dialogue is the priority representation, as shown in Figure A.8: Priority Structure Among Criteria for Evaluating Alternatives A and B.

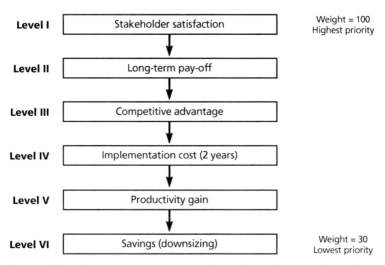

Figure A.8.   Priority structure among criteria for evaluating alternatives A and B.

## Step Three: Assignment of Weights

After studying the priority structure, the stakeholders are engaged in a dialogue focused on assigning weights to the criteria. As shown in Figure A.8, the criterion of highest relative importance is assigned 100 points. In this particular example, the criterion "Stakeholder Satisfaction" was determined as being the most important in step three, and hence it was assigned 100 points. The remaining criteria were assigned lower number of points in accordance with their level of priority. The lowest priority criterion, namely "Savings," was assigned 30 points.

Following the assignment of weights to each criterion, the aggregate value for each of the two alternatives is determined and displayed in a histogram representation, as shown in Figure A.9: Trade-Off Analysis—Comparison of Alternatives A and B. In the particular example, the total number of points assigned to Alternative A is equal to 240, while the points assigned to Alternative B is equal to 150. On the basis of these results Alternative A, i.e., the Interactive, is the preferred design alternative.

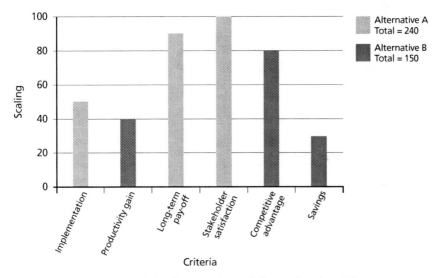

Figure A.9.    Tradeoff analysis of comparison of alternatives A and B.

## STAGE FOUR: ACTION PLAN

Having selected the preferred alternative the stakeholders are asked to transform the alternative into a temporal sequence for action. Since the *Interactive Alternative* is the preferred one, it is desirable to organize the options that have been selected and connected to the Tie Line for this alternative in a time sequence.

### Step One: Time Sequence Representation

For this step the dialogue focuses on the *generic question*:

"In the context of Alternative A (i.e. the Interactive), is it better
to start implementing:
(Option-X)
before we start implementing:
(Option-Y)?"

The outcome of this deliberation is shown by the representation of Figure A.10: Action Plan for Accomplishing the Strategic Vision of Our Organization. The action plan represents an architectural rendering of the collective wisdom of the stakeholders.

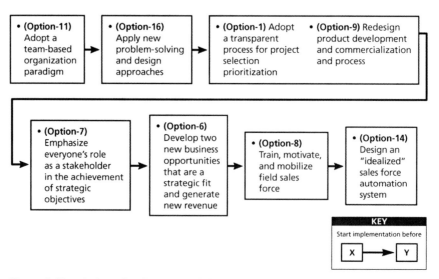

Figure A.10.   Action plan for accomplishing the strategic vision of our organization.

In some cases the stakeholders deem desirable to translate the architecture of the plan, as shown in the representation of Figure A.10, into a more detailed blueprint for action through the assignment of roles and responsibilities to individuals or specific organizational entities. In such cases, a Gantt Chart (see Chapter 5) or similar form of project/process management representation is produced either through a small team selected among the most relevant to this task stakeholders, or through a DELPHI questionnaire.

# APPENDIX B

# THE ROOTCAUSE MAPPING SOFTWARE

The RootCause Mapping (RCM) software is a component of the SDP process for managing complexity. It is a computer based group design support system deployed for identifying and analyzing the Factors that contribute to complex problems and discovering the root cause Factors. The development of this software has a history of 35 years, with the current version representing the fourth generation software.

The goal of RootCause Mapping goes beyond merely "fixing" the complex problem; it seeks to actually prevent it from happening again. This is accomplished by identifying the Factors, organizing the Facors in affinity clusters, determining the influences of each Factor on other Factors, and mapping the corresponding Influence Tree making the complex situation transparent. Included in the software are the proven problem-solving and consensus methods of SDP discussed in Part II.

Fundamentally, the software assists in capturing the Factors authored by the colaboratory participants, which are automatically displayed, stored and organized for ease of use. Displaying these Factors on a screen aids in the quality and efectiveness of the dialogue, which is an important component of the SDP process. The software is capable of producing automatically such reports as Table of Factors, Table of Clarification of the meanings of Factors, Prioritization of Factors as a result of voting, Options Field and Options Profile reprresentations, etc., with maximum flexibility of thought and structure.

*How People Harness Their Collective Wisdom and Power*, pages 239–240
Copyright © 2006 by Information Age Publishing
All rights of reproduction in any form reserved.

One of the products derived after the completions of the Definition Stage of the SDP is a RootCause map, or an Influence Tree, that shows the influences of selected Factors and a shared understanding of the most leveraged Factors to be addressed in the Design Stage and the follow-up implementation of the preferred action options for the resolution of the *Problematique*.

Ideally, a trained SDP Facilitator, along with a trained computer software operator and a recorder, makes the utilization of the software a very powerful tool for managing complexity, and converging on a Collaborative Action Plan (for methodological details please see Appendix A).

## LEADING DESIGN INTERNATIONAL (LDI)

The fourth generation RCM software has been developed and is being maintained by Leading Design International (*www.leadingdesign.org*). The vision of Leading Design International is to promote design cultures in organizations and communities to improve performance and accountability. This is being accomplished through the application of scientific methods, such as SDP, for addressing complex problems by engaging "the wisdom of the people" in disciplined dialogue for social system design and redesign.

The Principals of LDi have over 100 years collective experience in design theory, methodology, and practice in a variety of settings—including government and private sector arenas, and applications in areas such as Education, Health Care, Economics, Regulatory Policies and Practices, Patient Safety, Natural Resource Management, and Product and Process Development.

The Root Cause Mapping™ software became available for purchase in 2005. Pricing options include a choice of Limited Use License, Site License, Professional Services License, and Distributor License. The software includes a User Manual on CDROM, and Online Technical Support. Customized training options are also available. Leading Design International holds exclusive rights to the RCM software. For more information consult *www.Leadingdesign.org*.

# APPENDIX C

---

# CONSTRUCTING AGORAS OF THE GLOBAL VILLAGE

*Agoras—the vital centers of the Ancient Greek city-states,*
*With their outdoor markets and convention halls,*
*Were the hubs of the exchange of ideas and the birthplace of democracy.*
*The Institute for 21st Century Agoras*
*Revitalizes vibrant democracy in the Information Age.*

**S**ome of the best, most intelligent, motivated, and committed people are the backbone of the world's non-profit and community organizations. They put in hard hours to advance their goals, having some success, but often failing to produce the impact they desire.

These organizations generally lack funds. They need to concentrate their efforts on key leverage points and build working coalitions with similar-minded groups. Unfortunately, they often lack time for strategic reflection. As a result, scarce resources are often expended on activities that lack long-term impact.

The 47th annual conference of the International Society for the Systems Sciences (ISSS) in 2003 examined reasons why well-meaning and committed people have difficulty building livable, democratic, life-enhancing communities on the planet. They did so under the theme "Constructing Agoras of the Global Village," and they identified four basic activities that would vastly improve the agora-building success rate:

---

*How People Harness Their Collective Wisdom and Power*, pages 241–248
Copyright © 2006 by Information Age Publishing
All rights of reproduction in any form reserved.

- Provide methodology and facilities to continuously support the construction and sustainability of global agoras;
- Organize planetary networks;
- Identify stakeholders who may not identify themselves as stakeholders; and
- Link to an established entity that has the capacity to initiate agora construction activity (Hays and Michaelides, 2004).

The Institute for 21st Century Agoras is equipped to serve those needs. What it lacks are the funds that will enable it to aggressively "initiate agora construction activity." As specified in the attached budgets, $7 *million* over the next *four years* could establish *100 demonstration projects* around the world with the potential to spreading agoras like wildfire.

21st Century Agoras exists to serve the design and efficiency of progressive nonprofit organizations. It assists their efforts to construct livable communities on the planet. The organizations often lack significant funding. As a result they need to concentrate their efforts where they will have the greatest effect and they need to work in coalition with like-minded organizations. 21st Century Agoras helps these organizations locate their key leverage points and act on them in cooperation with other organizations.

## ORGANIZATIONS DESIRING AGORA ASSISTANCE

At the present time, Agora assistance has been requested for the following projects:

- Advancement of Global Indigeneity (AGI) wants to hold SDP sessions in Mexico, Bolivia, and Morocco.
- International Christian University wants a follow-up SDP session with students of Northeast Asia.
- The Cyprus Reunification Project requests assistance for additional SDP peacemaking sessions.
- The University of Flinders and the Neporendi Forum would like to use SDP to facilitate their efforts to promote Aborigine health and social inclusion in Australian society.
- Members of the faculty of the University of Buenos Aires and the municipal YMCA would like to employ SDP in conjunction with its National Council on Values.
- The Gaia Preservation Coalition will co-sponsor with 21st Century Agoras a Co-Laboratory that will enable its participating organizations to leverage their influence and collaborate to maintain a livable world.

These organizations and others recognize the need for internal cohesion and cooperation with like-minded people and organizations. They believe they can meet those needs by utilizing SDP. We thoroughly believe the same thing based upon SDP's distinguished history of achievement.

People who participate in the Structured Design Process are usually enthusiastic about the co-laboratory experience and even more enthusiastic about the results they achieve on their action plans. We anticipate that the participants and observers of these co-laboratories will be interested in using them in other communities and organizations. We propose to make them available to parties that could not otherwise afford to invigorate themselves in this way. To that end, we seek your support.

## AGORA-BUILDING PROSPECTUS

There are several scenarios, each designed to eventually enable groups to conduct co-laboratories on their own. They range from co-laboratories with an initial training session through co-labs with intern assistance, and co-labs run by new facilitation teams with Institute guidance. We support stakeholders as they learn to function independently as leaders of co-laboratories. The new facilitation teams are paid proportionally to their roles as assistants or as leaders backed by a consultant. The new teams are then given the SDP software (value $5,000) and are free to conduct co-laboratories, hopefully with financial support from the Institute for 21st Century Agoras.

## THE CRUCIAL COORDINATION FUNCTION

One of the greatest weaknesses in most group consensus and action plan processes is that after the initial agreement and surge of enthusiasm, other challenges and distractions creep in and the momentum is lost or new challenges arise which the group does not know how to address. To address this challenge, after a co-laboratory, local coordinators ensure that the agreed upon action plans are implemented and that this actually results in achieving the objectives set by the group. For three years, each project has a local follow-through coordinator who coaches everyone on meeting the project's goals, reports regularly on its progress, and manages operating necessities. Each coordinator receives both initial training and tools to carry out this function, as well as ongoing support from the Institute.

At the Global Agoras Institute level, we provide a master follow-through coordinator who:

- Trains and supports local coordinators;
- Communicates regularly with them;
- Summarizes local reports and produces quarterly Institute progress reports;
- Leverages local learning by sharing it with co-laboratories worldwide;
- Assists in production of action research and popular articles.

Follow-up coordination is crucial to both the success of the action plans and our ability to document their success. With this coordination, we ensure consistent followthrough, creating the successes that kindle enthusiasm, and assuring people that their initial work with the SDP process is supported. With systematic reports, we create benchmarks for gauging the success of various projects, and more importantly, learning from each one so that we can share those insights and learning with future groups using the SDP process so as to enhance their experience and their results.

We will publish action research articles and popular accounts of our successes so that practitioners of SDP and other group processes may benefit on an ongoing basis. We will publish so as to alert those organizations, communities or governments who would benefit from this process of its impact and availability. We will provide reports of results of these projects to those who provide financial support, so they will know exactly what is being accomplished with their money.

## ANTICIPATED ACTIVITY

We anticipate being able to conduct:

- Eight co-laboratories in the first year, including support for 8 local follow-through coordinators for three years.
- 20 co-laboratories in the second year, including support for 20 local followthrough coordinators for three years.
- 32 co-laboratories in the third year, including support for 32 local follow-through coordinators for three years.
- 48 co-laboratories in the fourth year, including support for 48 local followthrough coordinators for three years.

## Expenses For Co-laboratories, 2006 to 2009

|  |  | Total |
|---|---|---|
| **2006** |  |  |
| 8 co-laboratories with training session @ $42,000 | $336,000 |  |
| 8 Local Follow-Through Coordinators @ 6000 for 3 years | 144,000 |  |
|  |  | $480,000 |
| **2007** |  |  |
| 8 co-laboratories with training session @42,000 | 336,000 |  |
| 12 co-laboratories @30,000 | 360,000 |  |
| 20 Follow-Through Coordinators @ 6000 for 3 years | 360,000 |  |
|  |  | 1,056,000 |
| **2008** |  |  |
| 8 co-laboratories with training session @42,000 | 336,000 |  |
| 24 co-laboratories @30,000 | 720,000 |  |
| 32 Follow-Through Coordinators @ 6000 for 3 years | 576,000 |  |
|  |  | 1,632,000 |
| **2009** |  |  |
| 8 co-laboratories with training session @42,000 | 336,000 |  |
| 40 co-laboratories @ 30,000 | 1,200,000 |  |
| 48 Follow-Through Coordinators @ 6000 for 3 years | 864,000 |  |
|  |  | 2,400,000 |
| **Four-Year Co-Laboratory Total** |  | **$5,568,000** |

## First Year Institute Operating Budget

| | |
|---|---|
| Train 10 additional facilitators in SDP, three day workshop | $25,000 |
| Salary—Executive Director | 70,000 |
| Salary—Master Follow-Through Coordinator | 35,000 |
| Salary—Secretary | 30,000 |
| Employee taxes, benefits, etc. | 27,000 |
| Rent, Phone, Web, Printing, PR, etc. | 57,000 |
| Travel | 20,000 |
| Professional and Technical Services | 12,000 |
| Contingency and miscellaneous | 8,000 |
| Furniture and Equipment | 20,000[a] |
| First Year Operating Total | $304,000 |

[a] Subsequent years would not require all new equipment, but because of inflation, equipment and materials needs of new staff, and wear and tear, this $20,000 is budgeted in each of the 4 years.

The operating budget will increase by roughly 25% each year to accommodate the increased workload and expenses as larger numbers of co-laboratories are conducted each year. This includes training additional SDP facilitators each year and adding additional Master Follow-Through Coordinators to work with the growing number of projects plus increased travel. The operating budget for each of the four years, calculated at a 25% increase each year.

### Composite Budget

|        | Co-Laboratories | Operating | Total |
|--------|-----------------|-----------|-------|
| **2006** | 480,000 | 304,000 | 784,000 |
| **2007** | 1,056,000 | 380,000 | 1,436,000 |
| **2008** | 1,632,000 | 475,000 | 2,107,000 |
| **2009** | 2,400,000 | 593,750 | 2,995,750 |
| **Total** | 5,568,000 | 1,752,750 | **$7,320,750** |

For $7 million we project:

- 100 organizations around the world will have experienced the efficacy of SDP.
- 140 Facilitation team members will have been trained.
- We will have local coordinators for 100 projects.

## TWO FUNDING OPTIONS ARE PRESENTED
## FOR CONSIDERATION

### Option One

Provide the $7,320,750 amount to support this four-year program. This will not only fund 108 Co-Laboratory projects affecting organizations, communities and possibly even government entities, but the benefit from these projects expands infinitely. Not only is there direct impact from each specific project, which alone is very substantial, but each person involved in any of these projects, and especially those who receive training in the process or as a local follow-through coordinator, now has a set of skills that can be applied repeatedly in other projects and situations to create positive world outcomes. Working locally to impact globally is a hallmark of the SDP process. The potential ripple effect from over 100 projects involving many people is incalculable, but unquestionably substantial.

**Option Two**

Create an endowment of sufficient size, based on a set of assumptions about management of the fund that will provide ongoing funding, at least at the level described in the four year project, so that this work can continue indefinitely. This will allow the Institute to leverage its expertise and experience repeatedly and expand the impact of the SDP process and training to hundreds of projects in health, education, government and wherever there is a significant advantage in providing this service. This is truly an opportunity for positive global impact and leveraging ongoing benefits of tremendous proportions.

## TEN-YEAR PROJECTION

Within 4 years, the Institute will have amassed a substantial reputation that should attract large organizations and even nations with very complex problems as clients. These situations would require several coordinated co-laboratories. Similar SDP projects have been completed by CWALtd with the World Health Organization, the State of Michigan Department of Education, and the U.S. Federal Drug Administration. In this more complex environment, we project that during the first 10 years for *$70 million*:

- 1,076 regular co-laboratories
- 31 complex co-laboratories
- 300 trained team members
- Local coordinators for 1,076 projects

## SUPPLY AND DEMAND

This proposal lays out a growth pattern for the supply of a uniquely effective method of participative democracy. It is based upon beliefs that:

- The demand for wise, communal decision-making is insatiable.
- This demand is most often frustrated by the difficulties inherent in "decisions by committee."
- These difficulties force most communities to resort to decisions by authorities, by representatives, and ultimately to decisions by experts and elites.
- In our Information Age:
    - Experts cannot sufficiently comprehend the complexity of particular situations.

- Only the collective wisdom of a situation's stakeholders (including experts) can do that.
- Democracy in its many forms, from its Athenian roots today's rule by experts and plutocrats, works slowly, often taking decades, centuries, and even millennia to effect its reforms. Traditional democratic dialogue works too slowly for our Age.

Co-Laboratories solve four big problems of democracy today.

- They actively involve all relevant stakeholders in decision-making and design.
- They radically speed up respectful, inclusive, and efficacious dialogue.
- They generate consensual decisions and designs that are enthusiastically embraced by stakeholders who create them.
- They follow up with coordination of consensual action plans.

We believe that the democratic effectiveness of co-laboratories when sufficiently known will release people's pent-up desires into a flood of real democracy around the world. Evidence of this pent-up demand is evident in all SDP sessions and in sessions with many other methodologies (cf. Bausch, 2004). Documentation of this demand and action research into how it is mobilized will be integral to the project described in this proposal.

## INSTITUTIONAL CAPABILITY

The Institute for 21st Century Agoras is a charitable, non-profit organization incorporated in California. It has federal 501(c)(3) status. The Institute has a large reserve of SDP practitioners who are committed to assist in developing agoras. 21st Century Agoras through CWA Ltd. (*www.CWALtd.com*), which has a long history of dealings with U.S. federal agencies such as FDA, EPA, NOOA, and the U.S. Forestry Service, numerous large corporate accounts, and international agencies such as the World Health Organization. It has always maintained fiscal and accounting responsibility. Their CPA-certified financial records can be made available if necessary.

The Institute can call upon a large reserve of SDP practitioners who are committed to assist in developing agoras. Further information on the organization, Board members, methodology, and activities of the Institute for 21st Century Agoras can be found at *www.globalagoras.org*, and *www.cwaltd.com*.

APPENDIX D

# CHRONIC KIDNEY DISEASE

## Discussion Paper for CKD Initiative
## Stakeholder Workshop

**Shari Rudavsky, PhD (CWA, Ltd.)**
**Peter Schwartz MD, PhD (CWA, Ltd.)**
**Nicholas A. Christakis, MD, PhD, MPH**
**(Harvard Medical School, and CWA, Ltd.)**

### INTRODUCTION

While End Stage Renal Disease (ESRD) is the tip of the iceberg of kidney disease, it is nevertheless imposing: the number of people with ESRD has steadily crept up to more than 340,000, and projections are that this number could nearly double by 2010. ESRD claims the lives of about 20 percent of those who have it each year,[1] and Medicare alone currently spends almost $18 billion a year on ESRD. Below the surface of this iceberg, however, lies Chronic Kidney Disease (CKD, also called Chronic Renal Insufficiency).

There is increasing evidence that the adverse outcomes of CKD, including kidney failure and premature death, can be prevented or delayed with appropriate treatment. In order to have a significant impact on the growth in numbers of ESRD patients, a concerted effort must be made to educate

*How People Harness Their Collective Wisdom and Power,* pages 249–267
Copyright © 2006 by Information Age Publishing
All rights of reproduction in any form reserved.

clinicians and the general public about early diagnosis and treatment of CKD. As one nephrologist in practice for more than two decades said, "When you go to see your doctor you should be aware that your blood pressure needs to be checked, that your cholesterol needs to be checked and that you don't have CKD. It should be a preventive medicine issue." Now the question that nephrologists must tackle is how to develop an action plan to get there from here.

*Scope of CKD Initiative Workshop:* To address this question, the American Society of Nephrology, the National Kidney Foundation, and the Renal Physicians Association are convening a Workshop on February 25–26, 2003, with physicians, nurses, patients, policy-makers, providers, payers, and others involved with the field of nephrology in order to discuss how the field should respond.

Members of CWA, Ltd. (CWA)—an interactive management consulting company—will facilitate the Workshop utilizing the *CogniScope*™ system methodology (*www.CWALtd.com*). This "Discussion Paper" has been prepared by CWA, Ltd., with the advice of the Steering Committee of the CKD Initiative, to orient participants to relevant issues, thinking and trends. It is based on interviews with 14 experts and leaders in relevant areas, along with a limited review of the popular and medical literature. The CKD Initiative Steering Committee has also reviewed this document.

This paper is a platform from which to begin the discussion. It is not intended to be a comprehensive document of the state of CKD. There is no intention to publish it. It is for the use of the Stakeholders only. In certain categories, it may not fully recognize the efforts of certain nephrologists, service organizations, societies, and companies who have been working diligently in this arena. Any omission is not intentional.

The review highlights a number of challenges the nephrology community must confront in any initiative to improve the care of CKD:

- The true number of patients with CKD remains the subject of debate, with estimates ranging from 8 to 20 million.
- Developing a CKD action plan may depend on establishing which lab tests and values are reliable predictors of risk of progression to ESRD or of risk for other causes of morbidity and mortality.
- The pool of nephrologists, already strained by the large and growing population of ESRD patients, will need the assistance of primary care physicians or other health care professionals or a different model of care to meet the needs of patients with CKD seeking treatment.
- The source for payment for increased screening and care of patients with CKD is unclear, as well as how this will impact on nephrologists' reimbursement.

- Individuals at increased risk for CKD, at the very least, should be tested for proteinuria, and have their level of GFR estimated. Which tests to perform, when, how often, and even who should do the screening needs to be better defined.
- Certain interventions that have been proven to slow the progression of kidney disease, including strict glucose control in diabetes, strict blood pressure control, ACE inhibition and angiotensin-2 receptor blockade, need to be more widely and consistently applied. Other therapies may exist as well. There needs to be a consensus on treatment and the best practices.
- The high proportion of patients with CKD from minority and low-income groups must be considered in attempting to improve the care of patients with this disease.
- Lack of clear data and consensus among practitioners about the proper treatment of CKD, as well as significant geographic variation, form important challenges.

These eight challenges contain much more complexity, as detailed in the report that follows. In addition, interviewees suggested possible actions for any initiative, described below and summarized on pages 24 and 25. This document aims only to lay out the important issues and stimulate thought, with the crucial dialogue and decisions to occur together as a group in the February Workshop.

## I. HEIGHTENING CKD AWARENESS

It is generally agreed that for this initiative to succeed it must be pitched not only to the medical community at large, but also to the general public. Engaging the public could prove challenging, however. Unlike other diseases that are linked clearly to treatment (e.g. diabetes and insulin), chronic kidney disease is not a recognizable entity for many members of the general population, as well as some in the medical community. "When you say chronic kidney disease, they probably don't think much of anything," said one physician interviewed about both laypeople and some professionals.

As the field moves from an era of focus on ESRD to a greater emphasis on the prevention and treatment of co-morbid conditions, the nephrology community, say some, has not sufficiently begun to emphasize this component of their practice. A number of kidney organizations have put forth initiaitives to address this but more can still be done, many feel. "Nephrology as a subspecialty was not taking the lead in terms of trying to figure out a plan," said one nephrologist.

## The Prevalence of CKD is Very High

### NKF-K/DOQI Estimates of Prevalence of CKD in the U.S.

| Stage | Description | GFR (ml/min/1.73 m$^2$) | Prevalence (000s) | Prevalence (%) |
|---|---|---|---|---|
| 1 | Kidney Damage with Normal or ↑ GFR | >90 | 5,900 | 3.3% |
| 2 | Mild ↓ GFR | 60-89 | 5,300 | 3.0% |
| 3 | Moderate ↓ GFR | 30-59 | 7,600 | 4.3% |
| 4 | Severe ↓ GFR | 15-29 | 400 | 0.2 |
| 5 | Kidney Failure | <15 or Dialysis | 300 | 0.1 |

*Prevalence Estimates.* One ready response to this challenge would be the sheer volume of people who have chronic kidney disease, the vast majority of whom remain unaware that they fall into this category. No one doubts that the numbers have increased dramatically in the past decade. Dispute remains, however, about how high those numbers are. Earlier this year the National Kidney Foundation published clinical practice guidelines that estimate that as many as 20 million people may have the disease while another 20 million are at increased risk.[2] Perhaps because this estimate was based on a complex statistical analysis of the Third National Health and Nutrition Examination Survey (NHANES III), it has been greeted with some skepticism. "I'm not sure that most people have a lot of confidence in the numbers. I think most people feel that there are a lot of patients out there but I think a lot of people wonder who really knows the dimension of it," said one interviewee.

The NKDEP program uses an estimate of 8 million for people with GFR< 60 ml/min, which is in agreement with the K/DOQI CKD figures. Debate still exists as to whether people in K/DOQI stages 1 and 2 should be considered to have CKD. "While there may be 20 million people with lowered glomerular filtration rates (GFR), not all of these necessarily have chronic kidney disease. An individual might need to display other risk factors before he or she would or should qualify as having CKD," one respondent said. "We haven't done all of the homework we need to do to know what low GFR means," she said. "There needs to be recognition that GFR is an important marker, but before we label people as having chronic kidney disease, that marker needs to be further described."

Many respondents advocated greater consensus on a working definition for CKD to hone in on a more exact estimate for how many people have the disease. They feel that, before taking a campaign public, it is critical to zero in on a more accurate number. "I'm all for finding everybody who could eventually need dialysis," said one respondent. "I just want to make sure that we're not crying wolf." For now, using a 10 rather than 20 million estimate might prove the safest course, another respondent said. "I think 10 million has shock value and is a realistically high number," said one respondent.

The appeal of restricting the number further will help on many fronts, other interviewees note. A more manageable population will prove more amenable to intervention and also allow more readily for the sort of outcomes research that still needs to be done, said one interviewee. "If we have only a couple million, we now have something that's more tangible that we can assess and monitor," this nephrologist pointed out. If one were to consider only the patients who have protein in their urine, that would scale down the sheer volume of patients that a more generous definition would include, another respondent said. "It's like a funnel. We're now getting further towards the neck," said one respondent. "You have another 20 million that are thought to be at increased risk. That's probably true but there's no way we can handle that. That's an unreasonable number to think we can address."

## II. HANDLING AN INCREASED PATIENT LOAD

At this stage of the game, any increase in patient load will cause concern among nephrologists. The profession already feels stretched to its limits with a further shortage predicted for the future.[3] Projections suggest the pool of nephrologists would need to grow from its current level of about 5,000 to 11,000 by 2010 to accommodate all the ESRD patients without taking into account an additional CKD population as well. Already there's a critical shortage of pediatric nephrologists to treat young patients with CKD, some of whom will mature into adults in need of care. "I don't think nephrologists have a way to accommodate all these people," one respondent said. "If internal medicine people were to refer all of their early kidney patients, I'm not sure the system could hold them." If a screening initiative were to identify a large group of previously invisible CKD patients how would the field respond, some wonder. Are there sufficient nephrologists to handle such a bubble? Are there clear treatment guidelines to follow?

*Costs and Payments.* Then, there's the nagging issue of cost. "Everybody's nervous that if we start screening, this many people will add a huge cost to the healthcare system," said one interviewee. The question then becomes who will pay this price. Interviewees agree that persuading the government to shoulder this burden will be difficult unless data can show that preventive care for CKD patients will save costs down the road. Such arguments may not be difficult to make, one respondent said. "You have to understand how expensive this patient population is. If you understand how expensive this patient population is, any cost [of preventing CKD] goes down."

Compounding the problem, many interviewees say that nephrologists, already overburdened with work, may have few incentives to squeeze CKD patients into their practice. Such care can be time-intensive with little financial rewards for practitioners. Dialysis and ICU care can be quite remunerative for nephrologists, many note. The less invasive primary office care that CKD management will require will not compensate quite as well, others note. "There's a very odd, negative feedback system where the better you are, the more in demand you are, and the more End Stage Renal Disease patients you accommodate," said one nephrologist. "There's no structure to pay for the time of a person to do this." Nephrologists will do what they can, said another interviewee, but it may not be enough. "We're not just driven by numbers, but we're not oblivious to finances either," he said. "If it means shifting 2 percent of my time that's ok, but 12 percent is not ok."

*Screening.* The first line of attack against CKD, nephrologists feel, must be better screening efforts to identify those who do not know they have the disease. The efforts currently in place are often limited in scope and intensity. Many patients learn that they have long suffered from CKD only when they show up in an emergency room, hours away from dialysis.

A 1997 retrospective chart audit reviewed the hospital records of nearly 600 Medicare patients with diabetes and hypertension. Although almost all of the patients had their creatinine tested, only 68 percent of those with diabetes and 59 percent of the hypertensives had a urinalysis. While almost a third of the diabetics had positive proteinuria by dipstick, they were no more likely to be receiving protective ACE inhibitors than other patients and 6 percent were prescribed potentially dangerous nonsteroidal anti-inflammatory drugs.[4]

CKD may fall through the cracks because, in some sense, it competes for attention with higher profile conditions, such as diabetes, hypertension, and hypercholesterolemia, nephrologists say. In many instances, the decision of whether or not to screen falls to primary care practitioners who

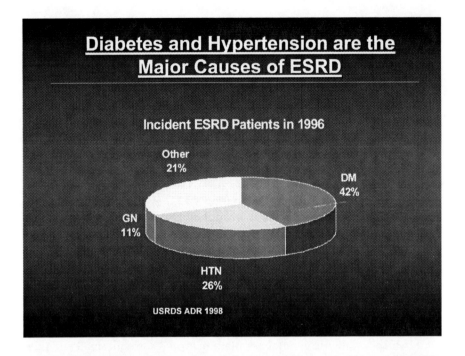

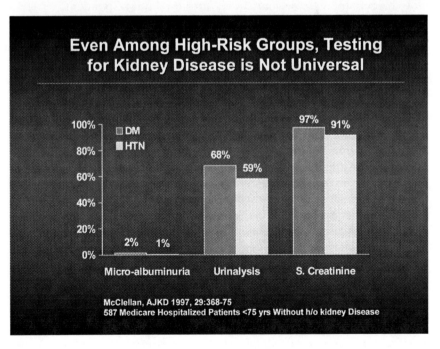

don't have the time to squeeze in yet another test. No more than 5 percent of most primary care practices consist of CKD patients, sending this problem under the radar of most doctors.[5] Family practitioners do not contest the assertion that the small amount of screening that is done "is not anywhere close to what the NKF recommends." Adding CKD to screening recommendations might help; "every society has its ideas for what people should screen for, but we go with the major recommendations and CKD is not included," said one family practice doctor.

Some nephrologists question whether wide-scale screening is warranted. Many suggest that any screening campaign be targeted towards those patients at the highest risk. This has been the approach successfully utilized in the National Kidney Foundation's Kidney Early Evaluation Program (KEEP). "Screening is okay in the highrisk population but the full-fledged screening of the entire population is not right," said one nephrologist. Long before anyone starts talking about universal screening, said this expert, nephrologists must examine the evidence to learn more about the real impact of low GFRs and whether everyone who suffers from such a condition will develop renal insufficiency. Another respondent proposed a *ramp-up approach* for screening where one begins with those at highest risk populations and then expands to include those at lower and lower risk until incorporating the general population. "You'd start out small and then move bigger and increase your circle," proposed this respondent.

Another way to telescope the population of prospective CKD patients would be to concentrate at first on *relatives* of patients already on dialysis, another respondent said. Studies have already supported the theory that kidney disease carries a strong familial component.[6] So, one place to start looking for patients in the early stages of the disease would be among relatives of those already in the ESRD system. "When your mama goes on dialysis, we ask whether anybody else in the family has kidney disease and we test their kidneys. This point is that kidney disease families are easily identifiable," said one respondent, recommending such a program be conducted nationally. Unfortunately, at present, relatives of people on dialysis tend never to have been screened to ascertain whether they have an early form of the disease themselves, research has found.[7]

Still, another way to narrow down a potential screening plan might be found in pilot programs that employ *data surveillance techniques* and that could provide a model for a larger-scale screening initiative. One disease management business that contracts with national health plans uses a combination of tools to identify patients with chronic kidney disease. Experts study laboratory work, clinical information, and any claim that suggests chronic kidney disease might be at play. Once the patients are identified they receive intensive care to prevent complications. Still, those familiar with the program know it will be difficult to persuade others to follow suit.

"The biggest challenge is finding the patient population that's at risk," said one. "There are no economic incentives to find them. They show up when they're really sick."

## III. IMPROVING PATIENT CARE

The overall care of CKD patients is not something about which nephrology can be proud, many respondents agree. Study after study has shown that very few patients with CKD today will actually see a doctor. One such study, conducted by Allan Collins, head of the United States ESRD Registry, followed a series of patients who had chronic kidney disease in 1996. In 1997, about 5 or 6 percent went on to dialysis and about 17 percent died. Of those who went on to dialysis, only about 45 percent saw a nephrologist beforehand. Of those who died, only about 10 percent saw a specialist. The following year, only about 10 percent of those with CKD who survived saw a nephrologist, prompting one participant familiar with the study to comment, "It's no wonder that if nephrology is trying to make an impact on this that they're not having much luck."

Many in the field feel that the nature of the patient population in part may explain why so few people receive care. Chronic kidney disease remains much more common among racial and ethnic minorities, groups that tend to be underserved when it comes to healthcare. In 1999, 953 per million African Americans had ESRD, 237 per million whites, and 652 per million Native Americans. Ten percent of all new ESRD patients were Hispanic, suggesting that the disease is rampant in this population as well.[8] These demographics, to the extent that they are compounded by poverty, may pose a further challenge to nephrologists, who may have to struggle to understand that CKD for this patient population is not necessarily a primary concern. As one nephrologist whose practice includes many minority patients noted, "when you have a silent disease, purchasing medication when you're worried about putting food on the table is just a low priority."

*More data needed.* Compounding the problem is the fact that the field has not reached consensus over what ideal treatment looks like. Over the course of more than a dozen interviews, it became clear that debate still rages in the field as to how effective available medicines are.[9] One respondent said that nephrologists have not enjoyed the luxury of having one medicine that appears to ameliorate the disease. Only recently have several medications come to market that physicians can agree are protective of the kidney. "Unlike high blood pressure and diabetes, there really is no medicine for kidney disease. That makes it more nebulous and more ill-defined," said one respondent. Other nephrologists agree it's not clear how to respond best to prevent CKD. "Physicians do believe that if you stop

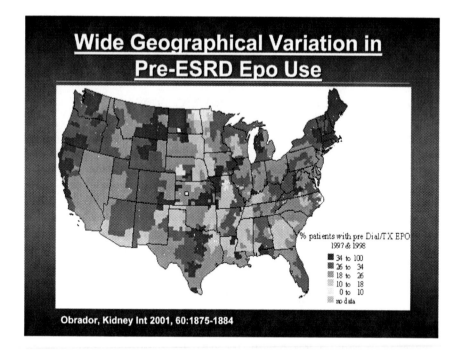

# Wide Geographical Variation in Pre-ESRD Epo Use

% patients with pre Dial/TX EPO
1997 & 1998

- 34 to 100
- 26 to 34
- 18 to 26
- 10 to 18
- 0 to 10
- no data

Obrador, Kidney Int 2001, 60:1875-1884

smoking, there will be much less cancer, but there's not the same conviction that if we go all out in kidney disease we can have much of an effect," said one respondent.

This may translate into many patients receiving what other nephrologists view as substandard care. One study found that only 40 percent of chronic kidney disease patients who were candidates for anti-anemia treatment received the medication and others have noted similar deficiencies in care.[10] Another, intriguingly, showed wide geographic variation in the use of erythropoeitin.[11]

Such distinctions may point researchers in three directions: What lies behind these regional differences? Can certain areas serve as models for their colleagues in the rest of the country to follow? Have those in more successful areas tapped into resources that providers elsewhere do not know exist?

But some feel that deficiencies in care transcend any geographic or professional boundaries. The problem can occur at any level of the interaction with the medical system, said one nephrologist, from a doctor to a dietician to a pharmacist. "There's a lag between our knowledge from clinical trials and our clinical practice," this respondent said. "It's very difficult to keep everyone up to date and I'm not sure that everyone who's involved in the kidney disease field is as up to date as they need to be." Additional research will help quell not only doubts about treatment regimes, but payers' concerns about what's reimbursable, said one respondent. "Insurers are often asked to pay for ineffective medical care," charged this respondent; "they prefer to pay for that which works."

*Guidelines.* Earlier this year, the National Kidney Foundation released guidelines for how to handle CKD. Prompted in part by the sense that the disease is under-diagnosed and under-treated, the guidelines aim to prevent adverse outcomes. Laboratory tests that can detect the disease in its early stages can lead to treatment that will slow the seemingly inexorable progression to kidney failure. The guidelines also aim to help the field arrive at agreement on a definition and classification of CKD stages.[12]

But some feel that the publication of guidelines has come too early. Without a clear notion of which healthcare professionals should be treating this large population of patients, any guidelines are just premature, said one respondent. "From my perspective they are way ahead of the game. It's great to have guidelines of care, but we've got to take a step back and have an organized approach. Otherwise it's hit or miss," this nephrologist said. Moreover, guidelines are often a blunt instrument for changing physician behavior to begin with, and are often unsuccessful since, in most cases, physicians are unaware of specific guidelines regarding a variety of topics.[13]

Further complicating factors, both the Renal Physicians Association and the National Kidney Foundation both issued new guidelines recently, which they developed in a collaborative fashion. Informal canvassing suggests that nephrologists have low compliance rates when it comes to providing patients in the early stages of CKD with appropriate therapies, said one prominent nephrologist. While the guidelines disagree on little, one thing that's clear from reading them both is the lack of strong data on chronic kidney disease, said one respondent familiar with them both. "The guidelines clear up what areas have been well-researched and just as importantly identify a lot of gaps," this respondent said.

Finally, an economic model that justifies the implementation of the guidelines is lacking. Who benefits and who should pay for screening and the attendant increased follow-up care? What new costs are created and old costs replaced?

## IV. INCLUDING CARDIOVASCULAR DISEASE

One gap in knowledge that demands further analysis is the trajectory for people who suffer from CKD. While much attention to date has focused on the undesirable CKD outcome of ESRD and dialysis, increasingly experts in the field express concern that such thinking masks another true outcome of CKD: cardiovascular mortality. New data suggests that CKD patients are more likely to die from cardiovascular disease than to require dialysis down the road. One study found that mortality for patients with high serum creatinine and left ventricular dysfunction was more than twice as high—36 percent—as for patients with low creatinine.[14] In addition, patients with CKD may be more prone to hospitalization for cardiac events than those in the general population, other studies have found.[15] These relatively recent discoveries, say some, require a "stark departure" from the way that nephrologists have treated CKD in the past. Now, said another nephrologist, "cardiovascular disease has emerged as a major issue."

This revelation, compounded by the fact that treatment of CKD could still use some fine-tuning, points to a need for additional clinical trials to determine the best way to handle treatment of chronic kidney disease. While the National Kidney Foundation's Kidney Disease Outcome Quality Initiative guidelines do address cardiovascular complications, many in the field state that more information is still needed. Once more, however, cost can prove an obstacle with few entities well-positioned to invest the type of funds necessary to support such trials. Based on the model of heart disease, one respondent recommended that the government, drug industry, and nephrology community partner on such studies to hone in on the best clinical practice.

Providing a corollary to this proposal, another respondent called for a clinical trial that would explore the best treatment for chronic kidney disease, studying a combination of treating any lipid disorders with statins, handling any anemia, controlling the blood pressure and offering ACE inhibitors. "Even though each of these things has been recommended, no one's put the whole package together. That's the trial that needs to be done." Noting that part of the cholesterol movement's success lay in the fact that data existed to back up the assertions, this respondent agreed that such investigations should predate any other concerted efforts. "The most fundamental thing is you need data that shows if you make this treatment modification you will have this impact," he said. "Then what you need is a way of making that intervention and educating people about what that data is."

Once the data has been developed, nephrologists can take further steps towards partnering with the heart and stroke foundations, others point out. Just this year the American Heart Association included an entire morning on kidney disease in its annual meeting, noted one nephrologist with approval. "It's coming into people's awareness, but the question is should we do anything to speed that up."

## V. ENLISTING PCPS IN THE BATTLE

Any such efforts, however, land the field squarely back in the problem of how to manage an overgrown patient population. Many nephrologists call upon primary care providers to serve in the front lines of the battle against CKD. However, nephrology had not had a good track record when it comes to enlisting these colleagues. "Our efforts in the past with primary care physicians have not been totally successful in terms of getting across a message about what to do with CKD." Other nephrologists warn that the subspecialty cannot blithely assume that primary care providers will serve as "their workhorse." "What they say is you guys are out of your mind," said one respondent, recounting how he suspects the primary care providers will respond if asked to assume the responsibility. "We have 10 or 15 minutes to see a patient and you want us to spend all of our time addressing your issue."

The lack of consistent guidelines coupled with the seriousness of the disease has played an integral role in this confusion, say many. "How does one manage a small number of patients that have a lot of risk. This is no small undertaking," said one respondent. One family practitioner who deals extensively with nephrologists reported a sense that specialists have reached no consensus on how to treat these patients. Consult two nephrologists on a case and you'll get two different treatment plans. With so many other demands on their time, primary care doctors do not appreciate such inconsistent messages. "We need one set of guidelines and a consistent message repeated again and again," said this family doctor. "If they have different ideas and we get our hands slapped once or twice in a row, then we're off the case." Afraid they will misstep, it's easy just to send such patients away rather than risk the scorn of their nephrology colleagues, this primary care provider said.

Contrast this situation with that surrounding the cholesterol movement, another respondent suggested. The NIH publishes guidelines that inform doctors about ideal cholesterol levels. "We don't have that yet with kidney disease," said one respondent. "You can look at the guidelines from the NKF or the RPA, but to a non-nephrology audience, seeing guidelines from a society and not the government is another level of rigor." In the long run, though, it boils down to primary care providers just not having the extra time to grapple with CKD patients, nephrologists concede. "It's kind of hopeless to think a doctor will spend 30 minutes with each of these patients several times a year. The numbers are against that happening. So some radical new care models have to be devised," one respondent noted.

## VI. BRINGING IN CKD EDUCATORS

That sentiment of needing what one responding referred to as a new "clinical delivery paradigm" cropped up over and over in interviews. Many endorsed the idea of specialized nurse educators and other physician extenders to handle chronic kidney disease. They envisioned individuals who would serve a role similar but not identical to that of diabetes educators. While diabetes educators already may discuss renal issues with their patients, most respondents advocated not merely expanding their role but creating professionals specific to CKD in their image. In their current incarnation, diabetes educators may pay scant attention to renal concerns, warned one interviewee, for instance, focusing extensively on the effect that disease can have on the eyes without even mentioning the potential risk to kidneys.

Preliminary research and pilot programs support the notion that physician extenders as part of a multidisciplinary treatment team could improve patient outcome, respondents say. They could monitor compliance, do regular check-ups, help oversee care, or take on a range of other activities related to CKD prevention and treatment. One disease management company developed a pilot project under which patients who appeared to have chronic kidney disease would first see a nephrologist. Then nurses, trained in a three-week course, would educate them and develop care plans along with them as well as conducting regular follow-up with them.

Other respondents mention academic clinics that bring together nurses, dieticians, pharmacists, social worker and physicians, both primary care providers and nephrologists in a multidisplicinary team approach. This variety of individuals working in concert with one another sends a critical message to patients, said one respondent familiar with one such clinic. "Patients say the psychological impact of seeing a doctor for 15 or 20 minutes is different from seeing a team for an hour and a half. I think we probably underestimate the double message that we give you: Your disease is so important that we've got to do all these things but I only have 20 minutes for you," said this expert.

Another piece of such a multi-disciplinary approach could include patient information materials. The American Association of Kidney Patients has an extensive public information campaign, complete with an Internet newsletter and conferences. Working with nephrologists, diabetes, and other patients with kidney disease, the association has developed a mailing list of nearly 50,000 chronic kidney patients who receive periodic updates. People with the disease tell the Association regularly that they learn more in 15 minutes of perusing this material than they do from their own doctors, suggesting that more could be done with printed materials to educate patients.

Here the model of breast cancer or cholesterol might prove a useful one, suggested one respondent familiar with the AAKP's materials. In the case of both those diseases, the general public was inundated with information. Before these campaigns, pointed out this interviewee, people only went to their doctors when they did not feel well. But these initiatives turned that dynamic on its head. Now people go for screening to catch breast cancer or high cholesterol early. A similar model might well work for chronic kidney disease, this participant suggested. "So much is pushing the general public to go to your doctor and get screened."

But such a concept is no easy fix, respondents agree. As many as 5,000 to 10,000 nurse educators could be required to address the situation and they would all require training, which would not be cheap. Estimated one pessimistic respondent: "The infrastructure to take care of this population is 10 years away if you think about how long it takes to train people. Either you're going to have to train more nephrologists which we're short on anyway, or you're going to have to train more nurses and physician extenders with guidelines on how to take care of this population on a routine basis."

While some practices or clinics may be doing this on their own, helping their own patients as much as possible, such a piecemeal approach in the long run will not serve the population as a whole, noted one respondent. First, it's hard for an individual practice to sustain such an initiative. Second, this diffuse system will not lend itself readily to data analysis, something crucial at this stage of the game. Not only is it critical to do this, said this respondent, it's necessary to collect data to show these programs are sound economic investments. "To do this in an organized way, which is pretty much pie in the sky, would be the ultimate homerun," this respondent said.

*Payment.* Even if sufficient numbers of such professionals could be identified and trained, the challenge of payment could still prove an obstacle. One family care doctor recounted her experience attempting to establish a chronic kidney management clinic for case screening and follow-up and care. Her colleague nephrologists at the medical center applauded the concept but she needed financial backup to realize her vision. So she turned to the drug companies, estimating it would take about $100,000 a year but none offered the support she needed. Now she's searching elsewhere.

Still, in the long run, say experts familiar with the problem, these seemingly expensive professionals will definitely save money for the health plans they work for. "We can't afford this for every individual who has a healthcare problem, but you can for people who are very expensive for a healthcare plan," said one respondent who works with national healthcare companies that have tested the nurse educator concept. "You have to understand how expensive this population is. If you understand how expensive it is, the costs will go down,"

One potential solution might come again from the experience of diabetes educators. Federal legislation mandated the creation of a training program and covered the cost of education, a model that insurance companies followed as well, recalled one respondent. The time may be ripe now for such an effort, said another respondent, given that kidney disease was included in Healthy People 2010 as a categorical disease for the first time. And, nephrologists may be in a better position to enlist high-level governmental support than those in other medical specialties because of governmental involvement with dialysis. One respondent familiar with government policies noted that a "dialysis caucus" exists currently in Congress. Any initiative should tap into this resource and try to bring along at least some of that group's members. "Ultimately if we want to do this right, we need to have laws passed," said this interviewee. "Clearly that's what's happened with other chronic disease efforts."

Another entry to finding and educating this burgeoning CKD population might be large employers who may have several examples of this disease lurking in their employee pool. Studies have shown that lost work days for employers who call in sick either to care for themselves or relatives incurs a major cost. "I would suggest we develop a compelling story for private industry to get on board with this issue," recommended one respondent. "In most workplaces they have diabetes awareness, awareness for breast exams, hypertension, cholesterol. This just needs to be one of those initiatives."

## VII. SUMMARY

This much is clear: Chronic Kidney Disease will not go away. If nephrology does not jump in to address this problem in the near future, it will pose even greater challenges for the field, something no one wants to see. A successful concerted effort, however, could perhaps save both dialysis dollars and lives that otherwise would be lost to cardiovascular disease. With so much riding on the community's response, all of the interviewees agree that a Workshop and initiative such as this one are clearly warranted. One interviewee said he hoped that the February Workshop would result in a blueprint that could be set into action within a year.

As this Discussion Paper has detailed, multiple challenges can be described for an initiative in this area (summarized as bullet points on pp. 2-3). In addition, some of the action proposals that arose can be summarized as follows:

- Collect better data on the morbidity and mortality of markers of CKD and better data on the impact of aggressive treatment in various groups. Is this data available through various sources: insurers, labs, pharmaceutical databases, etc.?
- Increase public awareness of CKD and the availability of patient-information materials.

- Explore use of PCPs, interdisciplinary teams, nurse-educators and other physician extenders in providing care for CKD. One commonly mentioned model is diabetes educators.
- Given the clear connections between CKD and cardiovascular disease (including CAD and strokes), attempt to partner with groups involved in providing care for these diseases. Establish the economic advantages of treating CKD, and make this clear to government, business, and health-insurance companies.

These challenges and proposals serve only as a starting point, of course. Participants in the February 25–26 Workshop should review this information and consider the situation from their own perspective.

## NOTES

1. Dave Cleveland, Kailash Jindal, David Hirsch, and Bryce Kiberd. "Quality of Prereferral Care in Patients with Chronic Renal Insufficiency," American Journal of Kidney Diseases 2002 July; *40*(30–36).

2. John O'Neil. The New York Times; February 19, 2002, "Catching Kidney Disease in Early Stages." National Kidney Foundation. *K/DOQI Clinical Practice Guidelines for Chronic Kidney Disease: Evaluation, Classification and Stratification.* Am J Kidney Dis *39*, 2002 (suppl 1).

3. In 1996, a survey of nephrologists found that most felt the profession already lacked sufficient numbers to handle an influx of End Stage Renal Disease patients. If anything, the problem has only increased in recent years. See W Mitch and Wm, McClellan. Patterns of patient care reported by nephrologists: implications for nephrology training. American Journal of Kidney Diseases 1998 Oct., *32*(4):551–556 and RJ Glassock, "Nephrology Workforce and Time Allocation: Important Issues for the Future, American Journal of Kidney Diseases 1998 Oct., *32*(4): 672–755.

4. Wm McClellan, DF Knight, H Karp, and WW Brown. "Early detection and treatment of Renal Disease in Hospitalized Diabetic hypertensive patients: important differences between practice and published guidelines." American Journal of Kidney Diseases 1997 Mar; *29*(3):368–375. The lag in care has even made it to prime-time television. In a January 23 episode of the sitcom "Scrubr," the head of the hospital reviews a nephrologist's case charts and determines that he has failed to stay current in his field. One of the tipoffs? That none of his diabetic patients have been prescribed ACE inhibitors.

5. National Kidney Foundation. "Attitudes of Primary Care Physicians Focus Groups and In-Depth Interviews," November 1994.

6. See, for instance, BI Freedman, JI Soucie, and Wm McClellan, "Family History of End-Stage Renal Disease Among Incident Dialysis Patients," Journal of the American Society of Nephrology; 1997 Dec;8(12):1942–1945.

7. C Jurkovitz, H Franch, D Shoham, J Bellenger J, and Wm McClellan. Family members of patients treated for ESRD have high rates of undetected kidney disease. American Journal of Kidney Diseases 2002 Dec;40(6):1173–1178.

8. Gregorio Obrador, Brian Pereira, and Annamaria Kausz. "Chronic Kidney Disease in the United States: An Underrecognized Problem." Seminars in Nephrology 2002; 22: 441–448.

9. This feeling is also reflected in the medical literature, in which experts are still discussing the ideal treatment for patients with mild to moderate chronic kidney disease. See, for instance, Chi-Yuan Hsu, Charles McCulloch and Gary Curhan. "Epidemiology of Anemia Associated with Chronic Renal Insufficiency among Adults in the United States: Results from the Third National Health and Nutrition Examination Survey." Journal of the American Society of Nephrology 2002 13: 504–510 and Allan Collins and William Keane, "Higher haematocrit levels: do they improve patient outcomes and are they cost effective," Nephrology Dialysis Transplantation 1998 13: 1627–1629.

10. Allen Nissenson, Allan Collins, Judith Hurley, Hans Petersen, Brian Pereira, and Earl Steinberg. "Opportunities for Improving the Care of Patients who Chronic Renal Insufficiency: Current Practice Patterns," Journal of the American Society of Nephrology 2001; 12: 1713–1720. See also, A Kausz, S Khan, R Abichandani, et al. "Management of patients with chronic renal insufficiency in the northeastern United States." Journal of the American Society of Nephrology 2001 12: 1501–1507.

11. Gregorio Obrador, "Trends in Anemia at Initiation of Dialysis in the United States," Kidney International, 2001 60:1875–1884.

12. National Kidney Foundation. "Clinical Practice Guidelines for Chronic Kidney Disease: Evaluation, Classification and Stratification. Executive Summary, : 2002.

13. DA Christakis and FP Rivara, "Pediatricians' Awareness of and Attitudes About Four Clinical Practice Guidelines," Pediatrics 1998 101 (5): 825-830; KA Roberts, "Best Practices in the Development of Clinical Practice Guidelines," Journal of HealthCare Quality 1998 20 (6): 16-20,32; DA Davis and A Taylor-Vaisey, "Translating Guidelines into Practice: A Systematic View of Theoretic Concepts, Practical Experience and Research Evidence in the Adoption of Clinical Practice Guidelines," CMAJ 1997 Aug 157(4) 408–416.

14. Al-Ahmed. "Unadjusted All-Cause Mortality Stratified by Renal Function," Journal of the American Society of Nephrology 1999 10:152A.

15. Samina Khan, Waqar Kazmi, Rekha Abichandani, Hocine Tighiouart, Brian Pereira, and Annamaria Kausz. "Health Care Utilization Among Patients With Chronic Kidney Disease." Kidney International 62 (2002): 229–236.

# APPENDIX

## List of Interviewees

Roland Blantz, MD
University of California, San Diego

Robert Brenner, MD
Amgen, Inc.

Allan Collins, MD
Nephrology Analytical Services

John Dickmeyer, MD
Renal Management Strategies

Cathy Dooley
Ortho-Biotech

Cynda Ann Johnson, MD
University of Iowa

Adeera Levin, MD
University of British Columbia

William McClellan, MD
Georgia Medical Care Foundation

Keith Norris, MD
University of California, Los Angeles

Brian Pereira, MD
New England Medical Center

Richard Rettig, PhD
Rand Institute

Kris Robinson
American Association of Kidney Patients

Barry Straube
Center for Medicare and Medicaid Services

Jim Weiss, MD
Renal Physicians Association

# INDEX

## A

Academy for Contemporary Problems, 9, 151

Action, types of, 129

Action phase, 38

Action planning (1989–1995)/interactive inquiry stage, 48, 70

Agency, and power, 20

*Agoras,* 241

  *See also* Global Village and *agoras* construction; Greek democracy

Application time phases, 37

  Action phase, 38

  Designing phase, 38

  Discovery phase, 37

Axioms of SDP, 155

  Cognitive Limitations Axiom, 156–158

  Complexity Axiom, 156

  Saliency Axiom, 158–159

## B

Belousov-Zhabotinski reaction, 132

Bernard effect, 131

Brainstorming, 25

  *See also* Nominal Group Technique (NGT)

Bryn Gweled international community co-laboratory. *See* SDP approach/

co-laboratory of democracy case example

Burns, James MacGregor, 192–193

## C

CATWOE. *See* Soft Systems CATWOE acronym

Change, 12

  fumbled opportunities (case examples), 20–21

  and importance of "science of complexity," 21

  *See also* Conscious evolution

Chronic Kidney Disease (CKD), 249–250

  application. *See* SDP methodology (customized application)

Clinton, President Bill

  Northwest forest conference, 20–21

  "reinvent government" goal/difficulties, 9–10

Clockwork/Hierarchy paradigm, 132

Club of Rome, 9

  and conscious evolution efforts, 205–206

  and group dialogue issues, 19

  *Problematique,* 31

  origin, 149

  original proposal/global *Problematique,* 150–151

*How People Harness Their Collective Wisdom and Power,* pages 269–277
Copyright © 2006 by Information Age Publishing
All rights of reproduction in any form reserved.

Printed in the United States
211957BV00003B/29/A

9 781593 114817